CHASING GHOSTS

FAILURES AND FACADES
IN IRAQ: A SOLDIER'S
PERSPECTIVE

PAUL RIECKHOFF

NAL
CALIBER

NAL CALIBER
Published by New American Library, a division of
Penguin Group (USA) Inc., 375 Hudson Street, New York, New York 10014, USA • Penguin Group (Canada), 90 Eglinton Avenue East, Suite 700, Toronto, Ontario M4P 2Y3, Canada (a division of Pearson Penguin Canada Inc.) • Penguin Books Ltd., 80 Strand, London WC2R 0RL, England • Penguin Ireland, 25 St. Stephen's Green, Dublin 2, Ireland (a division of Penguin Books Ltd.) • Penguin Group (Australia), 250 Camberwell Road, Camberwell, Victoria 3124, Australia (a division of Pearson Australia Group Pty. Ltd.) • Penguin Books India Pvt. Ltd., 11 Community Centre, Panchsheel Park, New Delhi - 110 017, India • Penguin Group (NZ), 67 Apollo Drive, Mairangi Bay, Auckland 1311, New Zealand (a division of Pearson New Zealand Ltd.) • Penguin Books (South Africa) (Pty.) Ltd., 24 Sturdee Avenue, Rosebank, Johannesburg 2196, South Africa

Penguin Books Ltd., Registered Offices: 80 Strand, London WC2R 0RL, England

Published by NAL Caliber, an imprint of New American Library, a division of Penguin Group (USA) Inc. Previously published in an NAL Caliber hardcover edition.

First NAL Caliber Trade Paperback Printing, May 2007
10 9 8 7 6

Copyright © Paul Rieckhoff, 2006
All rights reserved

Grateful acknowledgment is made for permission to reprint lyrics from "Bullet and a Target" by Citizen Cope.

NAL CALIBER and the "C" logo are trademarks of Penguin Group (USA) Inc.

NAL Caliber Trade Paperback ISBN: 978-0-451-22121-6

The Library of Congress has cataloged the hardcover edition of this title as follows:
Rieckhoff, Paul.
    Chasing ghosts/Paul Rieckhoff.
      p. cm.
    ISBN 0-451-21841-8
    1. Rieckhoff, Paul.   2. Iraq War, 2003—Personal narratives, American.
    3. Soldiers—United States—Biography.   I. Title.
    DS79.76.R5   2006
    956.7044'342092—dc22   2006002301

Set in Garth Graphic • Map by G. W. Ward • Designed by Sabrina Bowers

Printed in the United States of America

PUBLISHER'S NOTE
This book is a work of nonfiction. Because of the nature of its subject matter, however, in some cases, the author has replaced the actual names of persons with pseudonyms or otherwise masked identifying personal characteristics.

While the author has made every effort to provide accurate telephone numbers and Internet addresses at the time of publication, neither the publisher nor the author assumes any responsibility for errors, or for changes that occur after publication. Further, publisher does not have any control over and does not assume any responsibility for author or third-party Web sites or their content.

"Paul Rieckhoff is a unique voice of truth whose stories of his service in Iraq enlighten, inform, entertain, and capture the understanding missing on the war. Paul shows us that you can be a brave soldier and a brave citizen without compromising either. The sensory images he presents in his book, *Chasing Ghosts*, are vivid, vibrant, and unique. A must read that I could not put down."   —Serj Tankian, lead singer, System of a Down

"Paul Rieckhoff is a citizen in the classical sense. He went to war when his nation called, but his service didn't end when he came home. Paul poured his hard-won wisdom into changing the public dialogue about Iraq . . . and it's working. He's a patriot, a warrior, an organizer, and a leader. Paul's an inspiration, and you cannot put his book down without realizing that guys like him are changing Iraq, and America too."

—Nathaniel Fick, author of *One Bullet Away:*
The Making of a Marine Officer

"Powerful . . . an unabashed, succinct, and fascinating mix of shocking detail and humorous commentary. Must reading for those who care about the truth, *Chasing Ghosts* tells an engrossing and wise tale of well-meaning soldiers trapped in the wasteland of war."

—Bob Kerrey, president, The New School; Medal of Honor recipient;
Vietnam veteran; Navy SEAL; and author of *When I Was a Young Man:*
A Memoir

"Language that does not apologize for its raw candor." —*The Herald-Sun* (NC)

"Rieckhoff takes you to the stomach-churning streets, day by day, rifles and teenage soldiers in hand, nothing left to the imagination save the full fear. We had better heed Rieckhoff's brutally honest, strong, and unimpeachable scream."

—Leslie H. Gelb, former foreign affairs columnist for *The New York Times*
and president emeritus of the Council on Foreign Relations

"Powerful, heartfelt, and real. Anyone who cares about Iraq and the U.S. military—that is to say, anybody who cares about this country and where it's headed—should read this book."

—Janet Reitman, contributing editor, *Rolling Stone*

"Get it! It's a good book."

—John Gibson, *The John Gibson Radio Show,* Fox News Radio

"Rieckhoff writes sympathetically of troops and civilians alike."

—*Seattle Weekly*

"A most commendable eyewitness report on Iraq."   —*Booklist*

"[An] undeniably proud narrative."   —*Library Journal*

"Rieckhoff has a story to tell."   —*Publishers Weekly*

CHASING GHOSTS

**An uncensored and unrehearsed statement from a war veteran.
A candid grunt's-eye view of the bloody battles
on the streets of Baghdad.
A patriot's vision of where America has gone wrong
and how it can reset its path.**

"Alternately hilarious and tragic, the best reporting to come out of the Iraq War—possibly the best reporting to emerge from any war. No book since *Catch-22* has depicted this gruesome subject so compellingly. Rieckhoff should make room on his mantel for the Pulitzer Prize."
—Chuck Palahniuk, author of *Fight Club* and *Haunted*

"This book hit me in the gut. . . . It is the real story of how the lies, idiocies, frustrations, obscenities, and tragedies of the war impact those who fight it . . . full of courage, GI talk, humor, and pure patriotism . . . a must read for all of us struggling to understand the number one issue of our time."
—Senator Max Cleland, Vietnam Vet

"A hybrid of *M*A*S*H*, *China Beach*, and *Platoon*." —*Dayton City Paper*

"A clear-eyed, hardheaded, softhearted, and functioning-kidneyed account of our nightmare in Iraq. Anyone who would question Paul Rieckhoff's unquestioned authority on the war and its cost is dangerously dangerous."
—Al Franken, bestselling author, comedian, host of
The Al Franken Show, frequent USO tour host

"America has to thank its new war veterans for going into harm's way. But now America has to answer the questions of vets like Rieckhoff: Why were they lied to, why were they not given all the protections available, who will pay the price for the almost twenty thousand casualties? Rieckhoff's anger is the rage of a patriot." —Richard Clarke, author of *Against All Enemies*

"Paul Rieckhoff is a human being of true substance and character. These descriptions are tossed around too easily nowadays, but Paul is one of the few who is really striving for what is right, in our lifetime. His dedication to truth and life itself is clearly proven in his work—and now his word."
—Chuck D, Public Enemy

"A gripping account. . . . Rieckhoff writes with rare authenticity and passion. . . . Every American who professes to 'Support Our Troops' should read *Chasing Ghosts*." —Evan Wright, author of *Generation Kill*

"Masterful."
—Scott Ritter, AlterNet, former U.S. weapons inspector and author of
*Iraq Confidential: The Untold Story of the Intelligence Conspiracy to
Undermine the U.N. and Overthrow Saddam Hussein*

"Like a firsthand report from your coolest friend. . . . Rieckhoff totally nails the absurdities of American soldiers confronting mortality in aid of a failing mission. Anyone trying to figure out how the Iraq war went into the ditch needs to study *Chasing Ghosts*. With the eye of a seasoned novelist and the sensibility of a hip New Yorker, Rieckhoff brilliantly captures the American soldier's experience."

—Bobby Muller, chairman of the board for the
Vietnam Veterans of America Foundation

continued . . .

CONTENTS

To
the Soldiers of Third Platoon,
Bravo Company, 3/124th Infantry, 2003–4
and
the 44th President of the United States,
whoever that may be

Sector 17 Landmarks

1) Saddam Auditorium
   (B Co. (-), May 03)
2) Ministry of Labor
   (B Co., Jun. 03–Aug. 03)
3) Republican Guard Officer's
   Club (3rd BN, Aug. 03–Jan. 04)
4) Soccer Stadium
5) Turkish Embassy
6) Lebanese Embassy
7) Water Treatment Plant
8) Ministry of Defense
9) Medical City
10) Emergency Room
11) Saddam/Sadr City
12) Baghdad International
    Airport
13) Green Zone
14) Saddam's Wife's Palace
15) Abu Hanifa Mosque
16) Little Mogadishu
    (the elementary school)
17) Bridge—SPC Robert Wise
    killed by IED
18) Traffic Circle/Liberty
    Monument
19) Gunner Palace (HQ 2/3 FA)
20) The Ministry of Health

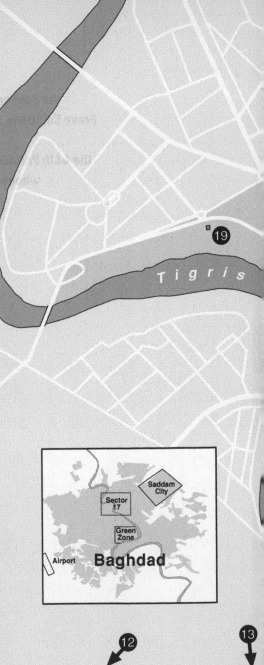

G. W. Ward

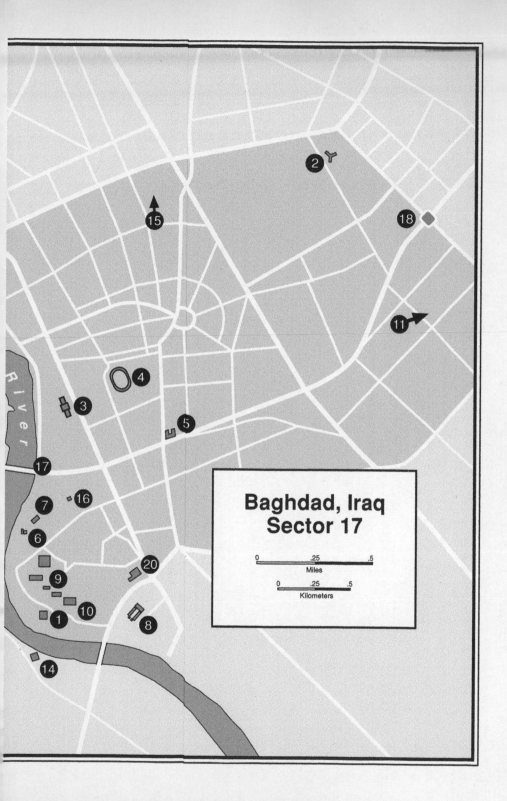

Baghdad, Iraq
Sector 17

0	.25	.5
Miles

0	.25	.5
Kilometers

River

CHAPTER ONE
GEORGE BUSH HAD BETTER BE FUCKING RIGHT

> If you don't like obscenity, you don't like the truth. If you
> don't like the truth, watch how you vote. Send guys to war,
> they come home talking dirty.
>
> —Tim O'Brien, *The Things They Carried*

George Bush had better be fucking right.

That's how I began my journal on April 3, 2003. Writing in pencil in an Army-issue notebook with mint green pages, leaning in on deliberate, hard letters, I underlined "better" and penciled over the words again and again until they wore through the tactically colored paper.

On March 19, just two weeks earlier, the United States had launched the first air strike of Operation Iraqi Freedom. Troops on the ground had invaded Iraq the next day. And now I was off to war for reasons that I feared were bullshit.

I reclined in the first-class section of a civilian 747 bound for Kuwait with an M16 wedged between my legs and my gut firmly stuffed with all the Krispy Kreme doughnuts I could scarf down in twenty minutes, courtesy of the old Red Cross ladies who had seen us off at Hunter Army Airfield, Fort Stewart, Georgia. It seemed a bad omen that the Red Cross was the last organization to see us off

1

to war: these are, after all, the people who send emergency notifications to deployed soldiers when something urgent happens back home—like when a sister is in a car accident or a grandmother dies. It was the soldiers' equivalent of a knock at the door.

Sitting in a cracked faux-leather seat with *In Flight* magazine's glossy pictures of Hawaii poking out of the seat pocket in front of me, I considered the absurdity of the situation.

"Gentlemen, please ensure your seat backs are in the upright position," an older woman's voice crackled over the PA system.

What? We were geared to the teeth with the essentials of combat: bullets, grenades, rifles, knives, rucksacks, scowls, Copenhagen chewing tobacco, cigarettes, hatred, the March 2003 edition of *Penthouse*, with Lilly Ann on the cover—the whole Army deal. I was cranked up and ready to run through hell, already bracing myself for incoming explosions, and going over indoctrinated checklists in my mind. And I had to worry about the seat back being upright?

I was going to war, with the greatest military force the world had ever seen, on a jet snagged from a recently bankrupted airline. I wondered if we'd get the little bag of peanuts.

I slid my CD headphones over my ears. I tried to shut out the endless cacophony of yelling, farting, gear rattling, spitting, and snoring with headphones streaming System of a Down, Linkin Park, and Jay-Z. The emotional oasis of a temporary musical vacation helped all of us forget we were constantly surrounded by thirty-eight other men.

Funny. These headphones were just like every piece of equipment issued to my Platoon: old and held together with nothing but hope and some twenty-mile-an-hour tape (green Army duct tape). I hoped these suckers wouldn't break before we got there. I needed my music to keep me sane—to buffer me from the men, if only for a song or two. Where the hell do you get new headphones in Iraq?

My men and I were National Guardsmen, attached to First

Brigade, Third Infantry Division, also known as 3ID.* We were shouldered with the task of taking over a foreign country, yet disallowed from smoking in the lavatories of the plane. Since the days of Troy, soldiers have pushed the limits of what little they are allowed to do—especially in pursuit of a vice. The Army has a saying: "Ask for forgiveness, not for permission." I was pretty sure that on this seventeen-hour flight one of the many chain-smokers in Third Platoon would test the FAA to see if it would really fine a soldier $1,000 for smoking a cigarette in a latrine on the way to die in Iraq.

I looked across the dimly lit aisle at one of my saw gunners. I'll call him "Gunner." Think of the most Johnny-All-American-Homecoming-King kid you ever met. With a white-blond flattop, blue eyes, perfect teeth, a chiseled jaw, and about 5 percent body fat, Gunner was straight out of a recruiting commercial. Perfect uniform, immaculate weapon, and always followed orders without being told twice. He didn't bitch, and maintained perfect military bearing.

Gunner was big on two things: God, and his beloved girlfriend. On the left side of his stomach, just above his kidney, was a meticulously scripted tattoo in flowing cursive letters: *Andrea*. He'd proposed to her just weeks before we left. He probably spent everything he had and then some to buy her the ring.

I thought of that tattoo as I glanced at him. It was buried beneath his BDU top now, but it stuck in my head. A lot of guys in the Army have tattoos around the same area—but a few inches

---

*A Division is made up of anywhere from ten thousand to eighteen thousand troops. It is subdivided into three Brigades, and each Brigade contains three or more Battalions, with five hundred to nine hundred soldiers in each. A Battalion is further subdivided into three to five Companies, and a Company is made up of three or four Platoons. Finally, a Platoon contains two to four Squads. Mine had four, each with a Squad Leader, who was a Staff Sergeant or NCO (Non-Commissioned Officer). We were Third Platoon, Bravo Company, Third Battalion, 124th Regiment, First Brigade, Third Infantry Division.

higher, and in a much different design. Soldiers call them meat tags. A meat tag is a copy of the Army dog tag you wear around your neck, tattooed on your torso, just below your armpit. A meat tag isn't just a hard-core status symbol. It's a way to identify your body if the torso is all that remains after you're blown apart. Name, Social Security number, and religious affiliation (if any). Call it thinking ahead. Prep for combat. Another safety measure, like an extra pair of socks.

As I scanned away from Gunner to the faces of my other men, time spun in slow motion. From the moment I got the call to go to Iraq, I felt like I was in a movie. Everything around me was a scene I was watching, rather than a moment I was living. When I walked with my men behind me, I felt like Mr. Blonde in *Reservoir Dogs*, wearing sunglasses, smoking cigarettes, walking toward the camera.

Sitting upright in my seat, I panned left to right across the cabin of the plane, taking in the pregame swell of fear, rage, anticipation, and urgency. I zoomed in on a foot tapping nervously inside a desert combat boot still wet with red Georgia clay. I cut to eyes darting, closed, or squeezed shut tightly. The maniacal screams of Korn's Jonathan Davis assaulted my head through half-broken headphones and amplified the emotional effect of the moment. My head bopped. Bass guitar thumped and drums pounded as I panned down to my lap, where my thumb tapped on the thick plastic buttstock of my rifle. "I'm feeling mean today . . . Not lost, not blown away. . . . Shut up! Shut up! Shut up! I'll fuck you up!"

Maybe I saw everything cinematically because I was part of a generation of soldiers who assumed war would be just like in the movies. Combat was etched in our heads as a series of slow-motion scenes featuring brave men firing guns and screaming triumphantly, with "Adagio for Strings" swirling around them. American combat classics like *Platoon*, *Full Metal Jacket*, *The Deer Hunter*, and *Saving Private Ryan*. Violent and inspiring underdog stories like *Glory*, *Gladiator*, and *Braveheart*. Movies with characters who fought the good fight. Movies with heroes.

I wanted to fight the good fight. I wanted to be a hero. When I was growing up in New York in the 1980s, most kids I knew dreamed of being Phil Simms or Don Mattingly. What I really wanted to be was a noble warrior who fought bravely for the good side. I wanted to be the ultimate American badass. I wanted to be Jed Eckert.

Played by a young Patrick Swayze, Jed Eckert was the lead character in the horribly fantastic modern American classic *Red Dawn*. If you've served in the military in the last twenty years, you've seen this movie. Jed, a former quarterback, drives a pickup truck and wears a baseball cap. He's an ordinary, straight-talking American kid until the morning the Soviets invade America and enemy paratroopers drop into his Midwestern town.

At the dawn of World War Three, Eckert leads his little brother Matt (Charlie Sheen) and a ragtag bunch of high school kids in a daring escape to the mountains, where they hide for the winter and survive by hunting deer and eating canned soup. After a covert mission back to town, they learn that their families have been killed or imprisoned in brutal work camps, and emerge from the hills with a vengeance. The film's tagline is *The invading armies planned for everything—except for eight kids called "The Wolverines."*

Jed and his band of guerrillas courageously take on the evil army of occupiers. They ride horses into battle against attack helicopters. With nothing left to lose, they rebel, inspiring others and giving birth to an insurgency that is emulated nationwide. They use creative unconventional tactics against a superior military force and incredible odds. And in the end, they win.

Red Dawn was entered into the *Guinness World Records* for having the most acts of violence of any film up to that time. When I was ten years old I thought it was the greatest thing I had ever seen. The first time I watched *Red Dawn*, I lay awake in my bed for hours. My thoughts raced. With total specificity, I laid out in my head how I would lead my little brother, our dog, Sugar, and the McGuiness boys if the Soviets ever made the fatal mistake of invading Peekskill and coming onto Arden Drive. We would be ready. Hiding in the big tree at the end of our block and on the roof of old Mrs. Hertz's house, we would set up ambushes and kill those bastards with rocks, BB guns, and M80s. The next day at school during recess, I ran around the playground carrying a stick like a rifle, climbing trees and screaming, *Wolverines!*

Now, with the roles reversed, I was on my way to invade and occupy someone else's country. America could soon create thousands of Iraqi Jed Eckerts in places like Mosul and Baghdad. We were going to kill Saddam and break his army. Dogs of war and all that shit. Ready to be unleashed. Grrrrrrrr. Warrior killers, steeled for death.

And served obediently by marginally attractive middle-aged stewardesses in cheap, ugly suits, with little tears welling in the corners of their overly made-up eyes. I could feel the other guys thinking the same thing I was every time the perfumed one with the long dark hair glided past my seat. We all harbored shamefully animalistic, testosterone-laden thoughts of taking her into one of the back bathrooms for a few minutes before we hit the ground. A sacrifice of purity for the gods of the Infantry. Or maybe just one last moment of fleeting happiness before I had my head removed by a sniper round or an RPG (Rocket Propelled Grenade).

When you get sent to war, you think about dying. What I worried about most was how my death would affect my family. Maybe a clinician will have a technical term for this condition in a few years. It could be called Modern American Soldiers' Guilt Syndrome. It's one of the burdens of the all-volunteer army that makes this generation of American soldiers different from those of generations past. We are not like many of our predecessors in Vietnam or World War Two, who were drafted. Their numbers came up and they put their lives on the line because they had to. We who went to Iraq *chose* to risk our lives doing this. We volunteered for this shit. And we volunteered our families for this shit.

The Army helps you plan for your death to some extent. And plants the seeds of the guilt syndrome. Right after you get your head shaved in Basic Training, you start filling out a series of mandatory forms. One of the first forms is the one that determines whether you want SGLI, and who gets it. SGLI is the Serviceman's Group Life Insurance Policy—the optional government-subsidized life insurance money your loved ones get if you take the big dirt nap. Your family gets the loot if you get fragged by a careless Private with bad aim on the grenade familiarization range. They get it if you fall off the obstacle course and land on your neck. Or if one of the psycho Drill Sergeants kills you in a fury during hand-to-hand combat training. Or if the civilian transport plane you're sitting in gets hit by a Scud missile on approach into Kuwait.

The Army recruiter told me so.

My recruiter was a slick, fat, middle-aged Italian-American Sergeant. He smelled like a dirty ashtray and called me "kid." Everyone in America knows that recruiters work like used-car salesmen. This guy actually looked like one. He was sweaty and beady-eyed, and wore a thin mustache that looked like it was drawn on with a Sharpie. Not exactly the face of the Army I had seen in the commercials that ran constantly on MTV.

In a moment that was easily one of my dad's worst nightmares, I had walked into a strip mall recruiting office during my senior year at Amherst College. Before the recruiter could put down the comics section and pull his fat ass from behind the tiny government-issue desk, I stood over him burning a hole in his face with my eyes.

"I am graduating from college in a few months," I told him flatly. "After I graduate, I want to be a soldier."

Sergeant Super Mario almost shat himself. This was 1998. A full three years before 9/11. College kids weren't exactly lining up to serve in defense of freedom. People didn't think much about patriotism, especially not in the liberal collegiate well-heeled part of Western Massachusetts where I went to college. But that's why I wanted to join. I loved my country. I had been afforded tremendous opportunities in this country and I wanted to give something back. In a democracy, the military should be representative of the population. Just because I didn't *have* to go didn't mean I *shouldn't* go. I felt that if, God forbid, my generation went to war and I didn't do my part, I would never be able to look at myself in the mirror or be a good father to my future children.

I also wanted to do the hardest thing I could do. I needed a trying experience that would test my mettle. I didn't exactly wish for war, but I wanted to travel to the apex of human experience: combat. It may sound sick, but war is the oldest, and ultimate, extreme sport.

I wanted to learn to be a leader in an environment where courage mattered. I didn't care what any Human Resources robot from Goldman Sachs tried to tell me, being a midlevel manager at an investment bank is not leadership. Bond traders telling rich people what to do with their money is not leadership. Neither is going to graduate school and pushing paper for a few years. Real leadership is motivating others under tremendous adversity. True leaders are forged by leading men in combat.

Everyone was telling me that because I went to Amherst, the sun shone out of my ass. Well, I wanted to go to a place where that sun didn't shine: either the Army or the Peace Corps. Both were demanding and intense. Both involved travel. Both were opportunities to better the world and participate in something larger than myself. Both offered shitty pay. The Peace Corps had women. But in the Army, you got to shoot guns, jump out of airplanes, and blow things up. No contest.

Clearly, Sergeant Super Mario did not know what the hell to do with me. A college kid had never walked into his office demanding to join the Army, and he was actually stupid enough to tell me so. His eyes darted around the room, like he was afraid he was on *Candid Camera*.

Every person I ever knew who had worn a uniform for the

United States had warned me about clowns like this. I was planning to defer a six-figure job on Wall Street to join the Army, and I was damn fucking sure I was not going to spend the next four years of my life peeling military potatoes in Alaska. Time lines, terms of commitment, uniforms, weapon systems, training—I wanted the details, statistics, legalese, and fine print for all of it.

After a few minutes of nervous paper shuffling, Mario recovered from his initial surprise. Like any soldier in a time of crisis, his training kicked in and he reverted to full fisherman mode. He had me on the line and focused on reeling me in. For every topic I raised, he and the Army recruiting machine were ready with materials, talking points, and a supercharged three-minute music video produced by Leo Burnett advertising. (Ironically, I had turned down a job offer from that firm only two months earlier.) America's tax dollars hard at work. The presentation was perfectly designed to target my precise demographic—middle/lower-class, MTV-watching, video-game–playing, Doritos-eating, action-hero wannabe.

Mario advertised a multitude of jobs for enlisted soldiers, each with its own terminology and signing bonus, determined by need (or lack thereof). He explained to me that in the Army, a job is called an MOS (Military Occupational Specialty). And each MOS has its own vocational follow-on school, sometimes at a different military base, with a unique curriculum called AIT (Advanced Individual Training). The school terms ranged in length from under a month to over a year.

Each MOS was assigned a different two-digit number and letter. A is Alpha, B is Bravo, C is Charlie, and so on. These fancy military-sounding names help mask the actual job specifications. So "21V/Twenty-one Victor/Concrete and Asphalt Equipment Operator" pushed a wheelbarrow; "92G/Ninety-two Golf/Food Service Operations" was a cook; "91R/Ninety-one Romeo/Veterinary Food Inspection Specialist"—the Dogfood Dude.

The multimedia assault and crafty acronyms even made playing the tuba in the Army band seem cool.

"And check this out, kid. Follow-on school for band is only two weeks long!" Mario proudly told me.

I was already in the door and it was his job to close the deal. But I saw through the pitch. I didn't want to join the Army to play the xylophone.

Mario was relentless. As soon as a question fell out of my mouth, he conjured the corresponding pamphlet out of thin air. Every one featured another multiethnic mix of Kool-Aid-smile-wearing soldiers.

And when I asked whether my little nephew would be paid in full if I were smashed to bits when my Oldsmobile stalled on the tracks and was hit by a Metro-North train full of suits headed to Manhattan, he smiled broadly and said, "No problem, kid! Happens all the time! It's covered."

So I left my SGLI $250K to my three-year-old nephew, Sean. I figured he would be able to pay for college if I died in some violent and unfortunate manner. One generation of my family would grow up with *some* kind of financial security.

As I sat restlessly on that plane to Iraq gnawing on a wad of Levi Garrett chewing tobacco, for the life of me I couldn't remember to whom I had designated the sorry task of the death notification. I wasn't sure who I had actually, *formally*, designated as my next of kin. I had been in the Army four years at that point. In those four years, I had changed my address three times at least. I'd signed up in September 1998. In January 1999, I arrived at Fort McClellan, Alabama, for Basic Training. Seven months later I was back in New York City, an Army Reservist. That fall I took a job on Wall Street. I knew jackshit about high finance, but my mom faced some big medical expenses and I wanted to help out. I figured that in the intense atmosphere of Wall Street I could make fast money and learn a ton about business. I only planned to stay on Wall Street for a few years, then go to grad school. I switched from the Reserves to the National Guard. In 2000, I went to Officer Candidate School (OCS), spent some time at Fort Benning, Georgia, got my commission, and chose Infantry as my branch. I also got fed up with Wall Street and quit. I spent six months back at Fort Benning, completing the Infantry Officers Basic Course (IOBC), and when I saw the war looming, I wanted in. I volunteered for active duty and the invasion of Iraq.

Before I was called up for the war, I was crashing with my girlfriend in Brooklyn, but I didn't get mail there. I had a post office box back home in Peekskill because I moved around so much. So Lord only knows which one of my "homes of record" the Army had listed in its jacked-up "notify if killed" files.

I wondered which of my parents they'd reach out to first. By 2003, my parents had been divorced for over ten years. It was a messy divorce; they fought over everything. But in all the fights between them, over custody and property, I was pretty sure they never discussed who got dibs on my death notice.

I hoped it was my dad. He was the more stable of the two. And he had been drafted for Vietnam. True, he'd been really pissed when I told him I'd enlisted, and even more pissed when I told him I'd volunteered for combat. A foreman for Con Edison, he'd always hoped my brother and I could avoid going into the service. After all, I was the first in our family to go to college. And not just any college, but one of the "Little Ivies." I worked the whole time to help pay for it, as a bouncer at local bars, working security—jobs that suited a six-feet-two, 240-pound football player. And then, in my dad's eyes, I went and jeopardized my college payoff by joining the military. "I just don't understand why you want to turn down a great job on Wall Street, and all that money, to roll around in the mud with a bunch of rednecks down south."

As mad at me as he was, my dad would be devastated to get my death notice. But he would multitask like a motherfucker letting the family know. That would be his way of coping. My grandmother (his mom) was one of eleven children in a huge Italian family from the Bronx, so I had a dozen aunts and uncles and throngs of cousins named Vinnie and Marie who would need to be notified.

But there was no guarantee that the Army would call my dad. It was entirely likely they would call my mother first. And that would not be pretty. My mother has never exactly been a pillar of emotional stability. When I left for the war, she sobbed inconsolably for days, and sold her TV to a pawnshop because she couldn't bear to hear the news coming out of Iraq. I thought about how she would react in the moment she saw the two fabled Army men, uniformed impeccably, in her doorway. My stomach curled into knots just thinking about it. Would she be alone? Would she faint? Would she attack the poor officers delivering the news? Who would she call first? My brother? My dad? Her psychiatrist?

Maybe if I died the Army would totally fuck up and call my eighty-six-year-old grandmother. She lived alone and could barely even walk. I could already see it unfolding in my head.

"Stop ya bangin'! Stop ya bangin'!" she would holler from behind the triple-locked steel door. "Hold ya horses! I gotta get my walka! I don't get around so good at my age. Hang on . . . . I'm comin'!"

My grandmother *has* always been a rock of stability. She kept the coolest head of anyone through my predeployment. When I told her I was going to Iraq, I expected her to be a wreck. But she was very matter-of-fact.

"Okay," she told me in her scratchy New Yawk old-lady accent. "I figured dat was comin' soona or lata. Ya know, honey, I've been t'rough dis before."

Twice.

World War Two: Her husband, my grandfather, was not planning on leaving his block in the Bronx. When he was thirty-two, everyone thought he was too old to be drafted. Of course, he was the first one. Perfect Army-dictated irony. But that wasn't the best part. My grandfather had emigrated from Germany at age seventeen, and spoke German. It would make too much sense to send someone who spoke German to help fight the Germans. No, the Army sent him to the other side of the world, where his background would be totally useless. He ended up in the Philippines, New Guinea, Guam. Drafted three years after getting married, he spent three years away from my grandmother. He called it his "all-expenses-paid world tour." He sent my grandmother rent money from his poker winnings, and ashtrays he made out of artillery shell casings.

Grandma's second helping of war came during Vietnam. This time it was her son, my dad, who got the call. They hoped and prayed his lottery number wouldn't come up. My grandfather told him, "If you get an envelope from the government with a subway token in it, you're going to Vietnam, Paulie."

In 1965 that one-way fare arrived, and my dad was out of the Bronx and off to Uncle Sam's School for Boys. Unlike my grandfather, he didn't speak German, but was sent to Germany anyway. He didn't see combat, but he did his time in uniform. He paid his citizenship dues.

After two wars, I guess my grandma was used to this routine. My little tour of the Middle East should be no problem. We weren't a rich family, so my service seemed like a part of the contract. For generations, the deal was this: If you were American and working-class, you served in the military.

And after all, this war was going to be short and easy. Just like the Gulf War in '91. All we had to do was take out Saddam and his regime would crumble like a house of cards. Vice President Dick Cheney said we'd "be greeted as liberators." I'd be home by summer. That's what they told me. But I knew the Army didn't know how long we'd be gone. The Army did to us the same thing we did to our families. They gave us a date so we'd stop asking.

I told my girlfriend to prepare for three to nine months, but I had no idea. I just wanted to give her a date to look forward to. I couldn't tell her that we could be gone for two years. I just couldn't put that in her head. It didn't seem fair.

I worried enough about counterattacks on New York City. I expected our enemies to try something, and I told my girlfriend to avoid the subway if she could for the next few weeks. This was truly a global war now, and my friends in Manhattan might be in more danger than I would be in the Middle East.

A few hours into our flight, Sergeant Thomas stood in the back of the plane and addressed the men. Sergeant Thomas was a real character. He had red hair, freckles, and a deep Southern drawl like Foghorn Leghorn. He was my second in command, my Platoon Sergeant.

"Men!" he boomed. "Get used to bein' gone! Get used to this shit. We gonna be gone a long-ass time. We already dealt with Afghaneestan. Now we goin' to Eye-raq to take care of this mothafucker! After that, we goin' to Sy-reea! Then we goin' to Ko-reea! The president ain't fuckin' around, men. Now that we got started, we gonna be kickin' everybody's ass from now on!"

Sergeant Thomas was almost always full of shit. But I knew that what he'd said could happen. We all knew that once we got to Baghdad, the order could come down from the Pentagon to make a big left turn and keep on going all the way to Damascus. Or a big right turn to Tehran. Our president was arrogant and single-minded, and that made anything possible.

I never thought America would make this mistake again. The Iraq war sounded too much like the Vietnam War. It had all the same flaws at its foundation: an unclear rationale, a guerrilla enemy that was virtually indistinguishable from civilians, a culture we didn't understand at all, and tenuous public support. Millions of people all over the world were already protesting the two-week-old war. In his book *The Long Gray Line*, Rick Atkinson describes how, after Vietnam, Ross Perot once proposed building a war memorial that could be seen from the White House and that bore this inscription: FIRST COMMIT THE NATION, THEN COMMIT THE TROOPS. That seemed particulary pertinent in 2003.

I really could not believe this was happening: American Infantrymen on a plane to a foreign land to execute the will of our president, and supposedly the will of our people. I guess I was out of touch with "the people," because a lot of people I knew were not gung-ho about this war—especially people with family members going to fight. If the president was going to take America to war, I thought he should have more of the public behind it.

Using the 9/11 attacks as a justification for this war just didn't hold water in my opinion. The president had failed to prove to me that the Iraqis were in any way connected to the attacks on the World Trade Center. Yet he continued to use the emotional power of 9/11 to gain support for his controversial war—and tons of guys bought the rationale. More times than I can count, soldiers in the Battalion would say something like, "Hey, L.T." (short for for Lieutenant). "Maybe they sent you down here from New York to get some payback for your city. Maybe they sent you with us so that you can be up front when we take out Baghdad. They'll roll you and the other New York guys in just in time for the pictures. It would make a great front page for the papers!"

The men had lots of conspiracy theories about why I was the only guy from New York in Bravo Company. A Yankee officer in a Florida National Guard unit made up almost entirely of deep-fried Southerners, with a very light sprinkling of African-Americans, Hispanics, and a few other ethnicities. There were only four New Yorkers in the whole Battalion. The best theory went like this: When the decision was made to send National Guard units into combat for the first time since the Korean War, the spin doctors in D.C. thought the glory of toppling Baghdad should go to Guardsmen from Florida, where President Bush's brother Jeb happened to be the governor. Having some guys along from the 9/11 state was a publicity bonus. I had volunteered for combat, making it a no-brainer.

One thing I knew for certain: the White House was pretty damn good at creating photo opportunities to galvanize public support for military endeavors. I remember when the president came in for his first big one at Ground Zero, three days after the attack. I was there. I had quit my job on Wall Street on September 7, 2001. For days, I worked in "the pit" alongside everyday New Yorkers trying to save their own. I worked with three firemen, a Port Authority cop, and a guy who looked like a steelworker. We were all covered in a coat of fine powder that a few guys called "the dust." A combination of incinerated drywall, soot, and the dead, the dust blanketed everything in sight and covered the streets six inches deep like fine gray doomsday snow. I never in my life have seen human dedication like I did during those days. Amidst the unimaginable horror, the way strangers worked together was a thing of beauty. I witnessed Americans exhibiting a pure and selfless human devotion to help their fellow man. I was surrounded by ordinary people under extraordinary circumstances who emerged as heroes.

And we all wanted payback. But we had to be sure we were counterattacking the right country.

But Colin Powell was on board. And his opinion held serious weight with me. He made the case for war before the United Nations and the world. He told us that Saddam had dangerous and extensive chemical weapons capabilities. I trusted him more than any other public figure in politics. Our president may have been a draft dodger, but Powell was a guy who walked the walk. He was a Vietnam combat veteran. I read his autobiography cover to cover at least twice. Powell showed me that being a soldier was a noble and honorable thing. His story taught me to have enormous respect for the profession of arms, and to care for my men. I wished he was our president, and deemed him one of the most impressive American patriots alive. He knew the tremendous human cost of war. If he was on board with the plan, it must be sound.

Powell once said, "We must not . . . send military forces into a crisis with an unclear mission they cannot accomplish—such as we did when we sent the U.S. Marines into Lebanon in 1983. We inserted those proud warriors into the middle of a five-faction civil war complete with terrorists, hostage-takers, and a dozen spies in every camp, and said, 'Gentlemen, be a buffer.' The results were 241 Marines and Navy personnel killed and a U.S. withdrawal from the troubled area."

American soldiers were not designed to be buffers. I held on to the faith that Powell would never push America into another war that didn't adhere to this standard. As the chairman of the Joint Chiefs of Staff after the 1991 Gulf War, Powell outlined his requirements for decisive military action, later popularly referred to as the "Powell Doctrine." Essentially, the doctrine expresses that military action should only be used as a last resort, and only if there is a clear risk to America's national security and only if there is a clearly attainable objective. When force is used, it should be overwhelming and disproportionate to the amount of force used by the enemy; there must be strong public support for the action; and there must be a clear exit strategy from the conflict.

America had a moral obligation to use its tremendous military power to help the helpless. And Powell got that. He gave me reason to think that Saddam might actually have WMD.

Beyond the threat of his WMD capabilities, Saddam had proven to be an evil and oppressive monster. He and his sons brutalized an entire nation into submission. The world knew of Saddam's atrocities. He had gassed his own people. Taking him out and freeing the Iraqi people were the only parts of the war that I saw as fighting the good fight. And all American soldiers want to fight the good fight. Every one of us on that plane wanted to be the soldier who avenged millions by firing the fateful 5.56 round that would make Saddam's head burst like a watermelon. He definitely had it coming.

Bush said killing Saddam was not the primary reason he was

sending us. He was sending us to find weapons that were threatening America.

I prayed that Bush was right about Saddam's WMD. He had abandoned diplomacy and essentially told the world to fuck off. I wanted weapons of mass destruction to exist in Iraq, because if they didn't, there would be hell to pay for us all. America's reputation would be irreparably damaged for generations. If Bush was wrong, thousands of American troops would die for a mistake, and the Iraq war would be one of the greatest foreign policy disasters in our nation's history. The decision to invade Iraq was the mother of all poker games. Bush was betting the house on this one hand. "He must have the cards to back it up," I wrote.

So my entire role in the war was a paradox: against the war from the beginning, I volunteered to go fight in it. I feared that President Bush's decision to invade Iraq was not in the best interest of our country, but I desperately wanted be a part of that invasion. I was torn in half, wrestling with my hunger for combat and my distrust for the president. But I would not let doubt drive me to sit on the sidelines for the biggest game of my generation. On the contrary, I volunteered to be one of the first to fight. This war was happening whether I liked it or not. Protesting the war in Washington or New York wouldn't stop it from happening now.

America was angry. And America was scared. Little old ladies in Kansas worried that Saddam would reach out and blow up their Bingo games on Friday nights. When people are angry and scared they sometimes make rash decisions—especially when they don't fully fathom the consequences. I just wanted everyone in America to step back and think about it all a little harder. Once you fire that round out of the chamber, you can't take it back. Senator John McCain once said, "War is wretched beyond description, and only a fool or a fraud could sentimentalize its cruel reality." I just didn't understand the rush to take on that cruel reality, and I thought we needed more debate.

I printed out some things to take with me to Iraq. One was a speech made by Senator Robert Byrd on the floor of the Senate in February 2003. Senator Byrd expressed concern about the lack of debate and the rush to war:

> To contemplate war is to think about the most horrible of human experiences. On this February day, as this Nation stands at the brink of battle, every American on some level must be contemplating the horrors of war.
>
> My wife says to me at night: Do you think we ought to get some of those large bottles, the large jugs, and fill them with water? She says: Go up to the attic and see if we don't have two or three there. I believe we have two or three there.
>
> And so I went up to the attic last evening and came back to report to her that, no, we didn't have any large jugs of water, but we had some small ones, perhaps some gallon jugs filled with water. And she talked about buying up a few things, groceries and canned goods to put away.
>
> I would suspect that kind of conversation is going on in many towns across this great, broad land of ours. And yet this Chamber is for the most part ominously, dreadfully silent. You can hear a pin drop. Listen. You can hear a pin drop. There is no debate. There is no discussion. There is no attempt to lay out for the Nation the pros and cons of this particular war. There is nothing.

But if you say something enough times, people begin to believe it's true. Saddam had WMDs and America was going to take him out. The decision was made, the war machine was rolling, and I was a part of it. I remembered a quote that hung on the wall of my high school classroom: "No one made a greater mistake than he who did nothing because he could only do little." By volunteering to command a Platoon on the ground, I could at least have an impact on how things turned out. I didn't have a crystal ball, but I knew that there would be a time when the combat would settle down, and my Platoon could help people. That was my mission: to ensure that my thirty-eight men made a difference, served as a positive reflection of America, and came home alive. It would be great if we could kill Saddam in the process.

So my men and I were on a plane to kill another country's sons and fathers where they lived. In their own houses. Most of the men had never been out of the United States. Most of them had never even been out of the South.

Overhead, lights dimmed as we slid downward into milky dust and landed in the Kuwaiti kingdom.

Nobody was shooting at us yet, but we all felt a rush of adrenaline. After months of waiting, we were in the desert. "The Sandbox." In the excitement, a few cheers and some nervous conversations broke the silence. Of course Fat Stew, the resident smart-ass, piped up. He was like Jimmy Kimmel with a Southern drawl thick as gravy. Always reliable for timely sarcasm, he called from coach, "Are we there yet?"

Outside, in the darkness, a stairway rolled up to the fuselage with a bang. Footsteps clanged up to the hatch; a waft of hot air and a beefy black NCO rushed inside.

"All you motherfuckers shut the fuck up!" he shouted. The plane fell silent. Our CO was clearly not going to interrupt this dude, and neither was anybody else. Regardless of rank, he was in charge.

"When you get off this plane, you lock and load and move double-time directly to the trucks that are waiting outside. No flashlights. No cigarettes. No bullshit. Keep your pro mask with you. There could still be Scuds coming in. Any questions?"

Silence.

"Okay, then. Welcome to the fuckin' war!"

CHAPTER TWO
HURRY UP AND KUWAIT

How much of human life is lost in waiting.
—Ralph Waldo Emerson

We landed in Kuwait expecting it to be a quick stay, like stopping in a gas station to fill the tank and take a last piss on our way to the real action. Instead, it was more like our car had broken down in Bumfuck, and Cooter the gas station guy was telling us it'd take a week to get a new fan belt. After three months of rushed and intense training, we got to the desert cranked up and ready to shoot some bad guys, but our orders were to sit and wait for further orders. Hurry up and wait, the oldest saying in the Army. We had come down with a bad case of combat blue balls.

In the desert of Kuwait, I quickly learned that war is often tedium.

I wrote a letter to my girlfriend on the back of a piece of cardboard from an MRE (Meals Ready to Eat) box:

Dear Bama,

Today we are in a new camp called Camp Spearhead. It is a huge motor-pool-type compound sandwiched between a festering ship port and a looming, disgustingly sparkling oil refinery. The British have nicknamed it "Camp Cancer" due to all the chemicals that are saturating the air around us. Dozens and dozens of tanks, Bradleys, fuel trucks, ambulances, all shifting and shuffling on a putrid swath of desert. 110 degrees today. The winds swirl and sway the desert dust into a burning dance of skin and eye irritants. The sun is setting behind 200-foot-high smokestacks with billowing flames on top. They look like huge tiki torches. God, what we do to this planet disgusts me—I'm glad you can't see this place.

We have good chow here—actually ate lobster tail and shrimp last night. They get good seafood from the nearby port, I assume. Fattening us up for the slaughter maybe. We move with a large convoy of 20 vehicles or so north tonight. We'll drive north for about 3 hrs to Camp Virginia near the Iraqi border.

My guys are basically bodyguards for some really expensive missile systems that may or may not actually work—the Patriots. We guard the flanks, rear end, front of the convoy with my thirty-eight grunts and me. This place looks like some kind of post-nuclear wasteland from a Mad Max movie.

When I woke up this morning at about four, we were covered and caked with a layer (or five) of this super-fine desert dust. It plays hell on our weapons. My boys are still in good spirits—eager to push forward. The bullets are real now. My boys seem to be more focused than before—which pleases me. We are the only Infantry unit around here—and walk like it. We are like wolves among the sheep. They are timid around us—we lurk, growl, scratch and snort—like only grunts do. Please understand that I am OK. This is where I need to be— but you already understand that. Hope you are finding beauty every day—I will promise you that I'll do the same here.

Love, Paul

I loved the hell out of my girlfriend. Her name was Laura Thomas, but everyone called her "Bama"—short for Alabama.

We'd met only six months before I left, in a sketchy dive bar on the Lower East Side. I had just gotten back to the city after six months of training in Fort Benning, Georgia. A round of whiskey shots and two Heinekens into the night, I noticed a girl leaning forward from a dark stage like she was on a rope. She sang and played an acoustic guitar that looked almost as big as she was. Between songs she yelled aggressively over the half-listening, half-drunk crowd, with a glass of white wine in her hand like a prettier Janis Joplin. I was instantly devastated by her voice, her power, and her presence. She had a beautiful, distinctive sound like a jazzy Ani DiFranco and the body of Jessica Simpson. And attitude for miles. She drew me in like I was trapped in a tractor beam.

Six months later, we were living together in a tiny apartment across the street from a gas station in a shitty area of Brooklyn where most of the residents didn't speak English. As I left for the war, I gave Bama power of attorney over all my affairs. I missed the hell out of her and knew that staying connected with her any way I could was going to keep me sane.

We passed time in Kuwait City with our backs against our bulging rucks, reading books, telling stories, waiting for orders, and sleeping. Sleeping around Infantry guys can be a tricky business. Even if you're tired, you keep your eyes open to watch for the can of shaving cream or the bug in a jar. Tricks befall the guy who's unlucky or careless enough to be the first to close his eyes.

A few days after landing in Kuwait City, we finally left Camp Cancer and pushed north to an area where the coalition had built a constellation of large, remote desert bases just south of the Iraqi border. We drove through a vast expanse of flat, featureless desert, past dusty little towns and villages of what looked like adobe. Bedouins standing by the road and staring with blank faces. Some in scruffy Western-style shirts and pants, others in the ankle-length shirt-robe the guys had taken to calling a "man-dress." They often had a few camels or sheep or goats, and they always had a dirty cigarette in one hand. Sometimes, bizarrely, men in dusty business suits would appear, walking by the road out in the middle of nowhere. Probably the foreign workers the Army calls TCNs (Third Country Nationals), employees of the numerous corporate contractors who drill Kuwait's oil, build its cities and airports, and so on.

Eventually the convoy turned off the main highway onto a system of long dirt "roads" snaking through flat emptiness past makeshift airports and vast graveyards for Iraqi military hardware—tanks, armored personnel carriers, and artillery pieces confiscated or destroyed during the Gulf War. Spines of twisted metal and artillery barrels poked the sky like giant porcupine quills.

A wooden sign greeted us at the formidable sandbagged gate of Camp Virginia: WELCOME TO THE SUCK. Thanks for the heads-up.

A vast network of long dusty tents stretched to the horizon, with Humvees, troops, and helicopters bustling among them like ants in an ant farm. An immense tent city, with a huge berm around it for protection and guard towers every five hundred meters or so. The wind whirled up a dusty grayish-brown haze that obscured the sun like a smog cover. Black Hawks slid in and out of the gloom. It was impossible to tell where the earth ended and the sky began. Thin lines of soldiers wearing Army-issue black PT (physical training) shorts and gray PT shirts ran in circles, made clumsy by the M16s or M4s they carried and the green pro masks (gas masks) strapped around their waists like oversized fanny packs. Doing PT with the mask was necessary, but relentlessly annoying.

I stepped out of the Humvee and dropped a sweaty boot onto the packed desert floor. I was surprised at how hard the desert was. I had always envisioned it being much softer, like the sand at Jones Beach. This was solid as the blacktop in Brooklyn, veiled with a thin layer of constantly shifting dust.

Uniforms, colors, and accents collided as units and vehicles from all over the world mashed tensely together. Marines slick in their newly introduced digital camouflage uniforms, Air Force Pararescue Jumpers with gee-whiz gear clipped to their chests, Kentucky National Guardsmen with woodland green BDUs (Battle Dress Uniforms), and British soldiers lounging in front of their tents in shorts and sunglasses, tanning like lifeguards.

The Commander and mortar section had arrived ahead of us the night before. I searched for them and our assigned tent, feeling like I had ventured into another world. The alien terrain, the strange characters, the different accents—I was like Obi-Wan Kenobi looking for Han Solo on Tatooine.

I had imagined war in Iraq would be hell, but I never realized Kuwait would be purgatory. Our days overflowed with extreme boredom and drudgery as they stretched on into a week, two weeks, three. I remembered the painful vigil of waiting described in *Jarhead*, Anthony Swofford's classic Gulf War memoir. We passed the excruciating hours with similarly reckless football games, idiotic formations, and endless conversations about girls back home. For guys primed to step across the line and go to war, the wait was maddening.

We lived in long tan tents, each half the size of a basketball court, that rested on wooden-slatted pallets. As the sweltering sun climbed the blank sky, the heat inside those tents rose like the inside of a Jiffy Pop wrapper. In the Army, and especially in the Infantry, you maximize space at all times. Every man had been limited to three bags when he left the States. Two he carried, and one followed somewhere behind in the mysterious chasm of the supply trains. In the tent, men stacked themselves next to each other like used cars in a lot, with only two feet between each cot. Sergeant Thomas screamed at his NCOs, ordering them to ensure that everything was "dress-right-dress," Army-speak for lined up and organized in a method that projected total uniformity. "I will not have our area lookin' like a doggone refugee camp!" he shrieked as every newly arrived Squad Leader led his men into the tent.

We placed bulging rucksacks at the foot of our cots, and crammed our Army-issue duffel bags, called "A-bags," underneath. Weapons were kept in hand or on the rack, next to slimy spit bottles. Each soldier slept facing the feet of the man next to him, to decrease the chances of spreading sickness and disease. The health benefits were compromised by the annoyance of smelling a buddy's unwashed feet every night. Tent-city life demands a level of intimacy only soldiers and prison inmates can truly appreciate.

After a few days, the desert started wreaking havoc on our bodies, and on our minds. Sergeant Gipson, Third Squad Leader, came down with some kind of stomach virus that left him puking uncontrollably and nearly paralyzed with a dangerous 102-degree fever. One of my Specialists was with the medics for two days with a case of jock itch gone wild, both legs covered with sores and pus. At least he provided the boys with something new to talk about besides whether NASCAR driver Jeff Gordon was gay. The guy always had some kind of physical problem, real or imagined. He was consistently irresponsible and probably hadn't washed his ass since we left the United States. Maybe he actually thought this affliction would be bad enough to send him home. Well, there was no way in hell that was going to happen. Oh, the challenges of leadership. The Platoon leaders in the war movies certainly didn't have to contend with this type of management challenge. Let the real suck begin.

We fought a losing battle with the sand. We only showered about once every five days, and the second I got clean, I was covered in a layer of sand particles again. It formed a film that looked like spray-on tan. A sandstorm rolled through one night and toppled five tents. Soldiers scrambled in the dark, desperately trying to keep the tent posts from snapping.

"Sand is so deep in my ears that I'll be shitting out sand from this place for years," a soldier shouted.

We were now seven thousand miles closer to the war, and only miles from the border, but the Army had yet to decide what to do with us. The original plan had called for Bravo Company to invade from Turkey in the north, but the Turkish government abruptly decided not to let coalition forces use its soil as a jumping-off point, which threw a monkey wrench into the whole invasion plan. Our vehicles were still heading in that direction on a ship somewhere in the Mediterranean Sea. Not that we needed them yet. While the Marines and the rest of 3ID rolled northward, we sat and waited. The 101st seized Saddam International Airport, 3ID entered Baghdad, Saddam vanished . . . and we waited some more. Instead of Kuwait, the guys started calling it "You-wait . . . and wait. And wait."

We spent the bulk of our days sitting on MRE boxes playing spades, reading, watching DVDs, talking shit, and consuming mountains of cigarettes and chew. Ammunition, weapons-cleaning kits, water—they were all important. But at the top of this list of combat necessities was always tobacco.

For generations, no single product has been more critical to the morale of the American serviceman. In today's Army, the vice of choice comes in two main forms: with smoke and without. Of those that burn, Marlboro, Marlboro Light, and Camel are the most popular brands. Field and Flag-Grade officers are infamous for chomping fat, dubiously acquired Cuban cigars. And once in a blue moon, I saw a Swisher Sweet—the truck-stop and mini-mart favorite, plastic-filter-tipped cigar choice of rednecks everywhere.

And then there's smokeless tobacco, popularly known as chewing tobacco, chew, dip. Chewing tobacco is good for a soldier. It keeps him awake, passes the time, and gives him that wonderful nicotine buzz without the nasty tactical downside of cigarettes: every good Infantry soldier knows that sniper hits are more often in the jaw area than any other part of the body. An enemy shooter can spot the lit cherry red tip of a cigarette from a hundred yards away. Don't think you'll see a warning about that on a pack anytime soon.

The only thing that got our pulse up in Kuwait was losing three guys in a convoy. They were not dead—we literally lost them. We didn't find them until the next morning; this is exactly how some American POWs had gotten captured back in Bosnia. The guys we lost were driving a Humvee filled with top secret electronic hardware for the Patriot missile systems when it broke down on the side of the road. Twenty million dollars of electronics almost lost because they didn't have a twenty-five-cent hose for a Humvee engine. Like many of our broken-down vehicles, this one was older than the soldier driving it. Lack of supplies and equipment posed serious problems. It started to look like the swift invasion was outpacing the Pentagon's original plans.

The broken-down Humvee incident highlighted bureaucratic stupidity, and the type of shit that happens when a war is done on the cheap. A year and a half later (December 8, 2004), at a press conference in Kuwait, Secretary of Defense Donald Rumsfeld was confronted by a brave young soldier who complained of his unit having to rummage in scrap heaps and garbage piles to properly armor his Humvee. Rumsfeld famously said, "As you know, you go to war with the Army you have. They're not the Army you might want or wish to have at a later time." He then made the incredible statement, "If you think about it, you can have all the armor in the world on a tank and a tank can be blown up. And you can have an up-armored Humvee and it can be blown up." Then he climbed into an armored vehicle and was whisked away. Writing a week later in the *Washington Post*, the conservative pundit William Kristol blasted Rumsfeld for his casual arrogance, declaring that America's combat soldiers "deserve a better defense secretary than the one we have."

In the National Guard, the Army we had was broken, underfunded, and had been neglected for decades. The Army we had was never readied for the war. That should have been expected, since for years Congress had spent money on JDAM (Joint Direct

Attack Munition) missiles instead of Humvee cooling hoses. Awarding government contracts to the lowest bidder is like under-paying your babysitter. Many of the problems we faced seemed so avoidable. I realized that we were in for a very long war.

In the oppressive heat of Kuwait, rumors were the only thing that moved quickly. Forget the Middle Eastern oil—we could have run our country on the power of the rumor machine alone.

One night I went to sleep after making the rounds and check-ing on my guys on guard duty. I awoke to the frantic, sweaty face of Specialist Marvin Rydberg, near hysterical.

"Wake up, L.T.! You are not going to believe this shit!"

I sprang to my feet and grabbed my boots and weapon, ready for action, listening for Scud alarms and incoming mortars.

"What is it, Rydberg? What's wrong?"

Rydberg was my RTO (Radio Telephone Operator). He was my consigliere. A tall former high school basketball star from Ken-tucky who had been on active duty in the Marines for four years, Rydberg was another of the Platoon jokers, like Fat Stew, and also among the smartest soldiers in the Company. He got shit from the guys for a lot of reasons, but mostly because his job required him to carry the Platoon's SINCGAR (Single Channel Ground and Air-borne Radio System) radio and follow me around constantly. The RTO is often referred to as the PL's bitch. The job was a cross be-tween bodyguard and secretary. I was a young Platoon Leader, and there were few things that could make my job easier than a good RTO. And Rydberg was the best I could have hoped for.

"You're not gonna believe this shit, L.T.! Ben Affleck and Jen-nifer Lopez were in a car accident in Miami yesterday!"

"What?" My shoulders slumped and I fell back onto my sweaty cot.

"Terrible crash! J.Lo was killed and Ben was paralyzed!"

Everyone was flabbergasted. The story must have been passed

to thousands of soldiers before noon. I couldn't believe it. This was without a doubt the most devastating news we had gotten—the biggest loss of the war so far.

Everywhere we went, for days, it was:

"Man! Did you hear about J.Lo?"

"Yeah, man! It's true! Some MPs just confirmed they heard it over the radio. For real!"

"Really, L.T.! I was on guard duty and an Air Force pogue coming through the gate confirmed it!" (A pogue is any soldier who is a non-combat MOS or branch.) "They were in an accident on the 405 in L.A.! The Air Force pogue says the shit was all over CNN!"

Damn.

That really sucked. I liked watching J.Lo shake her ass on TV. Third Platoon was seriously depressed. I thought I might have to order a bereavement period for these guys. The idea of J.Lo's ass being gone was killing them—especially Hernandez. "Hernando" was a nineteen-year-old Latino kid who ran a car-stereo business back home. He had a forty-five-minute argument with Fat Stew about whether J.Lo's death would be a greater loss to the Latino community or to thousands of American white guys who don't know the name of another Latina.

The First Sergeant (aka "Top") called the entire Company to a formation and started chewing ass, screaming so hard he lifted himself onto his toes.

"I have had it, goddamn it! Stop the rumors. No more damn rumors! Do not believe any rumors that you hear. They only breed discontent. No more goddamn rumors."

The tirade continued for a good fifteen minutes as the men stood in formation at parade rest. Exhausted, the First Sergeant asked if there were any questions.

A notoriously wise-assed Sergeant in Second Platoon raised his hand. "Hey, First Sergeant, is J.Lo really dead?"

First Sergeant went ballistic.

"No, goddamn it! J.Lo is not dead! This shit is what I'm talking about. This is how bullshit starts! J.Lo is not dead!"

In the back of the formation, Rydberg whispered, "I didn't realize Top was such a big J.Lo fan."

The J.Lo rumor spread all over the country, until some Colonel who'd found his way to a satellite phone debunked it. Leaders actually announced the good news at formations to keep up morale.

It's tough to stay motivated and keep a positive attitude in the face of frustration, but the prospect of combat kept us eager. Speculation about the next mission was always the number-one topic of conversation. For soldiers, bullshitting is an art form. But like most arts, not everyone appreciates its value. Long, hot days spent in cluttered, smelly tents can fry nerves until the mere voice of another person is like fingernails on a chalkboard. Before long, I was deadly tired of it all. I was ready to move.

I once heard that on a first date, the two topics of conversation that should always be avoided are politics and religion. The same should be said about conversations among soldiers entering a controversial war. But I let them debate. I thought it was healthy and important that my men think a bit about why we were where we were. Despite their impact on my blood pressure, I stayed out of the debates as much as possible by pretending to listen to music or sleep.

Every soldier was a barracks politician to some extent, talking shit about pop culture, music, geopolitics, religion, and the world. Subjects for discussion ran the gamut, from "What breed of dog was Scooby-Doo?" to "Who is the most fuckable chick on *Gilligan's Island*?" to "Would Jesus approve of the Iraq invasion?" Arguments ranged from enlightening to frightening. They sometimes ended in blows. As a political science major fascinated by politics, I always found Third Platoon's debates to be extremely entertaining.

One night there was a heated argument over whether each member of Third Platoon was a superhero or a sidekick. Some were definite sidekicks; some were absolutely superheroes; some were heavily contested. The men had decided I was a superhero with two primary sidekicks. The first was obviously Rydberg, my RTO. Sergeant Thomas was the other.

The dynamics of an Infantry Platoon are a lot like those in a fraternity house. Everyone in our Platoon was given a pejorative nickname. I was no exception. My label was established after a training exercise the Platoon conducted back at Fort Stewart. Each of us was rigged into a support harness that was attached to a wire, like Peter Pan. The exercise required each soldier to conquer any fear of heights and demonstrate a degree of dexterity by climbing a wobbling telephone pole twenty-five feet high, standing with both feet on the flat top, and leaping outward to slap a hanging cowbell. The little guys scaled it with ease, hardly making the pole move. Balancing my bulky frame on the top of the pole was a different story entirely. With the Platoon waiting below, the pole swayed terribly from side to side as I struggled to keep from falling. It was apparently a sight to see.

That's when Specialist Collins came up with my nickname. He was a good-looking kid, but had huge ears that dwarfed his otherwise normally sized head. The guys called him Koko, after the sign-language gorilla.

Collins hated being called Koko, and was always looking to pin a nickname that would stick on other people. With me swaying overhead, he jumped at the chance to brand me.

"Hey, guys! L.T. looks just like a Pooh Bear trying to get some honey out of a tree!"

Lieutenant Pooh Bear was my nickname within the Platoon from then on. My sidekick Sergeant Thomas was "Piglet."

Trash-talking sessions among the guys were more mental PT than anything else. The Army is full of blowhards with much more passion than information. Kind of like the White House. The verbal jousting kept them from going crazy, and gave them something to do besides playing the 4,777th game of spades or counting the grains of sand on their hands. But after a few weeks I started to feel like these enlightening talks actually made us all stupider by the hour.

Music was always my escape. A CD player in a Ziploc bag was my personal treasure. One song a day. A four-minute vacation to preserve my sanity. A brown leather zippered case held thirty carefully selected CDs, ranging from Miles Davis to Metallica. A CD for every mood. Three of them were of my girlfriend's music: one studio album, one recorded live in a New York bar, and one solo acoustic from a Washington, D.C., club. They were the CDs I listened to the most. Her music kept me close to her in spirit, and the sound of a female voice was foreign and soothing. In the tent each night before I fell asleep, I found a new appreciation for the power and depth of her rich voice. Listening to my girlfriend perform in an East Village bar while I sat on a cot in the Kuwaiti desert was surreal. Missing her energy pained me. I never realized how much she kept me sane until I left her. I tried to send her a letter daily, with something from my exotic desert life enclosed, like the Arabic labels of a Snapple or water bottle. The day I arrived, I wrapped some desert sand with duct tape in a bottle cap and sent it off. A few weeks later, it was returned with a stamp that read: SAND SENDING NOT ALLOWED. IT IS ILLEGAL. Apparently I was not the first soldier to try to send a piece of the desert through the postal service. But I was not discouraged. If Bama and I were going to make it through the deployment, we had to keep finding creative ways to maintain a connection to each other's distant world. I planned to fully test the limits of the postal system.

I thought of what must have been going on in New York City at the time. The weather was probably getting warm. In Brooklyn, it probably didn't much look like there was a war going on. People weren't thinking about it unless they had someone serving in it— and few did. Less than 1 percent of Americans were sent to Iraq. In World War Two it was around 12 percent. And New York doesn't stop to think about anyone or anything. I loved and hated that about my home. Central Park would be nice soon—soccer games, dogs playing, lunatics dancing wildly, joggers bopping, cyclists jamming by. Thousands of New Yorkers getting back into shape. Again. I thought about baseball starting at Yankee Stadium. Cool breezes of the garbage-and-hot-dog-scented night air whirling by people as they stepped off the platform of the uptown 6 train. I coveted the thought of a place where people would, very much unlike Kuwait, leave me the hell alone—an environment where I could melt into the anonymity of everyone else.

One night, as I read Thomas Friedman's *From Beirut to Jerusalem*, I overheard what I considered a pretty frightening, though not surprising, conversation on the other side of the tent. It began with a Sergeant passionately arguing that the U.S. forces should not stop with the invasion of Iraq.

The Sergeant was a slim, slow-talking First Squad Leader from a rural town outside Pensacola, Florida. Even the self-proclaimed rednecks in the Platoon made fun of the way he talked. Promoted to E-6 just before we left, he was one of the youngest Staff Sergeants in the Battalion. On our weapons systems, he was as savvy as they come. Cultural awareness was another story entirely. Like many of the guys, the Sergeant had never in his life left the United States.

"When we get to Baghdad, we should just keep on going and invade Iran! Why not? We're already over here! Take them out too. We can do a world tour, with North Korea after that!"

Sergeant Thomas must have gotten into his head. It was not an unpopular view. But the rest of his argument was what really concerned me.

"It's all about God. That is what these Mooslem people need, a bit of Jesus in their life!"

The hair on the back of my neck stood up. The Sergeant continued in his trademark drawl, "When I git to I-rack, I am going to spread the word of the Lord. Got a whole stack of little Bibles in my ruck . . . and I intend to pass them out to all them little I-rackie kids. They need some Jesus! And I'm fixin' to bring it to 'em."

He was convinced that our time in Iraq would be spent like a Brigade of Billy Grahams, handing out the gospel and converting the heathens. I had spent time in third world countries, and I knew he would be in for a rude awakening once we crossed the border.

From a far corner of the tent, just before I drifted off to sleep, I could hear a soldier rail on angrily that the Kuwaitis should be friendlier when serving him in the mess hall.

"We sure saved their asses from Saddam last time! If not for us, they'd be speaking . . . uh . . . what language does Saddam speak?"

That sort of ignorance was common. Sergeant Thomas and I invented Kuwaiti Quiz Night while stuck on a twenty-four-hour Battle Captain duty. We asked the soldiers a variety of questions and bet each other cups of coffee and tins of chewing tobacco on the results.

Question: Who is the vice president of the United States?

Answers included Joe Lieberman, Donald Rumsfeld, George Bush. Most of the Platoon, about 60 percent, got it wrong.

Question: What is the capital of New York?

New York City was not an unreasonable guess, but Connecticut? Only about 5 percent got that one.

Question: What is the capital of Kuwait?

More than one soldier answered Iraq. Most didn't have any clue. After a night of this, I was seriously concerned about America's ability to invade the correct country.

As our time idling in Kuwait dragged through the second week, I hoped every day would be the one my Platoon and I had waited for—the day we got "the word," Army vernacular for orders from higher. With people saying the war would be over in a few weeks, morale was really sucking. Our blue balls turned purple. Rumors began to float that President Bush had said all Guard and Reservists would be home by July Fourth. About a thousand times each day I heard, "Hey, sir! You get any word?"

I had never in my life been as frustrated as I was during that time. I had so much control over everything below me, yet so little impact and what was above. Nobody taught me in OCS how to continue to keep my men motivated after they had been dicked with for so long. We had been told to hurry up and wait, hurry up and wait countless times since the unit had assembled four months earlier. The Army had tested me to my limits before, but this was without question the most agonizing experience of my military career. I hoped the Army hadn't sent us all the way to Kuwait only to send us back home.

The absence of information, compounded by the enormity of war, is maddening. It leaves a man jumpy, edgy, and chomping at the bit. From a four-star General to a Private First Class, a soldier always feels like he's missing key facts. The lower his rank, the more he dwells in mystery, and the more he struggles to connect the dots. If this frustration level rises, it builds and festers into an environment of nastiness and hostility.

Sleep was impossible and the days seemed endless, broken only by a mile-long hike through a maze of tents to a saunalike super-tent for breakfast, lunch, and dinner. Getting a hot meal was a two-hour commitment. Rarely was it worth it.

Except for one day in early April, when Geraldo Rivera came swaggering into the mess hall with a goofy grin. The word was that they had kicked his happy ass out of the Division because he was disclosing troop movements on TV. Idiot. He seemed to think he was doing play-by-play at the Super Bowl. Our war was just another car chase or celebrity trial for him to cover. Fucking press. I wanted to rip that cheesy mustache off his face and feed it to him. But then again, I was just an angry Infantryman stuck in a sandstorm shit hole. Overcharged and undersexed.

I read a number of books in Kuwait. Before I left, my good friend Peter gave me *Siddhartha* by Hermann Hesse. Peter was a fierce world traveler who had almost died of malaria in Myanmar, and told me it was the book that most changed his life. It's the story of a young man's search for meaning and peace—painfully ironic given my current fate. I tore through it in three hours. In an attempt at balance, I also read Bill O'Reilly's *The O'Reilly Factor*. I had just finished Michael Moore's book *Stupid White Men*, and figured O'Reilly's would be a good counterweight. An easy read, O'Reilly impressed me with his working-class success story—and his arrogance. I was surprised to learn that he had left television to earn a master's degree from Harvard's John F. Kennedy School of Government. He pulled a quote from President Harry Truman that seemed fitting in a time of war: "Men often mistake notoriety for fame, and would rather be remembered for their vices and follies than not to be noticed at all." I wondered if that quote would one day apply to our president's bold choice to invade Iraq.

The study of literature has always been encouraged by the Army. Although expressly forbidden in both Kuwait and Iraq by CENTCOM (Central Command) for reasons of cultural sensitivity, porn magazines were almost as plentiful as Bibles. In any Infantry unit, porn was as close as the men got to naked women. New issues were highly coveted and made great gifts to subordinates or superiors on birthdays.

Despite popular opinion, soldiers can read. Some read nonstop. John Grisham and Tom Clancy books were passed around the Platoon like viruses. I had a few books stuffed deep in the bottom of my A-bag below my extra boots. As soon as I finished one, I passed it off to the rest of the Platoon, starting with Rydberg. That way the two of us had something to discuss on late nights spent guarding a radio or waiting for a commo check. It was like a two-man Oprah's Book Club. I often tried to introduce the Platoon to something other than *Maxim*. I passed them authors like Gore Vidal,

Joseph Conrad, John Fowles, and Thomas Friedman. Rydberg liked *Lullaby*, the latest by Chuck Palahniuk, one of my favorite authors. It quickly became the Bravo Company book club book of choice, even surpassing Harry Potter. Palahniuk's violent and twisted satires had powerful appeal to every Infantryman.

His most famous work, *Fight Club*, inspired one of our most popular Kuwaiti recreations: Fight Night Kuwait. One night, dozens of soldiers gathered in a circle between two tents to create a makeshift boxing ring, screaming and snapping pictures with disposable cameras. Thankfully someone had been smart enough to pack some gloves. Otherwise it would have been much worse. Angry men of all sizes in DCU (Desert Camouflage Uniform) pants and sweaty brown T-shirts went at it. Red gloves flew as noses were busted and lips swelled. The frustration of being stuck in an insufferable shit hole fueled the fighters and flowed smoothly out of their clenched hands and into the faces of their opponents. Some were settling old grudges. Some were starting new ones. Sergeant Thomas and I let it go, monitoring the entertainment from a bit of a distance. It was fun as hell to watch. The longer we stayed, the more Camp Virginia looked like a demented carnival encampment.

We were a long way from home and wearing hard on each other's nerves. Our generation of soldiers had been raised to expect a ninety-hour war. This one was already weeks long, and most men were starting to fear we had come all this way only to miss out. We desperately wanted to get into the international ring for a piece of the fight before the referee called it.

As Fight Night was broken up by a female transportation officer of rank higher than mine, I sat outside the tent and looked at the stars above. They looked much brighter than any I had ever seen before. The men streamed back into our tent with sweaty grins and mischievous eyes. As they passed, they still drove me fucking nuts with questions. It was a Platoon joke at this point.

"Where the fuck we goin', L.T.?"

"When we pushing north, L.T.?"

"Yo, L.T.! Any word yet?"

"We goin' to get to shoot some ragheads soon, L.T.?"

On April 27, we received word that our Regiment's first soldier had been killed in action. A Corporal from our sister Battalion, the Second of the 124th, died when his Humvee overturned somewhere in western Iraq. The news made us all even more angry. Our friends were up north taking casualties, and we were sitting in the desert with our thumbs up our asses.

I picked up a *Stars and Stripes* to catch up on the news from back home. A top story reported that Secretary of the Army Thomas White was fired by Secretary of Defense Donald Rumsfeld. White had just spoken to us a few weeks before in Georgia, and now he was gone. I didn't like the sound of that. White seemed like a good man. I wondered if he knew he was leaving when he spoke to us in the hangar.

Anybody who had been fired by Rumsfeld must have been doing something right. It was clear that Rumsfeld was trying to get rid of anyone who challenged him. General Eric Shinseki would be out next, sometime in June. He got into trouble for disagreeing with Rumsfeld about the invasion plan. Both White and Shinseki were experienced military minds who had served in combat during the Vietnam War. That kind of experience would prove invaluable as our country faced the problems of Iraq. The firing of people with dissenting opinions in Washington was becoming a trend. And it certainly wasn't a positive one.

Not that you'd know that anything was awry from the way President Bush was acting. On May 1, he pulled some real John Wayne shit, piloting a fighter jet onto the aircraft carrier USS *Abraham Lincoln*, where he posed under a big banner that read MISSION ACCOMPLISHED and told the world that "major combat operations in Iraq have ended." He thanked all the troops for "a job well done."

What the fuck? Mission accomplished? The war was over? And Bravo Company hadn't even fired a round.

Senator Tom Daschle would later call the president's "Mission Accomplished" publicity stunt "one of the most significant embarrassments of the entire Iraq experience so far." Maybe the war felt like it was over out on the high seas, but even sitting on our asses in Kuwait, we knew this was bullshit. True, coalition forces had stomped the Iraqi army all over the country. True, we had taken control of Baghdad and sent Saddam into hiding. But there was still plenty of resistance. Our guys were being hit every day. The combat operations they performed daily must have been considered minor.

And then, to top it all off, the irony of ironies: that very same morning, May 1, after chow, our orders finally came down. At first we thought it was another chain-of-command jerk job, but it turned out to be true. Bravo Company was moving north to Baghdad.

Mission accomplished, my ass, Mr. President.

CHAPTER THREE
WELCOME TO SADDAM INTERNATIONAL AIRPORT

Men love war because it allows them to look serious.

—John Fowles, *The Magus*

Captain Bagpipes, as we called him, sent word
that he wanted to see the officers immediately for a briefing. As
the Commanding Officer (CO) of Bravo Company, he was tasked
with leading 140 men. The other officers and I met Captain Bagpipes in his cluttered, smelly corner of the Company tent. We
gathered a few boxes of water for seats as he sat spread-legged on
the corner of his cot.

"Men. This is it. We are finally going to battle. This is what we
have been waiting for. This is what we have been training for. No
more sitting around in the desert rotting our asses off. We are going north to do our job. And that is a good thing. I have no further
information."

Most officers consider Company Command the best job in the
Army, especially in the Infantry. A CO has his own ship to run. In
that little world, he is the king. He should be the smartest, most
badass dude in the entire unit of badass dudes.

Captain Bagpipes had gotten his commission via ROTC. He was

an Army dork. Army dorks are way too into the Army shit for their own good. He'd earned his nickname, Captain Hairy Bagpipes, partly because he really did play the bagpipes, and partly because one day when he was in a very deep sleep, some of the guys had depantsed him, and decided that his testicles looked like . . . hairy bagpipes.

Lots of guys played the guitar. Chesty, a crusty old Sergeant in my Platoon's Third Squad, played a mean harmonica. But who ever heard of a soldier playing the bagpipes? It was just weird. Especially in a group of Southerners. In Georgia, he would walk around Fort Stewart at sunset in his Army PTs carrying the bagpipes like a dead pheasant. It just didn't look right. Or he would sit by himself in a chair behind the barracks in the dark playing the thing. It was eerie. And not a pretty sound for anyone within a two-mile radius trying to get some sleep. You could hear soldiers from other units in nearby barracks screaming without regard for his rank every time he played.

"Who the fuck is the idiot playing the goddamn bagpipes?"

"Shut the fuck up or I am gonna shove that thing up your ass!"

Fat Stew snickered, "Hey, L.T. Where are your bagpipes? Don't they teach you officers that shit in ROTC?"

Company-wide, the men were convinced that it was super-dork activities like the CO's bagpipe playing that resulted in Bravo being assigned the shittiest missions time and time again. They were sure that the other officers in the TOC (Tactical Operations Center) wanted us, our CO, and his bagpipes as far away from them as possible.

The upside of being the redheaded stepchild of the Battalion was that we were free from some of the micromanagement and stupidity of our Battalion Command. It was like being a high school kid whose parents go away every weekend. The Battalion staffers were eating Kentucky Fried Chicken and tanning on an Air Force base somewhere back in Qatar. We were a bit jealous, but glad to be rid of them. The Battalion pukes could stay in the rear watching Air Force females do PT and pushing paper in defense of freedom.

On the morning of May 2, I stepped out of a bombed-out hangar into the blinding sun. Like all Infantry officers, I was taught that the Platoon Leader should always be the first one out the door and the last one to eat. "Lead from the front" is the mantra of the Infantry officer school. "Follow me" is the credo of the Infantry. Lead by example. Always.

"Let's go, Third! Ruck up! Our bird is here. Squad Leaders, get your men moving."

A hulking C-130 waited as we strode over with our weapons in a long snaking line. Every time we boarded an Army plane, we stepped into another abyss. The heaviness of our bulging rucks pushed down hard on our knees, as the weight of the war pressed even harder on our minds. I felt exposed on all sides, like a prisoner walking the plank of a pirate ship. It was just me and the boys now.

One soldier screamed, "Yeah, baby! Time to bring the fucking pain! Hey, Saddam, we're comin' to put a boot in your ass!"

Rydberg pulled alongside me on the walk and smirked with a lip full of chewing tobacco. "I got some good shit for you, sir. Check it out." He pulled out of his cargo pocket a tightly wrapped stack of Trivial Pursuit cards. We were on the same page.

"I swiped 'em from an Air Force rec room a few days ago. They won't miss 'em."

My RTO made me proud. Not because he was a thief, but because he appreciated the importance of keeping your brain from melting while in the Army. I spit a stream of chew juice and watched it float off, evaporating above the scalding tarmac. Sergeant Thomas had the men focused and ready. I was happy that our time had finally come. We were nervous, but upbeat. As the C-130 rumbled down the runway, a soldier asked me, "Hey, sir! Is this the flight to Hawaii?"

One of the blessings of command was that I didn't have much

time to worry about myself. I had a million things to go through in my head. Double-checking the radio frequencies; confirming the head count on the plane; confirming the time line. A successful Platoon Leader is a compulsive multitasker.

We landed in Baghdad with a thud. On a thickly dark night, ours was one of the first planes to land at the recently occupied Saddam International Airport. This was my first introduction to the fact that just about every building or monument of significance in Iraq was named after Saddam. He did one hell of a job at branding. Coca-Cola would be envious.

Our Platoon was the first of three on the ground in Baghdad from Bravo. The forward elements of 3ID and the 101st had taken the city just days before. I chugged away from the plane, dropped down my NODs (Night Vision Optical Devices, aka NVGs, Night Vision Goggles), and took a knee as the men quickly fanned out behind me. Signs of the recent fighting for the airport were everywhere. An Iraq Air civilian plane lay broken like a mammoth child's toy next to what looked like a blown-out passenger gate. Huge terminals and passageways were stitched with jagged bullet and cannon holes. Blackened carcasses of Iraqi tanks and BMPs (Russian-built armored infantry vehicles) smoldered in burned fighting positions. They had been destroyed when they met the wrath of the 3/7 Cavalry and the United States Air Force. Enemy bodies were still scattered in mounds. The pungent smell of death mixed with the vapors of vehicle fuel and fire. A stench I remembered well from 9/11.

Chunky Bradley Fighting Vehicles ringed the airport perimeter in entrenched fighting positions, silent but for the hum of their engines. I heard a turret buzz in the distance, revealing one of these hidden sentinels as my eyes adjusted to the dark. I remembered from my training at Benning that it can take the human eye ten to thirty minutes to fully adjust to the darkness. The stubby 25mm "Bushmaster" cannon barrel swung into my line of sight as it pivoted westward to give the gunner better overwatch with thermal sights. My ears opened wider as training kicked in and I started to assess the threat level. I was one giant exposed nerve holding an M16.

No one met us at the airport. It looked like no one was even expecting us. I grabbed a young soldier from the ground crew working on our plane to find out where to move my men. He hadn't slept in days and gave me a clueless shrug. The only thing I could ascertain over the roar of the plane was that we were definitely not in the right place. Planes landed and took off like roaring giants all around us. I did a quick GPS check and realized we were on the wrong side of the airport. Our rendezvous point was at least three kilometers away.

For the first time I noticed gunfire crackling steadily in the distance like rolling thunder. I ordered the Squad Leaders to get their men moving off the flight line. We rushed into an abandoned hangar about two hundred meters to our east. As Sergeant Thomas settled the men in place, I set out with Rydberg to link up with our point of contact.

Before I could give the order, my high-speed RTO was already trying to get the Company XO (Executive Officer), Lieutenant Luis Sierra (call sign "Wolfpack 5"), on the radio. "Wolfpack 5, this is Blue 6. Wolfpack 5, this is Blue 6."

Sierra was a quiet and easygoing former Special Forces enlisted soldier who was older than the Battalion Commander (BC) and usually called people "bro." He played lead guitar in a heavy metal rock band and seemed too smart to be in the National Guard. He weighed no more than 150 pounds, but was scrappy and respected by the men. Luis had left camp in Kuwait a few days before us with some elements from Bravo's Headquarters Company. Dangerously ambitious, they had barreled all the way up to Baghdad in the Army version of *The Cannonball Run*. Luis and his boys served as the Company advance element. Their responsibility was to link up with our higher command, find out our orders, and lay some groundwork for support.

After trekking around the perimeter for a few hours, I finally found Luis sitting with his back on the wheel of an open-back Humvee. It was the lead vehicle in a convoy from Bravo lined up alongside what seemed to be an executive hangar. His guys were clearly spent, sprawled out sleeping on and around the line of tired vehicles caked with sand. The only light came from the soft green glow of a few chem lights. Chemical lights were the Army's most trusted source of illumination. Clear plastic liquid-filled tubes made famous by roller skaters and house music ravers worldwide, chem lights were tactical, cheap, and reliable. Under the soft green glow, Luis looked like a hobgoblin.

" 'Bout time you guys got here. We were afraid you'd miss the party. This shit is pretty fuckin' crazy, bro."

It took a lot to get Luis upset. The only time I saw him show any real emotion was back in Georgia, when the CO told him there might not be room to store his acoustic guitar with the Company gear in the supply trains. Luis had been on enough deployments to know there would eventually be lots of downtime. A guitar was essential to the well-being and overall morale of the boys. We had spent many nights during the predeployment behind the enlisted soldiers' barracks, playing and singing as a group. Luis and a soldier named Lucky from First Platoon got some excellent jam sessions going, including an especially mean rendition of "Sweet Home Alabama."

"I am finding a way to bring it. I don't care if I have to smuggle it up my ass, I'm bringing my guitar!" he said. And he did. I was sure now that he had that guitar buried deep below the ammo and MREs somewhere in that Humvee.

Rydberg called back to the rest of the Platoon while a soldier showed him an area behind the building set aside for our Platoon. I walked with Luis, stepping through a shattered window into a bombed-out waiting area. Before the war, it must have looked like the airport lobby on the sitcom *Wings*. Luis laid out a tattered map on a broken ticket counter. I had printed a few satellite photos from the Internet before we left, but this was the first time I had been formally shown a map of Baghdad. Luis took a deep breath.

"Welcome to Baghdad, bro. Here's the deal. This is a map of the entire city. It's pretty fucking wild. We went rolling through it this morning from the south on our way out here. Civilians everywhere. They tried to run all over the vehicles like flies on shit. Bad guys were taking potshots from all over the place. We just kept the pedals down and hauled ass to get out here. Maps don't have street names. Shit, the streets don't have street names. The roads are like a maze. We got lost about five times, but we made it here in one piece.

"Battalion is still in Kuwait. Hopefully they'll stay there. Second Bat is somewhere out west near Syria. Our three Companies have been tossed like pick-up sticks all over the country. Each one is tasked out to a different element. Some guys from First Brigade got blown up by a suicide bomber this morning. Heard it was pretty bad. Charlie Company's been here for a bit. They now occupy one of Saddam's old palaces. One of their guys got his hand blown off picking up a booby trap. So tell your guys not to go picking shit up off the ground. Alpha is somewhere up north. Don't know where. You guys are going here."

He pointed to a spot east of the winding Tigris River.

"Sector 17. You'll set up in some big government building, just north of the Ministry of Defense. It is the highest building in the area and will give you excellent overwatch for much of the sector. It's about fifteen clicks away from where we are now. We will have the entire sector from here to the river. Once we set up shop, we are to locate, capture, and kill all noncompliant forces. Looks like things are settling down, but the area is still hot. You guys are headed in there tomorrow to take over for a Battalion from the 101st that—"

I stopped him. "Wait. Lou. What do you mean, take over for a Battalion?"

"Yep. Fucked up, huh? Check this shit out, bro. They have a Battalion holding the area now, with a full Delta Company. Good thing we left ours at home 'cause we wouldn't need 'em, huh? Idiots."

In an "Air Assault Battalion," like ours and the 101st, a Delta Company is an antiarmor mobile infantry unit. They have Humvees, stocked up with the good stuff—TOW missiles (Tube-launched, Optically tracked, Wire command-link-guided), .50-caliber machine guns, MK19 automatic grenade launchers. A Delta Company has all the things that are too much for us to carry. It allows a Light Infantry unit to bolster its firepower and mobility in a big way. Our Battalion was told to leave our Delta Company behind because we wouldn't need it.

"Tomorrow, the 101st guys are rushing out to the Syrian border. The word is they're going after Saddam. They're gone by the end of the day, so you better tell your guys to take this shit seriously. We're supposed to take it over with only a fuckin' Company. We are going to be busy. I told you this shit was crazy, bro."

The 101st currently controlled an area of sixteen square kilometers of urban terrain with about 500 soldiers. We would have to do it with 140. If we abided by U.S. Army doctrine, we'd need that many to properly take just one big building in that sector. Not a good way to start a war.

"That's all I got, bro. We're taking you in on deuce-and-a-halves at first light. I gotta get some sleep. I hope you guys have enough ammo, 'cause I haven't been able to find shit. Let's hope we won't need it."

I hit the light button on my G-Shock and checked the hour. It was dinnertime in New York City. We had about four hours until sunrise. I found Rydberg and briefed Sergeant Thomas and the Squad Leaders. We reviewed the planned route into the city and talked through the CasEvac plan. Sergeant Thomas broke up the Platoon into the two available trucks. I would be in the lead vehicle with half the guys and one 240-B heavy machine-gun team; he would be in the second with the rest of the men and another 240 team. You always spread out leadership like that during any kind of transport, in case one vehicle takes a direct hit. With surprisingly few questions, my Squad Leaders broke off to brief their men and prep for combat.

Sitting down for the first time in hours, I peeled open my flak jacket and leaned back heavily on my ruck. I broke out my weapons-cleaning kit and spit out a dead wad of chew. Time in the Army has a strange way of speeding up and slowing down. A day in Kuwait felt like an eternity, and the last few hours had ripped by in a blur. Glancing up, I noticed that the stars seemed much brighter in Iraq. Then I realized the stars were moving. The night sky was filled with red firefly tracer rounds dashing in and burning out, like a meteor shower. In Iraq, the stars were less plentiful and less powerful than the bullets.

with half the guys and one 240 B heavy machine-gun team. He would be in the second with the rest of the men and another 240 team. You always spread out leadership like that during any kind of transport, in case one vehicle takes a direct hit. With surprise ugly few questions, my squad leaders broke off to brief their men and prep for combat.

Sitting down for the first time in hours, I peeled open my flak jacket and leaned back heavily on my ruck. I broke out my weapons-cleaning kit and spit out a dead wad of chew. Time in the Army has a strange way of speeding up and slowing down. A day in Kuwait felt like an eternity, and the last few hours had zipped by in a blur. Glancing up I noticed that the stars seemed much brighter in Iraq. Then I realized the stars were moving. The night sky was filled with red firefly tracer rounds dashing in and burning out, like a meteor shower. In Iraq, the stars were less plentiful and less powerful than the bullets.

CHAPTER FOUR
INTO BAGHDAD

In the practical art of war, the best thing of all is to take the enemy's country whole and intact; to shatter and destroy it is not so good. So, too, it is better to recapture an army entire than to destroy it.
—Sun Tzu, *The Art of War*

We bumped and bounced down the highway from the airport with all our weapons pointed out of the stuffed deuce-and-a-half trucks like pins in pincushions. Off in the distance I saw the mammoth swords of the "Hands of Victory" arches, crossing high over the road at either end of Saddam's military parade grounds. They appeared untouched by the repeated bombing runs, despite being such easy targets—like, say, the World Trade Center towers or the Statue of Liberty in New York. Leaving them standing must have been an effort on our part to win the hearts and minds of the Iraqi people. Saddam had erected the arches as monuments to himself, but also to commemorate the Iraqi soldiers who'd died securing "victory" in his insane war with Iran, which dragged on from 1980 to 1988. We would have made more enemies than friends by destroying them.

I was shocked by the enormity of the structures. Resilient and proud, the swords towered hundreds of feet into the sky and loomed ominously between us and Baghdad. The guns of dead Iraqi soldiers had been melted and recast as the blades of the swords. Each one weighed twenty-four tons. Thousands of captured Iranians' helmets morbidly surrounded the base of each arch. The fists that held the swords aloft were replicas of Saddam Hussein's own hands. Every American had seen news footage of rockets, tanks, missiles rolling menacingly under them for Saddam's approval, an impressive show of force that only the truly legendary enemies of America could stage. The day before the first bombing run on Baghdad during the 1991 Gulf War, Iraqi soldiers had marched beneath them to the theme music from *Star Wars*.

Awe set upon the faces of my soldiers, mouths agape, eyes wide. I felt a tremendous gravity, a sense of history, knowing that we were the liberators of a nation that was not our own. It felt extremely heroic. We rolled closer and I thought of the newsreels of American soldiers proudly marching down the Champs-Élysées past the Arc de Triomphe, liberating Paris during World War Two.

As we rolled forward, Baghdad revealed its depressing lack of color. All the buildings were brown, all the cars white. Butterscotch-colored dust blanketed a vast sprawling city dotted with green palm trees. The tallest buildings were maybe twenty stories high, but most were much lower. The city reached out as far as the eye could see, looking like L.A. without the skyscrapers. Or the beaches, luxury cars, and breast implants. The heavy hot fog of the sky pressed down, and the dusty heat of the city pushed up, until the two blended into one.

Our trip into the city quickly devolved into something less like Patton's march and more like a Bizarro Mardi Gras parade. It was a scene of utter chaos. We rumbled into a cluttered intersection exploding with yelling and cheering people, yet AK gunfire rolled through in echoing waves, close enough for us to hear the metallic ching of shell casings hitting the asphalt. Heavy American machine-gun fire responded from not two hundred yards to our left. These crowds may have been cheering our arrival, but clearly not everyone in Baghdad was happy to see us.

Choking clouds of exhaust fumes mixed with dust. A twenty-story building that had collapsed on top of itself like a squashed concrete accordion smoked at one intersection, clearly the lucky recipient of a JDAM (Joint Direct Attack Munition). Ratty black wires were strung from the roofs of every building and across the streets in cluttered webs. Fruit stands were stacked with rotten produce. A red-and-white Viceroy Cigarette umbrella stood out. Just about every block revealed the dome and minaret of a mosque.

I couldn't believe how many people there were. Thousands scampering and bustling chaotically like insects in what could just as easily have been a street in New Delhi or São Paulo. Smiling children everywhere. Cars honking. All the men smoking cigarettes. Mobs with dark hair. Beards. Bad teeth. Women wobbling around in their dark burkas. "They look like penguins!" a soldier yelled from the front of the truck.

We drove straight through the biggest market in Baghdad. Kids bounced on the hoods of cars, waving and smiling. Crowds pressed closer to the trucks as we slowed for the congestion. Third Platoon rolled through town like rock stars on a float at the Macy's Thanksgiving Day Parade. At this stage of events, the majority of people in Baghdad really did see us as heroes, liberating them from the madness and tyranny of Saddam, his Republican Guard, and the fedayeen, his personal army of "martyrs." They believed we were bringing them liberty, democracy, peace, a return to normality, and tons of humanitarian aid. After all, our president kept telling them so. Old men watching us pass took off one shoe and banged it on the ground, a sign of extreme disrespect in Iraq, chanting, "Bad Saddam! Bad Saddam! Good Bush! Good Bush!"

But the precarious balance felt like it could be shattered in an instant. The fedayeen especially made everyone nervous. They were fanatical Saddam loyalists, and probably tens of thousands of them were still at large and responsible for daily attacks on our troops. The taxi driver who'd recently driven up to a checkpoint in the town of Najaf and detonated a bomb that killed him and four soldiers of 3ID had been fedayeen, and everyone knew that many more potential suicide bombers were out there. We could still hear gunfire in all directions. Two Black Hawk helicopters swooped up from behind us. The convoy accelerated as the traffic tightened.

Sergeant Thomas yelled over the roar of the convoy, "Keep your eyes open, fellas!" My senses overwhelmed, I scanned thousands of eyes and hands, looking for weapons and the bulge of a suicide vest.

Every soldier squatted down and grabbed something to hold on to as we banked into a hard turn and left the market area. My right hand gripped my rifle tight, finger on the selector switch, and my left hand clutched hard on a wooden canopy bar arching overhead. As the truck banked again, the wood snapped in my hand and I saw the street coming fast. Rydberg and another soldier snagged the back of my LBE (Load-Bearing Equipment) just in time, saving me from tumbling off the vehicle into a sure, noncombat-related death. The truck was so old that the wooden bar had actually rotted. I imagined what the engine must be like. It didn't have a reverse gear. If we needed to back up, the guys had to get out and push. We were at war with the Army we had. The one the Department of Defense created for us. Thanks, Don.

The road networks were surprisingly modern. Overpasses weaved and off-ramps jutted from the highways, all still intact and usable. Everything in Baghdad was top-of-the-line—if this were 1976. The architecture, the cars, the technology. Saddam and the sanctions imposed on him after the Gulf War had held the city and its people frozen in time. Like Seaside Heights, New Jersey, or Myrtle Beach, South Carolina, Baghdad was a shining jewel that time had sadly passed by. There was very little noticeable collateral damage, however. The air strikes were precise. Many Iraqis in Baghdad told us that we'd bombed the city much more ferociously in '91 at the start of the Gulf War. They were surprised at how careful and precise our targeting was this time.

As we approached our apparent destination, a crowd of dozens of chattering Iraqis gathered, peering at us from outside a fence. The driver sounded the horn angrily, and as we pointed a few dozen weapons at their heads, the crowd dispersed. Four haggard soldiers from the 101st on guard duty pulled back the recently broken gate, and we rolled into the parking lot. A bronze statue of Saddam, maybe ten feet tall, lay facedown, toppled from its pedestal. His head and uplifted right arm had broken off. We later found the arm. It was maybe four feet long and heavy as a motherfucker, but we carried it around Baghdad with us like a trophy. We heard that the 101st did the same with the head. Guys joked about auctioning them on eBay when we got home.

The Ministry of Finance building towered over us. The Iraqi version of Wall Street. Too damn ironic for me. The Rakkasans of the 101st Airborne Division, Fort Campbell's finest, were pretty shocked to see the Dirty Guard arrive as their relief. My men started unloading gear, and I went in to do a Leaders recon.

Air Force bombs and the 101st had done their part, but it was really the looters who had trashed the place. Papers, drywall, and broken glass were scattered a foot deep, like leaves in the New England fall—or like the shattered buildings at Ground Zero on 9/11. A massive smirking portrait of Saddam with a shotgun loomed over the entrance lobby. His eyes had been shot out. Soldiers bustled, stacking ammunition in corners and behind broken desks, where Iraqi businessmen had bartered just a few weeks before. I picked up an official piece of paper that bore a Third Reich–looking bird in its letterhead—the official Iraqi symbol. Most official documents bore letterhead in both Arabic and English—a result of the old British Empire. The edges of the paper were singed. The writing curled in the smooth squiggles and dots of Arabic.

No elevators on this tour. Taking the elevator in a bombed-out building is not exactly tactically sound. With Rydberg and a fire team from Third Squad, I began to climb the long stairs twenty stories to the roof. Walls were collapsed and missing; the windows were all blasted. The looters had stolen anything of value before U.S. forces had arrived. The locals knew where the money was. The ministry building was one of the tallest in the city, and the stairs seemed to last forever.

"Fucking great! We came seven thousand miles to do more fucking PT," Fat Stew groaned.

Li'l Mac snorted. He was a gritty little dude and a hell of a sharpshooter. He had a brother in First Platoon who was known, of course, as Big Mac.

"You need it anyway, Fatty," Li'l Mac snapped.

Fat Stew certainly was not fond of physical training (PT). In the Army, pain is mandatory, suffering is optional.

Twenty stories later, through brutally dark and steamy stairwells, we emerged on the roof to set up machine-gun and sniper positions. Burning buildings and smoke smudged the landscape of the sprawling city. Gunfire crackled from all sides below. Sounds reverberated around Baghdad like pinballs. You could only tell where the shots were coming from if they were close enough to hit you.

The panoramic view revealed a limitless maze of dusty adobe-looking buildings, most less than three stories tall, and a scattering of government towers. It was a city basted in chicken noodle soup and battered in dust. Saddam's crossed swords peeked out in the distance to our left. We were all speechless for a moment, taking in the vastness of it all. We were actually in Baghdad. Time seemed murky, like my eyes were being pulled through the scene my brain was recording.

But we were an Infantry unit. And this was the wise-ass Platoon. So the only silence left unbroken was strictly mission-related.

"*Fuck!*" Fat Stew spat. "I don't see another unit anywhere! No MPs. No fucking Red Cross. No food for all these fucking people. L.T., where the fuck is everyone else?"

"Good question, Stew. Good question."

General Shinseki testified before Congress that a successful occupation of Iraq would require troops "in the vicinity of several hundred thousand." Paul Wolfowitz, the deputy defense secretary, called the estimate "wildly off the mark." Rumsfeld also tried to discredit Shinseki. He and his gang of civilian planners with limited or no personal combat experience decided to dismiss the guidance of the best military planners in America and conduct the Iraq war on the cheap. They chose to invade Iraq with a mere 150,000 troops.

I was just beginning to see how thin we would be stretched.

"Good question, Steve. Good question."

General Shinseki testified before Congress that a successful occupation of Iraq would require troops "in the vicinity of several hundred thousand." Paul Wolfowitz, the deputy defense secretary, called the estimate "wildly off the mark." Rumsfeld also tried to discredit Shinseki. He and his gang of civilian planners with little or no personal combat experience decided to dismiss the guidance of the best military planners in America and conduct the Iraq war on the cheap. They chose to invade Iraq with a mere 150,000 troops.

I was just beginning to see how thin we would be stretched.

CHAPTER FIVE
SECTOR 17

> When you disarm the people, you commence to offend them and show that you distrust them either through cowardice or lack of confidence, and both of these opinions generate hatred.
>
> —Machiavelli

Sector 17 covered the neighborhoods of al-Wasiriyah and Maghreb, and cut across part of

the wealthy Sunni neighborhood of al-Adamiyah. It was bracketed by two bridges that crossed the Tigris to the north and south, and contained a number of key strategic targets. Three ministries—Finance, Health, and Labor. Four international embassies—Italian, Indian, Lebanese, and Turkish. And the gem of the sector, Medical City, the largest medical complex in all of Iraq. The ministries had been effectively taken out by the Air Force. The embassies were totally untouched. Medical City was somewhere in between.

Alpha Company took over Sector 17 North; Bravo took Sector 17 South. For the first few days, all of Bravo Company stayed in the Ministry of Finance. Then my Platoon and Second Platoon, led by Lt. Andy Berrey, split off and set up inside Medical City, along the banks of the Tigris. About seventy of us moved into a glass-

59

and-concrete conference center called Saddam Auditorium. At the core of the building was a plush red theater that looked just like a movie theater back home. Cool cement floors made it the most insulated room in the otherwise sweltering building. Guys camped out there just to get out of the brutal heat—and away from the annoying tinkering of our Commanding Officers.

We converted the projection room, film still in the projectors, into an interrogation room. The room had no windows and was safe from bullets and rocket fire.

Around the rest of the building, almost every window had been smashed, or at least decorated with the stitching of bullet holes. Medical pamphlets were sprinkled everywhere. Some were written in English. As I read from a few of them, I learned that a prominent Iraqi cancer surgeon had hosted a conference of doctors here in April, just a couple of weeks before the invasion. In a matter of days, this building had gone from hosting doctors practicing medicine to housing soldiers practicing warfare.

Difficult to defend, the building wouldn't have been my first choice, but choice isn't exactly a hallmark of military life. The high rooftop gave us a solid overwatch, but the river to our west provided the only natural barrier from attack, and across that river were hundreds of places where snipers could hide. Three sides of the structure had ceiling-to-floor glass windows that left us extremely exposed to anyone who would do us harm. Everyone within miles could observe our operations. It felt like living in a fishbowl.

Our guys teamed up with a few departing 101st troops and created a brilliant ad hoc defensive barrier for the perimeter of our new home. Rydberg used an old forklift to move a few dozen wrecked cars into a ring around the three exposed sides of the auditorium. They stacked the cars two high on the sidewalk, and lined them with razor wire. The makeshift wall of twisted metal and glass provided a solid barrier to car bombs. And the razor wire and 240 machine-gun positions would slow down any enemy dismounts who might try to storm our Alamo.

A long blue-lit sign flashed the name of the building in white block letters, SADDAM AUDITORIUM. It was like a big Mobil gas station sign. There seemed to be no shortage of reasons for the locals to shoot at us, but we noticed that gunshots came with special regularity to the front of the building—around the sign. The locals were so eager to vent against Saddam that they would fire their guns at anything with his name or face on it. After our third day there, we unplugged the sign, and the shooting diminished.

We stationed two-man machine-gun teams on each of the four corners of the auditorium rooftop. From up there we had a clear view of the area for hundreds of meters. The muddy, swirling Tigris River curled off to the west. On jagged rooftops, colorful, cruddy blankets hung from the windows. The Baghdad water treatment plant and the Lebanese embassy were just to our north. A mini-palace that belonged to Saddam's wife was just across the Tigris. Locals told us that while Saddam was in power, if a person even pointed or gestured at the place, he was put in jail and beaten repeatedly. One man told us his brother had his tongue cut off by Saddam's police for looking at it for too long one night years ago.

The dusty, cramped streets were jammed with tattered cars. No matter what direction I looked, I could see a mosque. Some were in the next block, some were a mile away. Five times a day the booming voices of the muezzins called the faithful to prayer, every single fucking day. No matter where you were in the city, you heard the amplified voice of a cleric:

"AAAAAAAAAAAAHHHHHHHHHHHHHHHHHHHHLLLLLLLL
LLLLLAAAAAAAAAAAAAAAAAAAAMAAAAAAAAAAAAAAAA
AAAAAAAAAAAAAAAAAAAAAAAAAAAAAAA. . . .
OOOOOOOOOOOOOOOOOOOOOOOOOOOOOAAAAAAAAAA
AAAAAAAAAAAAAAAAAAAAAYYYYYYYYYYYAAAAAAAAAAA
AAAAAAAAAAAAAAAAAAAAAA. . . ."

It got to the point where I heard it in my dreams. I heard it so much that I didn't hear it anymore. When I was feeling paranoid, I would imagine that I actually understood what they were saying in Arabic:

"Praise Allah! Allah is most high! Praise Allah! Give thanks to the most high!"

Or maybe it was:

"Kill all the Americans! Kill that big fucker in Third Platoon who pissed me off last week and arrested Mr. Hassan down on Haifa Street! Blow him up, and all his friends! Send those infidel bastards back to their commercialized, morally devoid wasteland! Do it tomorrow at six AAAAAMMMMM!"

Our biggest problem was security—there was none. In Sector 17, shootings, kidnappings, and robberies were rampant. At a press conference, Donald Rumsfeld shrugged off the looting. "Stuff happens," he said. I couldn't be so dismissive. "Stuff" was "happening" all over our sector every day. We searched the halls and rooms of the medical complex, flushing out shooters from inside closets and from behind dying patients.

Nevertheless, for our first few weeks, most of the people in Sector 17 still seemed happy to see us. We hadn't quite brought peace, order, and the Red Cross with us, as they'd expected, but they still had hope—a cautious, fearful hope. They weren't sure what to make of us yet. When they heard we were National Guard, they thought of Saddam's brutal Republican Guard and shuddered. Saddam's propaganda had trained them to expect the invading Americans to be monsters. Rumors had swirled about our technology, killing prowess, and brutality. Abrams tanks had force fields around them to stop RPGs (Rocket Propelled Grenades). To be a Marine you must kill both your parents. Rank in the U.S. Army was attained via kill tallies. Our desert combat boots detected and defused enemy mines. American soldiers could see in the dark and through walls. Well, that one was true. But only when we paid a local kid or one of our interpreters enough money to scrounge up AA batteries for our night vision equipment on the Baghdad black market.

But the Americans weren't all seen as superheroes. In the nearby town of Fallujah, a group of soldiers from the 82nd had recently opened up on a crowd protesting the presence of coalition forces, killing over a dozen civilians. A soldier had thought he'd seen an RPG in the crowd. It sent shock waves of caution throughout Baghdad. Every Iraqi in our sector had heard the story. It was yet another reason for them to be cautious of us. A minor firefight on one of the bridges our first week in Medical City added to the tensions. A vehicle tried to run some soldiers down at a checkpoint, and our guys opened fire.

Amazingly, though, we didn't seem to scare the children. Exactly the opposite. Every time we set foot out on patrol, children ran into the streets in mobs. I felt like the ice cream man. My men handed out candy and gum until their pockets were empty. We smiled and took pictures as swarms of kids followed us everywhere we went, poking and touching curiously, probing at our clothes and equipment. They had stunning golden skin and gorgeous dark eyes. An American combat photographer who had been everywhere in the world told me the most beautiful children of all were in Iraq. They were playful and fearless, and many spoke surprisingly good English. If they didn't, they were eager to learn. Being surrounded by these kids was the greatest feeling I had ever had in my life. I never felt so loved and appreciated. We felt like celebrities, or even gods, waving everywhere like the Queen of England as we made our rounds. Kids would regularly run down a road at us from three hundred meters away, just to shake our hands and run back home triumphantly, like they had just gotten an autograph from Michael Jordan.

"Now I know what the pope feels like!" Fat Stew yelled over the screams of a group of little boys scampering for candy.

"Or a woman at Fort Benning," somebody fired back.

Some kids demonstrated a real knack for the hustle. Two brothers were like little Donald Trumps, permanently stationed across from our compound selling cold Pepsis for American dollars. I designated myself the market maker and determined the fair market price at two for a dollar. The mighty U.S. Army couldn't get my guys a cold soda, but two Iraqi fourth-graders could.

Not all kids were doing honest business. Adult criminals often used them as pawns for robberies and drug or weapons trafficking, assuming the warmhearted American soldiers would go light on them. We nabbed a thirteen-year-old thief with $3,600 in U.S. cash. He pleaded with us to give him the money back, telling us that his dad would beat him to death if he lost it.

In among all the kids, stray dogs and puppies scampered everywhere. The locals didn't have much love for them. They wandered the streets in packs, carrying disease, and both Iraqis and Americans shot at them. A couple of them attached themselves to us right away. We called one of them Bob, because his salt-and-pepper fur looked like Sgt. Bob Gipson's hair. We called the other Mojo for the good luck she brought us. They were scrawny, but we fed them MREs and they fattened up quickly. One of the guys rubbed them down with diesel to clear up their mange (a true redneck trick). Later, when we moved out of Saddam Auditorium, we loaded them onto the back of a five-ton truck while Iraqis stared at us like we were insane. The guys loved those dogs and they loved us back. They were loyal companions. A foot patrol couldn't leave the compound without those dogs tagging along. They were especially great to have along at night. Several times they tipped us off to someone in the streets or in the shadows long before we could have seen him, even with our high-tech night vision goggles. We called it "recon by K-9."

Anarchy ruled in Sector 17, as it did throughout Baghdad. The crime rate was beyond our control. Because we'd bombed the power stations, the electricity was off, and would stay off for a long time. Baghdad was one very dark and dangerous place at night. And not much safer when the hot sun shone. Everywhere we went, Iraqis ran up to us urgently, pointing and screaming, "Ali Baba! Ali Baba!" Ali Baba was the understood term for all bad people. Remnants of the Iraqi army, foreign fighters, criminals, political enemies—all were Ali Baba.

In the first few days, we pursued every lead with zeal. We stopped cars at gunpoint, pushed into houses, and interrogated aggressively. But after a bit, we realized that many Iraqis were using us to detain and harass personal adversaries and avenge grudges. Kids playfully motioned at the unpopular child in their group, hoping we would react and detain him. "He Ali Baba!" There was no law in Baghdad, and with us preoccupied watching our own asses, the Iraqis took full advantage of the opportunity to settle scores long harbored under Saddam. Banks were robbed, assassinations were common, and young attractive women were snatched from their homes. It was as though we'd popped the cork on Iraqi society after decades of repression, and it was ugly. We were instructed to leave looters alone. Even if we hadn't been, with so few troops there was too much for us to stop. I felt like Wyatt Earp in Tombstone.

On top of everything else, it was soon painfully obvious that our supply lines were in ruin. Apparently, there were crates of water floating somewhere in the Mediterranean, but we couldn't get to them, and they couldn't get to us. It seemed amazing to me that we did not have enough water. One of my guys collapsed from dehydration after an afternoon patrol. He twitched violently as his core body temperature reached a dangerously high point, his skin white and dry. As he lay on a cot with an IV stuck in his arm, I questioned the Battalion Executive Officer about the supply problems.

"Sir, my guys are doing patrols twelve hours a day. They're humping in 120-degree temperatures with one fucking bottle of water. This is ridiculous. We need to get better supply, or draw back on the tempo, sir."

"Your men are fine, Lieutenant," he sneered. "You keep doing what you're doing and let the S-4 deal with logistics. Stay in your lane."

"Sir, I got one guy unconscious with heat stroke and two Squads on the verge of collapsing. I am not asking for a nuke strike here. I am asking for a few cases of water."

"That's enough, Lieutenant. Some of your boys could use to drop some weight anyway. You should disappear." And he turned his back to me as he reentered the soft glow and cool AC of the Battalion TOC (Tactical Operations Center).

It was clear to every one of us on the ground in those opening weeks of May that the great minds in Washington had no solutions to offer for our day-to-day problems. They were our problems. And it was up to grunts like us to solve them.

First things first: we had a lot of ground to cover, and that required vehicles to get around—and Dick Cheney and Don Rumsfeld weren't sending us their limos any time soon. We had to patrol the sector, and we also had to venture out across the city to "acquire" items that were essential—like water, ammunition, and Copenhagen chewing tobacco.

I sent the men out to canvass the surrounding area for what we called "useful items." They came back with bolt cutters, gasoline, batteries, and a live chicken. I didn't even want to know what they planned to do with the chicken.

Two soldiers came running into the CP grinning and out of breath.

"Sir, you ain't gonna believe this!"

They'd come upon a huge underground parking garage filled with 150 brand-spanking-new sport utility vehicles.

"L.T.! It looks like a fucking showroom!"

"Yeah, L.T. These shits is brand-new! You think we can take 'em home? That would be sweet! I'd be pimpin' hard in one of these bitches back in Florida!"

I grabbed Rydberg and my gear and we tore out of the gate to check out the alleged bonanza. We climbed over two wrecked cars blocking the entrance to the garage, pushed back a busted lock, and yanked open a sliding metal door. It was unbelievable—rows of Land Rovers and Nissan Patrols. Dozens of them, all loaded, all brand-new, all white. Most still had the plastic shrink-wrap packaging stuck on the roofs and hoods.

The soldiers had gotten the tip from one of the kids selling Cokes on the street. He said that these were vehicles hoarded by Saddam before the war and hidden underground. Any Iraqi government property was now subject to U.S. confiscation. We weren't stealing from the Iraqi people. We were taking back from Saddam what he had stolen from the Iraqi people. Many of the vehicles had already been looted for batteries and gas, but most were left totally untouched.

After about ten hours of work, two of my craftiest soldiers with automotive experience, one a former mechanic and one a former carjacker, had done some clutch work. Bravo Company and Third Platoon now had wheels—four vehicles, full of gas and running, with Eminem and Disturbed screaming from their Bose sound systems. And more on the way. Monster Garage Baghdad was fully operational.

But there was one problem. Soldiers inside couldn't maneuver with the doors closed on the vehicles. The doors squeezed us in tight, and prevented us from moving inside when bulked up with our weapons and gear. The close quarters made it very tough to aim our weapons at a target from inside. Not letting convention stand in their way, the guys opened the doors to one of the vehicles, slammed the shifter in reverse, and drove backward, smashing the doors into a palm tree at about thirty miles an hour. No more doors. Axes and sledgehammers also worked. It was just like a scene from *The A-Team*.

We could get around more easily now, but that didn't much lighten the workload. We worked constantly. Twenty-four-hour shifts, and patrols all day long. I averaged about four hours of sleep per day , and rarely got them consecutively. After the first few days of it, we were gassed. I wrote my father and asked him to mail me some baby wipes, Gatorade mix, and a box of the zip cuffs his Con Ed electricians used to bind bundles of wiring. We were detaining people every day, and the Army had run out of zip cuffs. After the number of EPWs (Enemy Prisoners of War) U.S. forces took in the first Gulf War, you'd think they'd recognize we'd need lots of zip cuffs.

We even had to find our own translators, since the Army hadn't seen fit to send any with us or train any of us in even rudimentary Arabic. They came from the local communities. We paid them four dollars a week—and it was considered the best job in town.

We inherited the finest of them, Esam (pronounced "Ee-sam") Pasha, from the 101st when they pulled out. Twenty-eight years old, he was tall, well over six-two, and looked like a cross between Jesus Christ and Charles Manson. He spoke fantastic English, in addition to French and Spanish. He had a gentle, stately way about him, but was also the former Iraqi national judo champion. He seemed like a guy I could easily have been friends with in New York. But in Baghdad, even though he walked patrol by my side every day, I had to be careful how far I trusted him. I kept one eye out for the enemy, and one on him. It was a very hard balance to strike.

Our other main interpreter was Mohamed al-Mumayiz. "Mo" was a bit older than I, and came from a wealthy local family. Sergeant Thomas found him while out walking patrol one night. Mo loved telling the story.

"It was about ten p.m. and I was sitting with my mother and a neighbor on the porch, chatting about all the events that happened and how all Iraqis still unbelieved what happened in Baghdad," he said in his slightly fractured English. Still, it was a hell of a lot better than our Arabic. "The city had no power and the street was pitch dark. Suddenly three objects jumped up. All of us were in a surprise. My mother thought that it was women wearing Ab'bi." (That's the long black cloth that women wear from head to toe.)

It turned out to be Sergeant Thomas and a patrol. "One of the soldiers asked if I saw men with a bicycle passing by. Then he asked me if I knew what a bicycle is, and started moving his hands up and down how the feet do with the pedals. I laugh and told him yes I know what a bicycle is, and no I didn't see anyone riding a bicycle. I started to have a chat with him and the rest of the soldiers. He introduced himself as Sergeant Thomas and said that I must work with the Army as a translator."

Of course Mo knew what a bicycle was. Mo's father was a writer and professor, and Mo had studied at a school in Ireland for a few years when his dad taught there. He had even picked up an Irish accent, and a hot temper to match. Mo looked and acted like an Iraqi Tony Soprano—heavyset, with tightly cropped hair, and always in need of a shave. He loved to laugh, smoke cigarettes, and eat. Very smooth and immediately likable. Despite his relative wealth by Iraqi standards, he was a kid of the streets. Mo knew every corner and every person in the neighborhood, and he knew how to get things done.

Besides playing the sheriff of Medical City, I also had to act like the mayor. We weren't just the law, we were the only semblance of local civil government. For example, we were responsible for seeing that certain city workers got paid—I guess it was assumed that if the government's money had gone through Iraqi hands it would have vanished. I was tasked to pay area doctors and teachers, who made five dollars and three dollars a week respectively.

One day a Civil Affairs Colonel dropped into our zone without announcement. Whenever a full-bird Colonel "drops in," people scamper. He ordered our CO to give him a Squad to provide security on a mission to the nearby Baghdad water treatment plant, and they were off. They were given the mission on the way.

The Colonel had $40,000 in U.S. cash in a box. He and my men arrived at a run-down office building at the back end of a water treatment plant. Apparently, the workers of the city's water treatment department hadn't been paid in months. Today was payday. Within minutes, the crowds started to arrive. There were no phones in Iraq, but whenever there was money being handed out, people were like moths to a flame. I have no idea how word got around the city so fast. The Colonel left my Squad Leader with the cash, a Squad of soldiers, and hundreds of angry, hungry Iraqis. "Good luck, boys."

By the time I got the call on the radio to send reinforcements, my guys were mobbed. I rolled in with an additional Squad and two vehicles, and saw what looked like the scene at a Metallica concert. There was a sea of Iraqis, all pushing into one little two-story building. One of my guys was standing on the roof of a Humvee screaming and waving his SAW (Squad Automatic Weapon) like a traffic cop. Mostly, he was just trying to keep from getting trampled.

It was a dicey situation. Nobody wanted to be stuck explaining on CNN why we had killed a crew of unarmed Iraqis. But my guys were nervous. They were being crushed and had limited options. It was a scenario they never trained us for in Infantry school. People were climbing in through windows, pushing into the doorways. We smacked a few of them, and butt-stroked a few more. It was like a scene from *Night of the Living Dead*. They were everywhere.

Two Iraqi dudes at a rickety table tried to keep track of who got paid and who did not, while my guys did crowd control. Since I had worked the door at bars and clubs in my younger days, this part was familiar to me. Everybody had some bullshit story to justify why we needed to let them in. Some workers went through, got their money, and tried to go through again for seconds. When we caught them, they'd change shirts and try again. This was long before we had any ink to color people's fingers purple. We had to settle for a Magic Markered X on the backs of their hands.

Finally, the crowd was gone and everyone had been paid. I told one of the Iraqi guys to do inventory. He told me there were others who had not shown up to collect their money, so he would keep the balance—some $12,000—and pay them later.

"Bullshit," I said. I didn't trust this guy to do anything with that money except buy himself a BMW. I didn't even have his name. I took down his address, made him sign a hand receipt, and took the money back with us. There was no way American tax dollars were going into this dude's pocket. After a mean look and the threat of detainment, he gave in. We took the money back to the vehicles and got the hell out of Dodge.

I had never seen $12,000 in cash before. Neither had my guys. We joked about spending it on a weekend of women and whiskey in Las Vegas. It was pretty amazing to see that much money in one place. A few guys took pictures of themselves with it. It was about a third of a Private's annual salary.

Of course I caught hell from the CO for retaining the money. He didn't want to do the paperwork and be responsible for custody of it. I told him that was fine. I'd just take it to the nearest school. It could do a ton of good there. A few stacks of Benjamins are often much more useful than an M16. I learned early on that American dollars were the best social and professional lubricant in Iraq.

The money stayed in a back room until the boys at Battalion generously agreed to take it off our hands. We couldn't get them to come out of their air-conditioned digs any other time, but funny how quickly they showed up when we had some booty.

ers who had not shown up to collect their money, so he would keep the balance—some $12,000—and pay them later.

"Bullshit," I said. I didn't trust this guy to do anything with that money except buy himself a BMW. I didn't even have his name. I took down his address, made him sign a hand receipt, and took the money back with us. There was no way American tax dollars were going into this dude's pocket. After a mean look and the threat of detainment, he gave in. We took the money back to the vehicles and got the hell out of Dodge.

I had never seen $12,000 in cash before. Neither had my guys. We joked about spending it on a weekend of women and whiskey in Las Vegas. It was pretty amazing to see that much money in one place. A few guys took pictures of themselves with it. It was about a third of a Private's annual salary.

Of course I caught hell from the CO for retaining the money. He didn't want to do the paperwork and be responsible for custody of it. I told him that was fine. I'd just take it to the nearest school. It could do a ton of good there. A few stacks of Benjamins are often much more useful than an M16. I learned early on that American dollars were the best social and professional lubricant in Iraq.

The money stayed in a back room until the boys at Battalion generously agreed to take it off our hands. We couldn't get them to come out of their air-conditioned digs any other time, but funny how quickly they showed up when we had some booty.

CHAPTER SIX
KA-BOB

Peacekeeping is not a job for soldiers, but only soldiers can do it.
—Dag Hammarskjöld, Secretary General of the United Nations, 1953–61

The Medical City complex included a teaching hospital, a blood bank, what they called a "nursing home," a dental college, the Ministry of Health building, a main ward, and an ER. The key was that ER. At the time, it was the only ER in Baghdad functioning at night—and that was only when my men kept it that way. The windows were blown out, and electricity was sporadic at best. Sanitation was not even a consideration. Doctors all smoked cigarettes constantly, even during surgery. An old woman cleaned blood off the floor with a dirty sponge and a bucket of rancid liquid. Body fluids congealed on the floors in puddles. Corpses were left on tables in corners under bloodstained sheets.

About a week after we arrived in Medical City, an English-speaking doctor came to the gate of the compound and asked to speak to an officer. He told me that there was a woman who worked in the nursing home who was a girlfriend of Saddam Hussein's. There was no shortage of Iraqis looking to get paid for info on Saddam and WMD, but he seemed credible, so I heard him out. He told me the lady was middle-aged and had blond hair. Anything that might be a lead to Saddam was worth checking out, so I grabbed a Squad and headed out to pay her a visit.

She didn't really work in a nursing home. It was a hospital for the wealthy. "Chemical Ali"—Saddam's cousin Ali Hassan al-Majid, number five on the Defense Department's list of "Iraq's Most Wanted"—was rumored to come to the facility in the middle of the night to get kidney or cancer treatment, but we could never substantiate that. To be honest, Chemical Ali could have been sitting at the reception desk and we wouldn't have recognized him.

A portly doctor with greasy, slicked-back hair greeted me at the desk. He had gone to college in Michigan in the 1970s and was eager to brush up on his English. After introducing himself, he insisted that I meet the rest of the doctors. He gathered about ten of them, and translated loudly.

"This is Lieutenant . . . Reekoff." Close enough.

"And this is?" he asked me, pointing to Rydberg.

"Specialist Rydberg," I answered.

They all gasped. And whispered angrily. The doctor blanched. *"Ryd-Berg?"*

Shit. They thought they recognized the name as a Jewish one, and they were not happy. This was my first introduction to how much most Iraqis hated Jews and anything remotely associated with Judaism or Israel.

My normally fearless RTO, who was not actually Jewish, whispered urgently to me, "Fuck, sir! Call me Jones!"

"Jones!" I yelled. "Not Rydberg, *Jones*! This is Specialist *Jones*! I confused him with another soldier. They all look the same. This is Specialist Jones. Marvin Jones."

"Ah, good. Jones. You and Mr. Jones, please follow me."

He escorted me and Specialist Jones/Rydberg up a flight of stairs to his office. After some chitchat about New York and his studies in Michigan, I told him we were looking for Saddam's girlfriend.

"I do not know anything about that," he told me flatly. And immediately I knew he was lying. If I had heard these rumors all the way inside my compound, he had heard these rumors in his hospital. I wish the Army issued us portable polygraphs. Rumsfeld should have called up Lockheed Martin and ordered them to come up with one of those. It would have been a much better use of taxpayer dollars than another billion-dollar missile defense system in Alaska that didn't work. Every day I faced countless situations where I had to figure out if Iraqis were lying to me or not.

"Look, Doc. We can do things the easy way, or we can do things the hard way." Baghdad was making me sound like a character from *The Sopranos*. Unsolicited, Rydberg chambered a round in his weapon behind me.

"Okay, okay. Don't kill me! Please! She works on the second floor. I'll take you to her."

I knew it. But that was much easier than I expected. Rydberg and I would use this round-chambering technique effectively in the future.

A few minutes later, we found the lady. She seemed to be expecting us. Mid-forties and large-chested, she had the worst bleach job I had ever seen. Twenty years earlier, she had probably been very attractive. Now she wore incredibly thick makeup—lots of blush, dark red lipstick, and eyes lined with black drawn beyond the eyelids in an upward curl, giving her the desired Cleopatra look. It was terribly unflattering. She looked more like a drag queen than the queen of the Nile. But I learned that this type of heavy Tammy Faye Bakker makeup was common among wealthy, modernized, fashionable women in Baghdad.

Well educated and quite charming, she calmly told me that the charges leveled against her were lies. According to her, some of the conservative-minded doctors in the hospital did not approve of her dress, her modern ways, and the fact that she was unmarried. They told her she was too outspoken for a woman. When she refused to tone it down and cover up, they started spreading the Saddam rumors and labeled her a whore. She told me she feared for her life, and planned to quit working at the hospital within days to move to Jordan. It sounded like office politics taken to a whole new level.

I wasn't exactly Columbo in camouflage, but I believed her. Iraqi Wahabists, the most extreme and conservative of Muslims, wanted to turn Baghdad into a Saudi Arabia, where women live under cover and follow their men. In the post-Saddam chaos, groups of men all over Iraq were threatening women—even killing them—for failing to conform to their idea of religious appropriateness.

Rydberg and I said good-bye to the woman, thanked her for her time, and wished her well on her trip. I was sorry to see her go.

As I turned away, she called to us.

"Boys," she said smoothly, almost without accent, "thank you for freeing my people. Things are bad here now, but it is good that Saddam is gone. Especially for educated women. We all prayed that you would come one day. We are very grateful."

For days, every time I came through the ER I noticed a skeletal, wrinkled woman lying on a gurney just inside the doorway. Always alone, she was calm and emotionless when we came in—except for a constant, gentle cough. Immobile, but following my face closely with her sad, yellowed eyes. She had no visible wounds, yet was clearly waiting to die.

I finally grabbed one of the doctors who spoke some English to find out what was wrong with her. The doctors hated being seen talking to us and did all they could to avoid it.

"Oh. That one? She has disease and no money," he said dismissively.

"Okay. What disease exactly does she have?" I was trying to be patient.

"A breathing disease. She have very sick chest." He pointed at his own rib cage.

I feared where this was going.

"Okay. . . . Do you know what the disease is called?"

"Ehhhhhh . . ." He was searching for the word in English, and took a long pull from his cigarette. "Ehhhhhhhh . . . Toobercolli-sis!" he yelled.

Doc Lewis, our Platoon medic, leaned in alongside me to hear the conversation. He was a quiet, chain-smoking, really squared-away guy, who the men nicknamed Doc Flamer for his red hair and mustache, which apparently made him look like some gay porn star.

I lowered my voice. "What? You mean tuberculosis?"

"Yes." He nodded happily.

My jawed dropped and I nearly choked on my chew. Doc Lewis chuckled, shook his head, and started to creep toward the doorway.

A squad of my guys panted deeply in the tepid night air not twenty feet away. I took a breath—a shallow one—and said quietly, "Look. This woman is highly contagious. You cannot just leave her here in the lobby of the ER to infect everyone else and die."

"Why? I have no room to put her. And she have no money."

"Listen, Doc. There are dozens of rooms in this building. You better find a place for her. Tonight. Not tomorrow. Not next week. Tonight. She had better be gone by the time my next patrol comes through here in a few hours. Either you get her out of this area, or we stop coming to this ER to protect your ass."

"But I am doctor. I go to school. You are just soldier." He was arrogant and incredulous. This was the way many Sunnis, who represented the wealthy and educated class in society, were used to talking to people they considered beneath them, like the Shias. (Think of the Sunnis as plantation-era Southern whites and the Shias as black slaves, and you won't be far off.) He pushed his shoulders back defiantly and said, "She is okay. She stay here."

Now I was pissed. This guy's ignorance had already endan-gered every soldier who'd come through here in the past two weeks—not to mention the countless Iraqi patients and their fam-ilies streaming through the lobby every day and night. Now he wanted to test me. I needed to convince him to move the infected woman without freaking out my guys or upsetting the dozens of civilians now watching closely.

I stepped toward the young doctor. Rydberg instinctively shuffled over to his right, boxing him in. I stood six-two and Rydberg was at least six-four, both of us more than six inches taller than the doctor. I leaned down into his face and said, "I don't care if you think you're fucking Hippocrates. She is highly contagious. You cannot keep her here. You are a doctor, and I may be just a soldier, but we are the law. And if I find her here next time I come through, I'll zip cuff you, take you back to our compound, and give you a long class on infectious diseases. Got it?"

Rydberg tapped his M16 with his thumb.

The doctor didn't understand every word I said, but he got my drift. He took a nervous drag from his dirty cigarette and nodded reluctantly.

"Okay, mister. No problem. No problem."

That type of ignorance combined with arrogance was common among the staff. One night while passing through on a patrol, I asked an Iraqi doctor the guys called "Liberace" if he was worried at all about the prospect of AIDS. Liberace's English was very good. He had flamboyant, effeminate ways, a gaudy fake gold ring on his middle finger, and loved to try to touch us—especially the young guys.

"Oh, no. We don't have AIDS," he said proudly. "Saddam made sure everyone with AIDS was killed or kept out of Iraq."

I was skeptical at best, and asked him what he used to test for AIDS.

"We don't have tests. But don't worry. No AIDS here in Iraq."

"Really? I'm pretty sure you're wrong about this one, Doc," I said.

But he was adamant. "AIDS is only a disease for homosexuals! And we don't have those either."

"Yeah, right, Liberace!" a soldier shouted from across the room.

"That's total bullshit. First Platoon saw two dudes fucking each other under the bridge with night vision. I heard them request permission to engage the targets over the radio net."

Homosexuality is not exactly accepted in the Army. It's almost as bad as being a Democrat. Soldiers love to label each other gay in ridicule. In Iraq, I frequently overheard them talking with surprise about "all the faggots" in Iraq. It was customary for Iraqi men to hold hands, and to kiss each other on the cheek during greetings, as in many other Arab countries. Some of the soldiers thought that all the men we saw kissing each other were gay. In the early weeks in Medical City, a few soldiers got very upset when they saw the practice. They could even turn violent when an Iraqi attempted to greet one of us that way.

I had lived in Manhattan for a while, where gay men and women hold hands and show affection openly all the time. So men kissing each other on the cheek didn't surprise or bother me a bit. Also, in my travels I'd seen straight men observing similar customs in other places, like Argentina. But many of the soldiers in my Platoon had never left the South, much less the United States. Their cultural ignorance scared and saddened me. It made communicating with a foreign people in a foreign culture that much more difficult. Preparing soldiers for this and the countless other cultural differences we would face in Iraq would have been a smart move for the Army. Not just because it was right, but because it would have made us more effective. But it was clear to me that cultural sensitivity training was not high on the DOD's priority list. They were too busy training us for chemical attacks that never came.

There was plenty to disturb us about the medical complex besides cultural differences. The lack of basic sanitation was appalling. Medical waste was thrown in corners with the rest of the trash. The smell throughout the buildings was enough to make you gag. Stray dogs, rats, and cats dug through flyblown piles and sniffed in doorways. One day the guys saw a cat roaming the grounds with a severed hand dangling from its mouth. The story became legendary. A few weeks later, a First Sergeant from another unit told the story to *Stars and Stripes* and claimed it as his own. My guys were furious. As National Guardsmen, we had been treated like second-class soldiers since our deployment began. But this was the last straw. Rydberg designated himself the unit spokesman, and sent a scalding letter to the editor. "This is either the same cat and it has a hand fetish," he wrote, "or there are multiple cats snagging hands from the hospital grounds." He was a little worried when the letter actually ran. In the Army, it's never good to sound off in public.

The ER was a magnet for all of the worst trouble in central Baghdad. Before the Americans came to town, twenty gunshot deaths a month were standard for the entire city. Now, in the "postwar" anarchy, there were five hundred a month. Anyone who had been wounded, whether by our troops or by another Iraqi (which was the vast majority of cases), came to our ER. Kids with missing and shattered limbs, pregnant women having babies, and local thugs with gunshot wounds to their chests all scrambled in looking for help. If an attack or assassination had been unsuccessful, the killers came here to finish the job. The bad guys didn't wear ID cards. So every incoming patient was viewed with skepticism.

Families who'd brought their loved ones in often responded to their deaths by attacking the well-meaning doctors, who had done all they could to save the victim. Imagine the *Jerry Springer Show* set in a run-down Brooklyn ER, with a power outage, under occasional small-arms fire. Add some Shia women screaming in the waiting room, tattoo-faced old ladies on their knees, screaming and bashing their heads on the floor, hands covered with blood, performing their unique mourning ritual, as a pickup truck full of fedayeen brandishing AKs drives up to the front door. Every few hours cars flew in with a newly broken body, or ten. Lots of kids. I don't care how tough you think you are, seeing the mangled bodies of kids will fuck you up. Some of the guys really took it hard. Especially the ones with children of their own.

One night on patrol we came upon a little girl in the back of a pickup truck. She was under a dark blanket and jerking uncontrollably. Blood filled the bed of the truck in a shallow pool. She apparently had taken shrapnel to the head and definitely had some brain damage. Grayish brain matter bubbled from her scalp and her body convulsed ferociously. Her brothers and father were having a hard time holding her down because her body was bucking so violently. It was tragic. They were desperate to get to the doctor, but in their desperation was hope that something could be done for her. They thought that as Americans we had the power to save her. She was going to die and I knew it, but they did not. I couldn't save her. I couldn't save most of them. I wanted to so badly, but it was just beyond my capacity. There is no worse feeling than helplessness. It really got to me.

Another night Rydberg and I made our rounds to check on the two-man teams posted at key points throughout the complex. We rounded a corner in the dark with weapons raised to see the soft glow from the cigarettes of two guys from Second Squad, pacing in front of a tattered ambulance.

"Check this out, L.T. One of the Haji doctors just showed us some crazy shit in that trailer over there." Guys had started using "Haji" as an adjective to describe anything Iraqi—usually because it was cheap, poorly made, or just fucked up. Haji food. Haji women. Haji cars. If the cheap batteries that Esam got on Haifa Street failed, it was "Fucking Haji batteries!" We'd bust into some family's apartment, searching for weapons on a tip, and see how the whole family slept together on mats on the floor. "They were hiding this AK under the Haji mattress, L.T.!"

As he pointed, I panned my flashlight through the hot darkness, revealing a burned gray trailer parked alongside a warehouse loading dock. The soldiers led me toward the trailer with crooked smiles, and I knew Rydberg and I were in for something interesting. The hulking and crooked trailer had dented walls and gooey, melted tires. All of Baghdad smelled like a horrible stew of shit, smoke, and death that reminded me of Ground Zero. The wretched stench was so constant you almost forgot about it. But as I walked along the side of the trailer, my eyes began to tear as the stench grew stronger.

The two soldiers paused at the steel doors for effect, like Monty Hall before opening door number three.

"You guys ready?"

"Open the fucking door already, dude," Rydberg snapped.

As the doors swung open a blast of death-smell hit me hard, pushing the helmet back on my sweaty forehead. My eyes struggled to focus through tears, as waves of ghastly air made me impulsively gag and taste the vapors of my own stomach. The first thing I saw looked like a bone. It shone black and sharp in the artificial light. It was long and straight—likely a femur. Rydberg swung a light around from behind me to illuminate it. Next I saw teeth. A huge set of crooked, charred teeth, grinning menacingly at me from behind lips half eaten away by rats. A demented, defiant, frozen smile of pain. It lay perched on a pile of burned blood, scalloped muscle, and frayed fabric. The front half of a leather sandal lay beside it. It hardly even looked like a body. It looked more like a melted stack of Freddy Kruger masks. I couldn't even tell how many bodies there were in the mess. Flies swarmed loudly within the metal walls of the trailer.

"This is our new friend. We call him Ka-Bob! Get it?" the soldier said proudly. "Ka-Bob! That's some funny shit!"

"The Haji doctors told us that the morgue downstairs is full. They had nowhere else to store the bodies, so they started piling 'em up here. Nasty, huh, sir?"

That was an understatement in so many different ways.

"Yeah. Nasty. Don't touch anything," I instructed them. "You guys haven't been given enough shots to protect you from all the contaminants flying around inside of this thing."

I felt horrible leaving the bodies there, but I wasn't about to have my guys putting their hands on the stuff and puking blood for the next four weeks, or going blind ten years from now. I couldn't help but think about the long-term effects of the constant exposure to an understaffed, overwhelmed, and antiquated hospital full of death and disease. The morgue trailer was like many of the dilemmas we faced. There was no good solution, just a few that were less bad. We had limited men and limited resources. Some things we could fix, but most we could not.

"Keep the Iraqis away from this thing if you can. Except for the medical staff and folks who have a legitimate reason to be here. I don't want the locals upset because they heard American troops were messing with their dead. Got it?"

"No problem, sir. We already took some pictures. Nobody back home is ever gonna believe that we saw this kind of shit."

I plotted it in my GPS and labeled it "Ka-Bob." Rydberg copied the coordinates into a notebook and relayed them back to the CP. As we walked to check on the next pair of guys, I turned and shouted a final order.

"One thing, guys. In the unlikely event that any of the officers from Battalion stop by, be sure to show them this shit. Maybe it'll give them a bit of a reality check."

"No problem, sir. We'd love the chance to see the BC puke on himself. That would make our night."

Since Medical City was the only functioning hospital complex in Iraq, the Iraqi people who worked there held tremendous power. Corruption was rampant. From the surgeons to the ambulance drivers, everyone had an angle and was trying to make a buck. The blood bank was no exception.

Around midnight one night, we were patrolling through the parking lot behind the hospital when one of the exhausted-looking young doctors approached me.

"Please, mister. I need your help."

I recognized this doctor and liked him. He was about my age, and was always working himself to the point of exhaustion. The medical coat he wore had stopped looking white a long time before. Although I could tell he didn't like us, he seemed to understand the necessity of our presence, and was always honest with me.

Many of the experienced doctors had left Baghdad, or refused to risk working under such dangerous conditions. Most of the doctors who worked in the hospital were young, idealistic, and inexperienced. Add that they rarely slept and were scared as hell, and I often got the feeling that behind the ER curtain was Frankenstein's workshop.

We followed him through the back door of the ER to the surgery area. Half the squad stood guard in the ER while I took the other half to check it out. I could hear women wailing from fifty feet away as we approached, and knew I was in for an interesting sight. You never knew what you were going to get. Gunshot wound? Pregnancy? Amputation? My men and I had seen more carnage than most of the trauma surgeons in America by the end of our first week in Baghdad.

I followed the doc to the back corner of the ER. He pushed aside a curtain and yelled at a crowd to clear the way. Two old women in black burkas had their backs to us, crying. They made way as the doctor shouted. There lay a girl, about eleven years old, sprawled on her back. Her skin was pale and her bob-cut hair was sticky with blood. She was a beautiful little child, and her legs were completely mangled. I heard one of the soldiers gag behind me, and I had to swallow hard not to do the same. Her right foot was twisted completely backward and the left leg was full of tiny lacerations. Wrinkled bandages covered only about half her wounds. She was alive, but in very bad shape.

"She needs blood. She needs blood or she is going to die."

I figured as much, but I was confused.

"Okay. So get some blood, Doc."

"No. That is why I need you to help! The man who runs the blood bank will not give us any blood tonight. He says he cannot afford to give us any blood. He is corrupt. He is a bad man. He wants money. He sells the blood to rich people. He says he does not have enough blood for this girl."

"What?"

My soldiers were listening, riveted. I could feel their collective blood pressures rise with mine as the doctor spoke. A Staff Captain, the Battalion S-4, was with us for a walk-along. He was a good officer who wanted to see what the men were seeing. I had warned him he would see some fucked-up shit, but I don't think he was ready for this scene.

"Got it. How much does she need?"

"She needs at least three liters. And she still may die."

The blood bank was about a block away from the ER, in a long, flat building that looked like an elementary school. We stomped over there like ten angry bulls. I was gonna fix this. I wasn't sure how, but one way or another, we would get some blood.

Inside we passed an abandoned welcome desk and an empty waiting room of blue plastic seats. We had heard rumors for weeks that Saddam was sneaking to the place in the middle of the night for blood transfusions. Who knew? He'd made his last official public appearance in early April, as our first tanks rolled across the bridges. But like Elvis after he died, there had been numerous Saddam sightings all over the city since then. Not a day passed without some local coming to our front gate claiming to have spotted him somewhere. In a city of six million, he could be holed up anywhere.

An irritated-looking fat man came from the back as my guys fanned out to search the rest of the building. I knew this was the dude I was looking for, and his body language instantly told me we weren't going to get along.

I asked him if he spoke English, and he shook his head angrily. I started through Esam.

"Why won't you give the doctors at the ER any blood?"

"He says he can not give them blood because he only has six liters of blood left."

"Okay. They only need three liters."

"Yes," the man replied irritably. "But if I give them three, I only have three left."

"Wait a minute! You just told me you don't fucking speak English. Now you do. What the fuck are you trying to pull with me?"

He put his head down and turned to walk away from us. I grabbed him by the shoulder and spun him around.

"Don't fucking walk away from me! I'm going to ask you one more time. Why can't you give up the blood? There's a little girl with her legs nearly blown off who's about to fucking die over there."

"In Baghdad, little girls die every day." He shrugged dismissively. "I cannot give you the blood."

That was it. I lost it. I hadn't slept in a day, and I'd had it with fuckers like this guy. I reached out and gripped his throat. I lifted and squeezed. His eyes bulged as I pushed his head against a wall. From the second I saw him, my gut told me that he had some kind of crooked agenda. I didn't know what it was, but I didn't like it. I leaned in close and looked right into his eyes. I was close enough that I could see the smoke stains on his front teeth. He smelled terrible.

"Listen, motherfucker. You are going to give us the blood right now."

I squeezed harder as he choked. The bravado was gone. He didn't like it, but I was in charge of his world. I knew the S-4 was right behind me and felt his discomfort, but I didn't give a fuck. Welcome to our world, where little girls die because scumbag assholes want to make a buck.

"You are going to give the doctors more if they ask for it. And if you don't, my men and I are going to find you, and we are going to kill you. Do you understand me?"

He understood me, all right.

"Okay, okay." Even though he was capitulating, he was still reluctant and arrogant, giving me Sunni 'tude. He was moving slowly, just to piss me off. Then he muttered with disgust, "You are just like Saddam."

I was past rage now. I felt my pulse beating in my neck. I thought about the little girl and went Zen. I stuffed back my desire to unload a full magazine of 5.56 rounds into his groin.

"No, scumbag, you are just like Saddam. And those days are fucking over. Now give me the damn blood, or I'm gonna start spilling some of yours."

He opened the case with the plasma stored in it, moving slightly faster now. I passed it back to the guys and watched his hands closely, fully expecting him to pull out a pistol instead of the plasma. But it didn't happen. He just hemmed and hawed and cursed me in his head. We had the three pints, and the little girl would have a chance to survive.

On the way out the door, I promised the asshole that a patrol of my men would be through his building every day to check on him and say hello (especially in case the Saddam rumors were true). I didn't expect to change his heart or his mind, but I could disrupt his plans and keep him on his toes. And make his wicked life a little bit more miserable. The girl might already have been dead, but our point was made.

I had probably broken some kind of law. Taken out of context, this scene could have ruined my career. But we were the only ones there, and nobody else would ever understand the complicated dynamics of that moment. As American soldiers in Baghdad, we were placed in an environment where the entire moral structure was crumbling—a moral structure that was already built on shaky ground. Under Saddam, survival had always been the most essential part of every Iraqi's existence, especially the poor. The skill of wearing multiple faces and hedging all your bets was the key to success. Lying, bribery, and treachery were the most important tricks of the trade in the streets of Saddam's Iraq.

I knew every one of my guys was fine with my course of action in the blood bank. There were eight "battle drills" that formed the core of all Infantry actions according to Field Manual 7-8, "Infantry, Rifle, Platoon and Squad." A battle drill was defined as a collective action rapidly executed without applying a deliberate decision-making process. Infantry battle drills describe how Platoons and Squads apply fire to and maneuver through commonly encountered situations. They require leaders to make decisions rapidly and to issue brief oral orders quickly.

The incident in the blood bank illustrated a new amendment to 7-8, developed by necessity among Infantry soldiers in Baghdad. Battle Drill 9: apply intimidation.

I wasn't proud of myself and my tactics that night, but I wasn't ashamed either. They worked, and that's what mattered. Medical City was our turf. We patrolled it like beat cops and defended it like our home. We patrolled the halls, protected the doctors, checked the morgue, had men stationed at the entrances and a Humvee outside of the ER. It was absolutely critical that the hospital stay open to treat patients.

Sometimes we used the carrot, other times we used the stick. One of the guys summed it up well, borrowing a saying from the Marines and scrawling it on a wall:

3rd Platoon: No better friend. No worse enemy.

Not since September 11, 2001, had I witnessed the type of selfless service and brutal efficiency that my guys demonstrated in Iraq. Memories of 9/11 haunted me daily.

I had quit my job at JPMorgan on September 7, 2001. Four days later, I was planning to spend the day sleeping in late, going to the dentist, and taking the train up to the Bronx to play some golf. I tried to ignore it, but the phone on my bedside would not stop ringing. I figured something must be wrong, and I finally picked it up. It was an ex-girlfriend in Miami.

"Paul, turn on the TV," she said, calm but urgent. As I saw the first tower smoking on CNN, I went numb and heard her say, "Paul. This is what you have always been waiting for."

I had always complained that mine was a generation without a cause. Not anymore.

I bounded the stairs in threes to the roof of our building on East Twenty-fourth Street. As I slammed the rooftop door, the first thing I saw was the cloudless soft blue sky. It was a gorgeous day—a perfect day. The next thing I saw was the smoke smudging the sky's flawless color. I heard the cacophony of sirens and people yelling from Third Avenue below. I ran to the street from the roof and over to Broadway, where I could get a clear look at the towers.

Breathless and focused, I stood among a crowd of stunned New Yorkers with mouths frozen open, eyes wide. They were hypnotized. It reminded me of the scenes in *Godzilla* when everyone in Tokyo frantically jumped out of their cars, dropped briefcases, filled the streets and stopped everything to collectively freeze and look back—before running like hell as Godzilla crashed through the city.

Then the second plane hit. We were in awe. Petrified but unmoved. No one ran. No one panicked. They just stared and cried.

Game time. Back in my apartment a few minutes later, I pulled a crumpled BDU set from a duffel bag on my floor and moved quickly. Training kicked in as I assembled my web gear in fast-forward. I called my dad and told him I was going and ran out the door into the smoke and sirens. I got downtown sometime after the second tower fell.

In all my days of military training, I never imagined I'd be called on to serve in my own city. Grotesque scenes were everywhere. So was the heroism. Very little small talk. Just cooperative commands, grunts, and labored breathing. And the sounds of people trying to choke back rage, sorrow, and awe. Looking across the vastness of the wreckage, I remembered the first time I took in the magnitude of the Grand Canyon as a child. Pictures just didn't do it justice. Sirens roared so constantly that I stopped hearing them. A gigantic plane engine sat calmly uninterrupted on a street corner like a bizarre piece of modern art. My eyes were numb from the constant sting of the dust, and they had developed a scalding red color, just like everyone else's.

We were hunched and tired, and had just finished digging out the bloated body of a corpulent older woman in a black dress. A stocky older fireman in front of me stopped and gasped. "Oh God. Oh Jesus. It's another lady," he murmured and started to sob. Over his shoulder, I saw what he saw: a black pump on her right foot poking out from behind some concrete and rebar. And my head started to spin. I felt light-headed. But it cleared as I tried to focus on moving the twisted metal around her. As we cleared the bigger rubble to pull her out, we found her clutching a black purse. This was somebody's mother. Somebody's wife. And she was smashed so thoroughly that when we finally got her freed to lift her out, her body flopped like a giant rag doll over our outstretched arms. Her face was unrecognizable and almost seemed fake. I had never seen anything like this. The bones were gone. All of them. Lifting her body felt like holding a big bag of skin filled with water. I found myself guiltily amazed that the human body could withstand such trauma without tearing. Her body had almost no cuts or abrasions, and no blood. Just every single bone in her body broken.

Later that day, as the bucket brigades snaked into the smoldering chasm, a young guardsman, holding up a red paint bucket, called to me, "Hey, sir! What do I do with this?"

His question baffled me. We had been passing buckets back and forth for hours along the lines. Full ones were passed to the rear to be dumped near the Burger King.

"Pass it back!" I told him shortly. "Same as the others."

But he insisted, "No, sir! What do I do with *this*?" And as I looked at his face for the first time, his eyes swelled and his hands shook. He leaned his young frightened face forward to show me the contents. Inside was the right stockinged leg of a woman, severed below the knee, black heel still on the foot.

The long cold refrigerator trucks were parked next to the stacks of body bags. I stood on the pile and heard a man scream on the bucket line behind me, and turned to see his left arm erupt with blood. The swirling winds and helicopter rotors overhead had blown shattered glass off a building somewhere stories above us and sent it raining down like bullets. Architects and engineers warned us that at least three other buildings could still come down at any time and kill us all. Everything was totally unstable. The deafening sound of three horn blows from the trucks, a warning to all in the area that another building might be coming down any second. It was the signal to run like hell if you wanted to live. It seemed like a command from God Himself. Workers dropped their tools and gear and sprinted north, as they had done so many times that week. Despite the incalculable risks, they always came right back.

The firemen, especially, worked literally until exhaustion. They whispered, inquiring about the friends and brothers they feared were trapped under it all. And they knew every second was precious. They had to be ordered by superiors to eat and take breaks—and would still sneak back onto the pile minutes later.

By the second day, FEMA workers and fire department personnel from as far away as California and Oregon were on the scene. They led search dogs that wore booties on their feet to protect them from cuts. The dogs worked tirelessly and were never once wrong. Sometimes it would take hours of work, and the movement of tons of wreckage, but the bodies were always in the spot where the dogs indicated.

After some especially difficult digging, we found an older woman's body stuck beneath a mammoth block of concrete the size of a small house. In her wallet, she carried a New Jersey license and pictures of her grandchildren. The women were always so much harder to deal with. It just hurt more. Concrete and steel locked her into the pit. The lower half of the body was solidly trapped and immovable. We pulled and twisted in vain to try to free her. Men poked tirelessly with tools and yanked at different angles, but we couldn't get her out. We were locked in a gruesome tug-of-war with the wreckage.

We all knew how many people worked in the towers. There were thousands. And we had no idea whether another attack was on the way. F-14s roared, curving around the tip of Manhattan low enough for us to see the numbers on their tails. Terribly concerned about fires and secondary explosions, we had to move quickly. All day we worked at a frantic pace to find the living and recover the dead. There were so many more we needed to save, and this one body was slowing us down terribly. We worried that if a fire started, and we didn't get at least part of her out, her family would never know.

Firemen and cops are a lot like soldiers. Many are soldiers nowadays. When faced with a decision under pressure, we are all trained to think about the "80 percent solution"—a decent plan executed now is always better than a perfect plan later. We had no more time to spend on this one body. Limited on tools, a fireman had an effective and grisly idea. And we all agreed to it. It was a collective decision, and any possible repercussions would not be pinned on him alone.

Burned in my mind forever were the tears that streamed down his face as he raised a shovel high above his head and drove it thudding into her bloated midsection. He had cut her body in half at the waist. Half a dozen men wept in mournful awe as the young fireman continued to labor, until he realized the shovel was not sharp enough to cut through her spine. A young doctor rushed up and fell to his knees. As he lifted the scalpel, he fell in a heap, crying uncontrollably. The exhausted fireman with the shovel dropped his tool and put his arms around the doctor, saying, "Doc, you have to do it, man. You're doing the right thing. It's the only way we can get her out. You can do it, Doc." He nodded, choked back his tears and cut through the last resilient parts of her spine with his hands. It was the most macabre and selfless act I had ever seen.

CHAPTER SEVEN
THE MOTHER'S DAY MASSACRE

The most terrible job in warfare is to be a second lieutenant
leading a platoon when you are on the battlefield.
—Dwight D. Eisenhower

We heard that everyone back home felt pretty damn good about the progress of the war. In those first weeks of May, despite how grim things were, we were still optimistic that the situation was improving a little every day. Guys talked about the ticker-tape parades down Broadway in New York City after the Gulf War. I told my soldiers that they would all be welcome to crash at my apartment in Brooklyn. We'd go to some of my favorite bars and tear up the town. Higher was still telling us we'd be home by July Fourth. I wrote my brother, Mikey, and told him to get tickets for the Yankees–Red Sox series in the Bronx.

But even with things settling down, there were still a million different ways to die. And July was a lifetime away. Units flew into our sector daily from the palace thinking things were safe. Despite our warnings, Colonels and Majors would fly around carelessly with no body armor on and helmets off, wanting to get their pictures taken handing out candy to the kids. One morning a team of Civil Affairs soldiers were traveling in two vehicles on a "public health-related mission" when they got popped with small-arms fire from an Iraqi who approached their vehicles while they were stopped in traffic. Four of them were wounded, one seriously.

On May 11, 2003, most of the guys in Third Platoon weren't much concerned about missing the Mother's Day holiday back home. We had much bigger fish to fry right here in Baghdad.

Secretary of Defense Donald Rumsfeld had just ordered L. Paul Bremer—the recently arrived administrator of the Coalition Provisional Authority (CPA)—to disband the Iraqi army and civil service. This colossal blunder immediately created 400,000 disgruntled, unemployed Iraqi soldiers and civil servants. Many had military experience and weapons. And in Sector 17, we felt the effects instantaneously.

Thousands of the newly laid-off Iraqis moved directly from government to the ranks of the blossoming criminal elements. They also formed the foundation of what would later be known as "the insurgency." They were what Rumsfeld boldly referred to as "dead-enders." To us they weren't insurgents, they weren't dead-enders, they weren't Syrian freedom fighters. To us, it was pretty simple: they were the bad guys who shot at our compound every night and wanted to make sure we didn't make it home to see our kids grow up. Bremer struck me as an ignorant and out-of-touch civilian bureaucrat. When he made bad decisions with the bold stroke of a pen, my guys suffered and bled.

And so, on May 11, not even two weeks after the world had been told "mission accomplished," my Platoon saw our first major enemy contact in Baghdad. Like so many skirmishes, this one began in confusion.

I was in a planning meeting in a back room of the auditorium with the CO, Andy, and our Platoon Sergeants, briefing the CO on the status of the hospital, when I heard the 240 Bravo machine gun on the roof start to roar.

I looked behind Andy and saw the first rounds impacting right outside the window of the CP, about thirty feet away. Just past the sandbags outside, the windshield of a battered car popped and kicked glass violently. I knew we were in for an interesting day.

"Fuck!" Andy yelled, grabbing his weapon as we sprung to our feet. Spit bottles and notebooks flew as we all turned for the front of the building. Now I could hear multiple weapons firing from a number of points in front of the building. They sounded mostly like ours, but I couldn't be sure. My mind moved at light speed as I thought about how vulnerable the building was in so many ways. I feared that a small enemy element had made a serious play for our front door and caught our guys sleeping. We jumped up and ran out of the room to the front of the building to find our Platoons.

As I ran down the hall toward the firing, I chambered a round and checked my vest pouches for extra ammo magazines. First thing I saw through the lobby was Sergeant Gipson's twitching back as he knelt behind a flowerpot and unloaded rounds toward the river. Two soldiers from Second Platoon to his left were doing the same. My heartbeat pounding in my eardrums, I slammed my knee hard into the concrete next to Gipson to assess the situation.

"Sir, we got multiple enemy to the front!" he shouted during a magazine change. "There are lots of them! All along the bridge!"

I saw two Iraqi men with AKs scampering about two hundred meters out, firing wildly from the base of the bridge. Flashes cracked from their muzzles, but I couldn't determine the direction they were firing. I remember thinking it was not at all like the movies, when you can see the bullet leave the muzzle on its way to the target. For a second I thought the men were firing somewhere to the far left of our position. Maybe they weren't shooting at us. Then a shard of something hard and sharp kicked into my face and threw concrete dust into my eyes. I raised my weapon to my cheek and simultaneously glanced down at a section of flowerpot that puffed gray smoke just a foot in front of me. The motherfuckers were shooting at us, all right.

My finger pulled back on the trigger and the muzzle of my rifle threw rounds toward the bridge in response. It was pure reflex, like putting up a hand to stop a punch. I didn't even think about it. Heavy fire was coming from my men on the left as weapons roared above me from the roof. A man wearing a white shirt went down in the distance. Another one ran behind the SUV. The men were so far away, and so many other guys were firing, that I couldn't tell if my rounds had hit him or not. Bullets sailed at the bridge in waves like swarms of insects. I heard at least five weapons alongside of me firing in the same direction. I turned to see that there were more. Guys continued to pour out of the building and lined up like a firing squad. The firefight quickly turned into a shooting gallery. The maniacs on the bridge had disturbed the wasps from our very large and deadly nest. I turned back downriver to see puffs of smoke and water popping up all around the bridge like it was the middle of a rainstorm.

I tugged my trigger back again and again. I couldn't get the rounds out of the magazine fast enough. These fuckers were shooting at us. They were shooting at my boys. Fuck them. I wanted to see their heads pop open like watermelons. My shock and fear were now long gone. It felt good to shoot back. I felt powerful. I had thunder in my hand.

As the bolt of my rifle slammed open with the magazine empty, I finally took a breath and stopped myself. "What the fuck am I doing?" I thought. "There are enough guys firing here now." I quelled my insatiable thirst to continue to pour it on. My blood was hot, but I gulped it back and turned to find the rest of my guys.

A fat, bearded Iraqi detainee and his skinny kid, maybe eleven years old, in a dirty striped shirt, lay on the floor about thirty feet behind me. A slimy trail of perspiration and dirt crossed the tile floor from where we knelt to where they crouched beneath the welcome table of the Saddam Auditorium. Shaking with terror, they had been pinned down in front of the building in our makeshift detainee holding pen when the shooting started. Doc Owenby, First Platoon's medic, had run out, rounds snapping overhead, and dragged them inside under the crackling of inaccurate fire. Now he had his back to the firing, screening them from the threat with his own body as he checked them over. Their hands were still bound in front of them, dark purple and bruised from the zip cuffs. They whimpered uncontrollably and hugged each other for dear life. Gunfire all around, commands being shouted, and all I could hear was their whimpering. I just wanted them to shut the fuck up.

They were so confused and scared. The father gripped the boy like the end of the world was coming. Maybe it was. They looked at me with huge brown eyes, pleading for more than protection, pleading for their lives. They were terrified they were going to die right there and then.

"Shit. You and me both, dude," I thought.

I developed a methodical, pragmatic callousness in Iraq. It is not something I am proud of now, but it is not something I am ashamed of either. And I feel grateful to the Army for giving it to me. I was taught a lesson in IOBC by an NCO who had been in Somalia in 1991. He said, "Remember, gentlemen, that once the bullets start to fly, there are only two kinds of people: warriors and victims. You must decide to be warriors. Warriors are those who fight. Victims are those who are unprepared, unable, or unwilling to defend themselves."

Most Americans who've never served in combat will never understand that reasoning. The best-trained soldiers are not designed to be humanitarians. That is not what they are built for. Yet that is what the American people expected them to be in Iraq. American soldiers are trained to succeed on the battlefield with incredible proficiency. And in the generations since World War Two, the U.S. Army has gotten much better at making its soldiers more effective—more deadly.

Without the ingrained callousness, my men and I would have been toast. Without it, we would have stopped to dry tears instead of setting up the machine guns to eliminate the threat that could tear all our heads off with the next round. Without the detachment, I'd be writing letters to mothers.

I saw lots of grown men cry in Iraq. It seemed like every day some man begged, pleaded, and sobbed. It turned my stomach a bit in the beginning. Then, I just stopped caring entirely. I just went numb. Sometimes I was more than unfeeling of their pain—I hated them for it. I hated them for not having the dignity, or pride, to suck it up. I hated them for not caring how weak it made them look. I hated them for giving my soldiers an opportunity to mock them and brand them an inferior culture. "Fucking Hajis are pussies," I'd often hear one of my guys say.

And I have to admit, I thought the same thing at times. There were so many reasons for us to be angry: the heat, the shooting, the outdated flak jackets, the lack of information, the shitty chow, the IEDs (Improvised Explosive Device, aka roadside bombs), the sight of our wounded buddies, the lack of sex, the holidays missed, the boredom, the uncertainty, the complete and total lack of control over our own lives. So many reasons to be pissed. And only one group of people to take it out on—the Iraqis.

There was really not much we could do about most problems. American soldiers in Iraq got used to feeling helpless. We became accustomed to not being able to do all the things for the Iraqi people that our government had promised we would.

"No. I'm sorry. I can't turn your lights on."

"No. I'm sorry. I can't give you clean drinking water."

"No. I'm sorry. I can't save your daughter's leg."

The United States Army doesn't issue Platoon Leaders a magic wand.

The old man and his kid were probably detained by my guys for something minor, like stealing sheet metal so they could sell it and eat. But for all they knew, we were going to take them out back and put bullets in their heads for it. And now they were facing the End of Days. Hot rounds were flying at them, and their only protection was an ornery ragtag bunch of rednecks who hadn't gotten their paychecks from Uncle Sam in a month and wished they were home getting drunk in Pensacola.

"Doc, are they hit?"

"No, L.T. They're good." He was calm and stone-faced. Unlike me. His cool made me pause, take a breath, and regain my composure.

"Take care of them, Doc. And check on our guys in front."

He was already in auto mode. The last thing he needed was me telling him how to do his job.

I looked at the Iraqis one last time as I turned to run to my men. I will never forget the faces of that kid and his father. Unadulterated fear and total helplessness.

A Squad from Andy's Platoon was assigned to QRF (Quick Reaction Force) duty that day. I could hear the engines starting as guys ran for the vehicles downstairs. Running up the stairs through the Platoon sleeping area, I pushed open the camouflage poncho dividers and screamed for everyone to get to the front of the building or the rooftop to return fire. Some guys had been sleeping when it all started. A nice way to wake up. They grabbed their helmets and ran to firing positions in their flip-flops and PT shorts. All the guys moved quickly and rushed to get in the fight.

I raised Sergeant Thomas on my Motorola handheld radio. It was a piece of shit, and completely unsecure (the enemy could listen in on it), but it was the only semi-reliable method of communication we had. It was either the Motorolas or smoke signals. Sergeant Thomas and I had bought a ten-pack of them at Wal-Mart with our own money the week before we left the States. Good thing.

Iraqi fire continued in spurts, ours in waves. I reached the roof winded as all hell, while our side responded full throttle with a wall of American lead. It was the middle of the day and the top of the building was like a giant frying pan. Soldiers from both Platoons were flying out of the woodwork.

Best I could tell, about a dozen bad guys in a pair of white SUVs had stopped on that bridge over the Tigris River and fired on a car carrying some city officials. These shots were answered by Iraqis on the other side of the bridge. Those were answered by one of our rooftop gunners. We wanted no gunplay in our hood. The Iraqis, in a moment of brilliance, then fired on the auditorium. Not a smart move. We had them outnumbered four to one. And unlike them, we could shoot with accuracy.

Running to the south side of the roof, I found Third Squad hunkered behind their weapons like they were on a firing range in Georgia. I spotted Chesty, who had replaced Gipson as Third Squad Leader. Chesty was hard not to spot. He was a forty-year-old former Marine who looked like a grizzly. A huge, old, tattered, nasty soldier who should have been a frontiersman in the Davy Crockett days. He got his nickname because he reminded the guys of Lewis "Chesty" Puller, the legendary Marine hero of World War Two and Korea.

I asked Chesty where one particular soldier was, a fire team leader. He pointed a gnarled finger to his right. The sniper, sporting black PT shorts and no shirt, leaned in hard behind his long scope. He knew I was there without even looking at me.

"Hey, L.T.," he whispered as I sucked wind. "What took you so fucking long, sir? I got a shot."

He had an enemy fighter in the crosshairs of the Wal-Mart hunting sight he had bought on his own. Battalion had told us they didn't have enough sniper rifles to go around. Just as he'd been trained, he was meticulous and emotionless. He adjusted the windage knob with his left hand.

"L.T., he's standing up back of the second SUV. He's got an AK and a white shirt. I got the shot."

"Take him out," I responded.

Crack. He had pulled the trigger before I'd finished the third syllable.

The silhouette of the bad guy slumped behind the vehicle.

The 240 twenty-five feet to my right kicked in. "Tow Truck"

had that sucker humming. Tow Truck, a corrections officer back in Florida, was built like a power lifter and walked the earth like an elephant. His alternate nickname was Shrek.

"Pour it on, Tow Truck!" Chesty screamed as he peered through his magnified sights. "Raise it up! You're too low!"

I could see water splashing fifty meters short at the base of the bridge.

"That's better. Keep it on that spot."

"Another motherfucker in the open," the sniper reported. "I got a shot, L.T."

"Take him down."

Crack.

I saw a figure in black disappear behind the SUV, and assumed it was a hit.

Meanwhile, across the river, the only other American unit in our vicinity had Bradleys, but they couldn't communicate with us. Higher command had refused to give me the radio frequency I needed to call that unit, so we couldn't request help. We were two hundred meters away from each other, and we couldn't talk. We were supposed to call up to our Battalion HQ, who decided whether or not to relay our messages. That was how they could "direct" the action on the ground from a safe, air-conditioned distance. To make matters worse, that unit was from a different Battalion than mine, and my Battalion's HQ probably did not even know their Battalion HQ's frequency. I wasn't even supposed to cross the sector line, walk over to the other unit and *ask* them what their frequency was. It was a complete bureaucratic muddle that reflected the fucked-up patchwork of units—Marines, Army, National Guard, British troops, contractors, circus clowns, what have you—that our brilliant leaders in Washington had thrown into this war. And, as usual, it made life on the line more difficult and dangerous for us grunts. Guys from my unit took to using mirrors to flash our frequencies to the other side of the river in Morse code.

After a while our rain of fire was so deafening that I couldn't tell if the enemy had stopped shooting at us.

"Cease fire! Cease fire!" The command echoed down line.

"Anybody hit?"

No casualties on our side except for a few windows.

The skirmish formally ended when an armored Bradley Fighting Vehicle with guns blazing appeared from the west side of the bridge and rammed into the SUVs, sending Iraqis running like roaches exposed to the light. The Bradley crew must have seen what was going on during a patrol and decided to get some trigger time. I doubt they called up to Battalion to get permission.

I watched the smoke clear and listened to the ringing in my ears. Second Platoon had just been in our first major firefight. We'd drawn our first blood. No more blue balls. And honestly, all I could think was how *stupid* those Iraqis were to go up against our tremendously superior firepower with what amounted to peashooters. What the hell were they thinking?

I knew that similar scenarios had occurred since the beginning of the war. As American forces pushed north into Iraq, trucks and buses filled with Iraqi soldiers pointing AK-47s out the windows rushed our entrenched armor and were instantly smashed. Our guys called them "suicide buses." Out near the airport one day, we saw two Iraqis in a field—literally standing in the middle of a field—popping off at a Bradley with their AK-47s. The Bradley just chopped them in half. The attempt was so futile it was almost comical.

But there was a method to their insanity. Essentially, what they were doing is what's called "recon by fire." Testing our strengths and weaknesses, learning our habits, by suicidally throwing themselves at us. Over time, the insurgents realized they could not take American forces head-on. That's when they stepped up the creativity of their guerrilla and terrorist tactics. Suicide bombers, mortars, IEDs, decapitating hostages on video—all that. American leaders called them "savages." The same thing was said by the British when the Americans used guerrilla tactics in the Revolutionary War.

Though the firing had stopped, the confusion continued. Every guy seemed to have a different count, anywhere from one to twelve Iraqis dead. A number of the survivors had fled and the wounded were rushed to the hospital—the same hospital my men were assigned to guard.

I hurried to the CP to tell the Commander to send the QRF (Quick Response Force) to track down the enemy fighters to be killed or detained, but he refused. Battalion instructed him to keep all soldiers inside the compound until they could verify the events of the contact.

The enemy was right down the street, bleeding just a few blocks away, but we were forbidden from going after them. The incompetence of our higher command led to another missed opportunity. Any chance of gaining intelligence from the enemy fighters was getting slimmer by the second.

Minutes later, an Iraqi doctor ran to the compound gate, exhausted and out of breath, with news: the dead and wounded enemy in the ER were definitely fedayeen. They had the unmistakable tattoos on their shoulders, a large bird shape with wings outspread like a guardian angel, but instead of a head there was a heart, with three nails shoved into it. I called Battalion to report their location, but no one seemed interested. I finally spoke to the Battalion intelligence officer, who flatly turned down my request to bring these guys in for questioning. My men were furious.

A few hours later, a Special Forces Colonel strolled into the CP with an MP-5, looking to meet the officer in charge. With Andy and the CO at Battalion, that was me.

He smiled largely. "Your guys did good today, Lieutenant. The dudes y'all shot up were some of the baddest mothers in the city. That was a full squad of fedayeen on that bridge. They were on their way to assassinate the mayor of Baghdad and his family when they caught hell from your boys. Y'all killed a few of 'em. There are a few of them all shot to shit in the hospital right now. I suggest you get down there and bring 'em in, Lieutenant. Division could get some real good intelligence out of 'em."

"I hear you, sir. I explained that to my Battalion, but they won't authorize us to go get 'em. If I bring them in, I'll have nowhere to take them. And I'll probably be relieved of command."

His face tightened. He turned to Rydberg manning the radio.

"Let me have your radio there, high-speed. What is your Battalion call sign?"

"Warrior Main, sir."

The Colonel called our Battalion and spent two minutes screaming at the Sergeant on the other end of the line before finally slamming the receiver down on the desk. He was a full-bird Special Forces Commander, with probably decades of special ops experience, and our Battalion was blowing him off.

"Lieutenant, you and your guys are doing the best you can out there. And you're doing some good shit. If you don't take it to the enemy hard every time he exposes himself, we're all fucked. You can't fight with one hand tied behind your back. You go all the way, or you don't go at all. Your command is clearly full of idiots. You guys go with your gut and take care of each other."

He looked around the room at the three or four enlisted men cleaning weapons. He turned to them and sternly said, "Boys, it's guys like you who're going to win or lose this war for us. This is an enlisted man's war. Squad-level tactics are going to rule the day. This war isn't even close to being over. Mark my word, we're gonna be here for a while."

He shook my hand, wished me luck, and left me with a few cases of water and a box of much-needed SINCGAR radio batteries—in exchange for a few SUVs from the lot. That garage of SUVs had turned out to be a gold mine. Units came from all over the city looking to snag one. We traded the vehicles for everything from batteries to ammo to phone calls home for my guys.

But I couldn't trade them for freedom from the tactical handcuffs our Battalion officers had cinched on our wrists.

By the time the battlefield was secure and my men got to the hospital during a patrol a few hours later, the wounded bad guys had vanished.

CHAPTER EIGHT
KEEPING THE PEACE

> They say that guns don't kill people, people kill people.
> Well, I think the gun helps. If you just stood there and
> yelled BANG, I don't think you'd kill too many people.
> —Eddie Izzard

Now that the invasion had ended, the Iraqis were at war with themselves. And we were caught somewhere in the middle.

Sunni and Shia have been disagreeing with one another since Muhammad died in 632 and they split over who should succeed him. Among Muslims worldwide, Sunni are the majority, but in Iraq, more than half of all Muslims are Shia. Still, the Sunni minority has all the wealth, power, and education, and the social gulf between the two groups is enormous. Saddam, a Sunni Muslim, was ruthless about keeping the Shia down and executed dozens of Shia clerics, leaving countless scores to be settled when his regime fell.

Al-Azamiyah, the neighborhood north of Medical City on the banks of the Tigris, was mostly Sunni. Its residents were wealthy and well-educated doctors, teachers, military officers. They lived in six-bedroom mansions with Mercedeses in the garages, hidden behind huge concrete walls. Many spoke at least some English. They had done well under Saddam—or as well as anyone could during a mad and brutal dictatorship. In Baghdad, it was said that if you were rich, you must have done some bad things. It was a huge drop from the wealthy Sunni standard of living to that of the Shia poor.

Iraq's Sunni and Shia won't get along with each other peacefully any time soon. In Baghdad, my men and I couldn't get them to stand on a gas station line together. Sunni would butt in line ahead of Shia. They would say that they had never before, and would not now, wait behind Shia. They did not understand the fundamentals of equality under the law. Or maybe it was just that nobody ever made them care.

It's tough for me to communicate to people who have never been to Iraq why I don't think the different sects will be able to get along. One can't just take groups separated for decades, sprinkle some freedom on them, and create a Woodstock lovefest. I try to look for analogies or historic parallels that help break it down in a way that explains all the unexplainables. This is not perfect, but it's the best I can come up with: Iraq in the summer of 2003 reminded me of the American South around the time of the abolition of slavery.

Slavery formally ended in America in 1865. Imagine an outside nation walking into America a few years before that and telling slaves and slave owners to work together, forget their differences, and live happily in equality. They would have to work together as partners on a police force. Imagine a slave having command over a slave owner in a new army. Imagine them sitting next to each other as equals in a classroom. They would suddenly be told that despite their history of abuse and animosity, they had been deemed equals by an outside force. Slaves and slave owners had hated each other for generations. They were used to being superior and inferior, to having power and being powerless. They were accustomed to a framework and understanding built upon decades of abuse and divisions. There is no way it would work. There's just too much history there.

Change might happen, yes. But not in two years. When the South was subjected to an "everybody just get along" policy during Reconstruction, the whites rebelled, and the result was the Jim Crow era, when violence and hatred toward blacks reached their highest levels ever.

In America today, generations after the legal end of slavery, we still have divisions and animosity between the two races. If you don't think so, you're either sheltered or deluded. Incidents like the Rodney King beating and Hurricane Katrina fallout revealed America's hypocrisy to ourselves, and to the world. After more than two hundred years America hasn't overcome its own divided history. Yet in Iraq we expect Sunni and Shia to get along amiably two years after we knock out Saddam, because America says they should.

It will be a long time before people of different factions treat one another as equals in Iraq. Saddam had trained an entire nation of people to undermine, betray, and abuse one another. To create tolerance will take at least decades. The entire generation of Iraqis who lived under Saddam may have to die off. There's just too much history there.

The world will never know exactly how many civilians have died in Iraq by other Iraqis' hands. I am sure of it. I don't think there will ever be an accurate count of the dead. In 2003, Iraq was a dangerous, insecure cauldron of murder and mayhem with thousands of Iraqi civilians among the dead and wounded, most of them victims of other Iraqis. Iraq was not like California or Florida. The systems of accountability in Iraq were destroyed during the war, and the newly established ones just didn't work very effectively. Most Iraqis didn't carry ID cards. They didn't have Social Security cards. Record keeping was horrible, and most institutions were wrecked. In a place where life was cheap, keeping accurate track of deaths was not high on the priority list.

In the summer of 2003, most Iraqis were still deciding where to place their loyalties. They were hopeful about the U.S. presence.

But establishing security is the most basic element of any military operation. When we could not establish that, everything else was just treading water. There was a sweet spot—an opportunity to win the Iraqi people over—and we blew it.

American politicians, military commanders, and media personalities are preoccupied with numbers. They can understand numbers. They can plug numbers into an article or use them as talking points. They can slice and manipulate numbers. Self-proclaimed experts gauge whether America is winning or losing in Iraq based on numbers of U.S. troops in Iraq, or daily attacks on Americans, or Iraqi security forces trained.

All these numbers are useless without security. The most critical metric for determining success in the Iraq war is whether the lives of the Iraqi people are improving. And that doesn't happen without security. And security doesn't happen without enough troops. The more Iraqis suffer and die, the longer they have to wait for safety and security, the more likely they are to support the insurgency. If America cannot show the Iraqi people that they are better off with us than without us, then we lose. As Esam once told me, "The only reason Iraq was united was because of their hatred for Saddam—and soon they will be united again, by their hatred of you."

As the end of May approached, it was becoming clear to everyone, troops and locals, that the party was over. Looting and violence exploded. Sunni and Shia were settling old scores with deadly abandon. No humanitarian aid appeared. No Red Cross workers were on street corners handing out blankets. The Marines were headed home, and the 101st Airborne was moving north to the Syrian border. That left 3ID in charge of all of Baghdad.

In Sector 17, we found ourselves isolated, underequipped, and without instruction from higher command. No additional forces arrived. We felt like we were trapped on an island. No one seemed to understand what the hell was going on. General Tommy Franks's brilliant plan had come to a screeching halt. President

Bush and his boys clearly did not have a playbook for the fourth quarter of the game. Low on water and out of batteries for our radios, we lived smack-dab in the middle of Baghdad as its own people tore it apart.

The troop mix for preserving the peace was all wrong. Controlling a cluttered urban environment of six million people with a Mechanized Division like the 3rd ID posed constant challenges. The 3rd ID was perfect for destroying the Iraqi army in the vast space of the desert, but not so much for occupying the city. Mechanized Divisions move on wheels or tracks, with heavy armor. The 3rd was built and trained to operate primarily around the Bradley Fighting Vehicle, a massive, fifty-thousand-pound vehicle with an M242 25-millimeter "Bushmaster" Chain Gun cannon on top of it. It is a fully armored, fully tracked vehicle with a crew of three men designed to carry Mechanized Infantry into close contact with the enemy. Devastatingly effective in the desert, it was a tough beast to get down a narrow Baghdad alleyway. Mechanized soldiers were forced to dismount. And when the Infantry soldiers who ride inside were used to that kind of protection, they were more than a little reluctant to dismount. As a Light Infantry unit attached to the 3rd ID, 3/124 was different—and ultimately more effective.

In contrast to the Mechanized Divisions, a Light Infantry Division like the 10th Mountain or 82nd Airborne is built around a soldier who walks everywhere with a pack on his back. The 10th or 82nd could have been deployed to Baghdad to flood the city with a man on every street corner. Unfortunately, most of the 10th and the 82nd were already committed—some deployed to Afghanistan, some just getting home from there.

Across the board, the Army was woefully underresourced in preparing soldiers for the unique challenges of urban combat. Many of my men had never seen a city larger than Tallahassee. Before we left Georgia, I battled with the Battalion for weeks to get my guys time on the MOUT site before we left. MOUT stood for Military Operations on Urbanized Terrain. A MOUT site is a training center created to look just like a section of a real city, complete with multistory buildings, cars, and sewer systems. The Battalion operations officer told me not to worry, because we were going to the desert, and MOUT training wouldn't matter. So I bypassed him and contacted Range Control directly, only to find that there wasn't available space anyway. There was only one MOUT site on Fort Stewart for an entire Division, and it was already booked up by the Rangers. They had priority and would have it for weeks. Our failure to commit to full preparation for urban warfare illustrates the old saying that the Army is built to fight the last war, not the current one.

I owed my men proper training. And they were going to get it, even if I had to find it for them myself, despite Battalion. Finally I talked the Commander into allowing me to train the Platoon on Battle Drill 6, Entering Building/Clearing Room, using our run-down officer barracks. Andy and I even got some bored Special Forces recruiters to teach my guys a few new tricks.

These Special Forces guys, often called Green Berets, were high-speed and superqualified, and had been sitting idle while my soldiers got crap training from a forty-year-old truck driver who had never been deployed overseas or fired his rifle in anger. I was thrilled at the chance to train under these men. Becoming a Green Beret was my ultimate goal.

My Platoon learned from them that walls were thin in the Middle East, and therefore grenades could blow through them back at you, killing your entire Squad. The Green Berets predicted that we would be kicking in doors and detaining prisoners who didn't speak our language. They taught us useful phrases in Arabic, and explained that Muslim men don't like their heads pushed into the ground when detained—it is especially offensive in their culture. The training was good, and the forecasts sobering.

Finishing up our third day of solid training with the SF guys on the parade field, the men felt good. I was conducting an AAR (After Action Review) when the Battalion operations officer barked at me from across the lot. I left my men and ran over to stand before my least favorite officer in the Army. He tore into me in plain view of my entire Platoon, reprimanding me for "conducting unauthorized training." I took the tongue-lashing and badgering stone-faced. I could feel my men watching as a man who had never led troops in combat told me he was the boss, and that I would be promptly relieved of command if I did anything unconventional again. He made sure everyone could see him humiliate and berate me, finally dismissing me with "Get out of my face, Lieutenant."

As I jogged back to my men, I felt the fury in them. They were as frustrated as I was. The gritty SF Sergeant took a deep drag from his cigarette and smiled.

"Fuck him, sir," he said loudly with an exhale, intending for the Platoon to hear him. "When you guys get into the shit over there, that motherfucker won't be around. It'll be just you and your men. That fucker'll be comfortably sipping coffee somewhere in the rear while you're calling for a medevac. You keep training these guys however you can. We'll teach you all we know. When you get over there, you're gonna need it."

Once I got to Baghdad, I knew how right he'd been.

Our life in Sector 17 alternated between checkpoints, patrols, and guard duty. With only two Platoons to guard the area, Andy's men and mine were forced to maintain a grueling pace, our Platoons trading off every forty-eight hours between guarding the compound and patrolling the sector. Andy and I took turns serving as "Battle Captain." The Battle Captain "manages the fight." He's responsible for controlling and coordinating all elements of his detachment. For a forty-eight-hour shift, I'd do a pile of administrative crap and rarely leave the CP (Command Post), a sandbag-lined back room with maps of Iraq on the walls. Chem lights shoved in water bottles served as makeshift lanterns. A corner table was designated for the two radios, the radio log, and the RTO. One radio always monitored the Battalion net, while the other was on the Company frequency. Battle Captain was the position with the most power, but I abhorred it. Long nights and days of sitting around while the guys saw action outside the wire. It reminded me of detention in high school—but with no girls to flirt with. Endless hours spent checking the time, chewing tobacco, telling stories, and reading books. Andy and I referred to the job as "TOC Bitch."

Four heavy weapons, each with a two-man team, guarded the compound: one at the front entrance, one at the back gate, one to guard detainees in the holding pen, and one on the rooftop. For the Joes, manning those sandbagged gun positions was pretty close to torture. It was like cooking in a microwave. They could actually feel the temperature of their brains rising. Imagine wearing an entire football player's outfit (uniform, helmet, pads, and so on), then strapping twenty-pound rocks on your chest and back, climbing into a black car at high noon in Arizona in August, rolling up all the windows, and parking in the middle of a parking lot. Then turn on the heat. That's sort of what it felt like to be a soldier on guard duty in Baghdad. The heat rose from the black streets and the air temperature got so high that the wind in a moving vehicle actually felt worse than standing still. At high noon on hot days, touching the black metal of your weapon was impossible without callused hands or gloves.

While one Squad was on guard duty, a second one would stand by, geared up, ready and waiting to respond as the QRF. Usually that Squad was somewhere smoking cigarettes, bullshitting, complaining, and trying to stay cool. Calling for the QRF was like dialing 911—it was the backup when things got bad for the guys on patrol.

Most times, the third and final Squad was "down." The down rotation rarely consisted of much downtime. The bulk of it was spent performing weapons maintenance, completing a multitude of First Sergeant duties (perimeter improvement, garbage detail, paperwork, mess duties), and eating and sometimes sleeping—in that order.

The Platoon out on patrol got to have much more fun. One or two Squads would patrol outside the compound or "the wire," while the remaining Squad was down. The patrol Squads chased down intel leads, looked for bad guys, set up ambushes, and conducted patrols to show our presence in the area. They checked the bridges for bombs and searched the streets every morning for IEDs—roadside bombs.

Looking for IEDs was a terrible task. Nobody liked to do it. Whether in a vehicle or on foot, you felt like the enemy had you in his sights and was just waiting to unload. IED sweeps were our version of recon by fire, since the one sure way to identify an IED was when it blew you up.

There was often a suspicious item or two that you needed to check out. A piece of garbage, a dead dog, a cardboard box—the description varied, but the routine was pretty steady. Battalion would call with grid coordinates and send a Squad out to investigate. A visual confirmation from afar was usually not sufficient. Battalion wanted someone to walk right up to it and look for wires, like ordering a soldier to stick his head into a cage with a snake and let the fangs sink in to determine if it's poisonous. It felt like a suicide mission. I never saw a soldier above the rank of Lieutenant execute this kind of task.

The major upside of patrolling was the action. Everyone preferred the patrol rotation. It passed the time. It was more dangerous, but infinitely more exciting than sitting in a sweltering bunker behind a machine gun staring at a dusty street for eight hours, thinking about what your wife was doing back home. On patrol, the Joes walked the hospital hallways to protect the doctors, broke up angry crowds, and detained people who caused problems ranging from revenge killings to drunkenness.

The patrol Squad was also responsible for conducting the

nightly checkpoints. We conducted hundreds of flash checkpoints. They were a mainstay for any American Infantryman in Iraq. The Platoon or Squad Leader would check the map and pick a spot somewhere in the sector based on either intelligence from higher, local rumor from Iraqis, or just at random. Weapons flowed with regularity across the bridge at the south edge of our sector. Some nights we would confiscate boxes of thousands of dollars. Every night we'd find weapons: hundred-year-old German muskets and marble-handled, gold-plated pistols. Iraq had more guns than Texas. Small amounts of cash and weapons for personal and family protection were allowable. Crates of RPGs, stacks of AKs, and cases of grenades were not.

Hidden in buses, produce trucks, taxis, ambulances, coffins, and donkey carts, weapons filtered directly into the city, to be fired at innocent civilians (and at us) in the hospital complex. Our job was to stop that flow. So, at least once a day, we sprung a checkpoint like an animal trap.

Checkpoints worked best at night, when the majority of weapons trafficking seemed to take place. It was also when— because of our technology—we held the greatest advantage.

Checkpoints were among the most dangerous missions an American soldier could undertake. We had to impede the flow of weapons and engage any enemy that attempted to engage us. Pretty simple on paper. We'd roll out of the compound with at least two Squads crammed into the back of our lone deuce-and-a-half truck. Led and trailed by gun trucks, we drove hard and fast to the target. In the first few weeks, the bridges that spanned the Tigris and marked our sector limits to the north and south made for especially good fishing for bad guys. We'd leap out and scatter to preassigned positions as traffic tried to squeeze past us. Our trucks parked horizontally across the road to stop vehicles in both directions, with the turret gunners atop the vehicles peering into the flow of cars. As buses, cars, and trucks came streaming toward the checkpoint, we leered down the sights of our weapons, hearts pumping, fingers almost tugging on triggers.

We faced a litany of potential threats: car bombs, rockets, gunfire. We also dealt with a litany of potential disasters. Traveling at thirty miles per hour, a car covers fifty meters in three seconds. You have three seconds. Every one of us had three seconds to decide the fate of our Platoon, or the fate of a family of Iraqis. We have Rules of Engagement, and know that the enemy doesn't play by them. Shoot too late and your Squad is torn apart by a car bomb. Shoot too early and you kill an innocent family of five and end up rotting in a military prison for the rest of your life.

A scenario that happened more times than I can count: a sedan comes barreling toward us. The headlights are out. The car is not slowing down. Maybe the driver can't see the line of soldiers in the street. Maybe he doesn't notice the headlights of two Humvees facing him. Maybe he's extremely drunk. Maybe the car is filled with a hundred pounds of explosives. We wave our flashlights at the car. But he keeps coming. We scream, yell, and wave our arms. But he keeps coming. We fire warning shots in the air. But he keeps coming. The car is close enough now that I can see the outline of the three passengers inside the cabin. But he keeps coming. I think about the fact that last week, another Squad lit up a car and killed a little girl. The .50-cal rounds blew her head clear off her body. She was wearing a little blue dress. I saw the pictures. But the driver keeps fucking coming. Just a few weeks ago, four American soldiers were killed ten blocks away when a car loaded with explosives ran a checkpoint. One of the soldiers had five kids. Another was nineteen years old and had just gotten married. We fire rounds into the ground feet in front of the bumper. But he keeps coming. There are no alternatives left. The vehicle is close enough that I can see dents in the orange hood.

What would you do?

During my time in Iraq, my men and I were on all sides of the equation. But I never had a soldier killed or wounded on a check-point. Never.

Sometimes we shot. Sometimes we didn't. Sometimes we were right. Sometimes we were wrong. My dad told me before I left for Iraq, "Remember, son. It is better to be judged by twelve than carried by six."

I told my men the same thing.

"You always maintain your right to self-defense. You make the decision, and I'll back you up on it. I'd rather have you live your life with a mistake than have it end here because of one."

My enlistment photo from January 1999. I had graduated from Amherst about eight months before. Courtesy of the author

My men and me (front row, left) at Fort Stewart, Georgia, just days before we left for Iraq. 3rd Platoon, Bravo Company, 3/124th Infantry. Courtesy of the author

May 2003. Saddam Auditorium. The view from one of the machine-gun positions. Behind me is the western side of Baghdad and the Tigris River.

Courtesy of the author

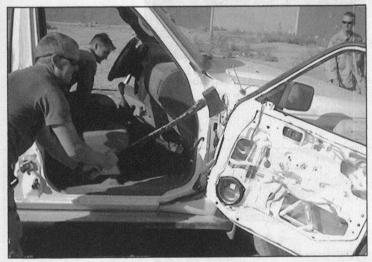

With our Humvees floating on a ship somewhere in the Mediterranean, our men had to improvise. Soldiers from 1st Platoon "customized" an SUV with an ax. We found dozens of Nissan Pathfinders and Land Rovers like these in a hidden underground garage and used them as our patrol vehicles for months in Adamiyah.

Photo by Roberto Carbonell

The finished product of our handiwork. The guys at West Coast Choppers would be proud. This is what we used to get around Baghdad for months. Needless to say, these vehicles did not have armor. An IED attack would have shredded this SUV in half.

Photo by Roberto Carbonell

Iraq was an environment overflowing with paradoxes. This picture captures the dangerous nature of operating every day in Baghdad. Specialists Pineta and Williams from 2nd Platoon (left to right) were stone-faced and cautious on patrol in a typically narrow Adamiyah street, as children smiled and played all around them. Photo by Roberto Carbonell

Some of the guys outside the MOL in summer 2003, gathered around our one and only Humvee. That's me on the far right and just to my right is our interpreter and friend, Mohamed.

Photo by Marvin O. Rydberg III

A few nights' work by Bravo Company on the checkpoints of Adamiyah. AK-47s, RPGs, and various other types of hardware. The flow of weapons in the city was constant.

Photo by Marvin O. Rydberg III

Some of my platoon and me with local Iraqi kids in Adamiyah. Our interpreter, Esam Pasha, is center with the beard. Esam was an amazing painter and taught my men and me about all things Iraq. He was our most critical weapon in Baghdad. I never imagined that only two years later, Esam would be living in New York City. Courtesy of the author

Specialists Stewart (Fat Stew), McQuiage, and Donaldson (Double-D) (left to right) in a pre-mission picture. Three of the best soldiers in my platoon, they could always be relied upon to do their job well—and add some humor.

Photo by Marvin O. Rydberg III

This little boy would always run out to meet our patrols—always wearing the same Bart Simpson sweatshirt. The Iraqi children were amazing and will always be my most fond memories of the war.

Donkey carts like this one were frequent on the streets of Baghdad. They were commonly used to carry produce and other goods into the city from outlying areas. They also carried metal containers of kerosene and diesel fuel. Photo by Marvin O. Rydberg III

Donkey carts are used to launch coordinated attacks on U.S. forces across Baghdad. In November 2003, a dozen rockets launched from the back of the carts slammed into Baghdad's two biggest hotels and the Oil Ministry. Our men captured this one filled with rockets parked across the street from our barracks just before it could be detonated. Surprisingly low-tech and uniquely frightening. Photo by Marvin O. Rydberg III

United Nations Headquarters bombing in Baghdad, August 20, 2003. Twenty-three people were killed and eighty-six seriously wounded. The ground shook and windows rattled across the city. This attack formally marked the emergence of the insurgency.

Photo by Marvin O. Rydberg III

Specialist Rydberg and me at a checkpoint outside the Turkish embassy. Turkey had recently announced a decision to send forces to Iraq and attacks were expected. We spent a week in and around the embassy in order to deter car bombs from attacking the site.

Courtesy of the author

October 14, 2003. A suicide car bomb detonated in front of the embassy just a few hours after we left the site, in roughly the same spot as we had been. The blast killed the driver and wounded more than ten people. Photo by Marvin O. Rydberg III

The view from the back of an Army deuce-and-a-half truck traveling through Baghdad. SPC Webb (Webigail) looks down on the crowd. We always had our hands on our weapons. The crowds were close and could turn on us at any minute. Photo by Marvin O. Rydberg III

The Humvee that carried Command Sergeant Major Eric F. Cooke. Cooke, 43, was killed on December 24, 2003 (Christmas Eve), after his unarmored Humvee was struck by an improvised explosive device just a few meters in front of my platoon.
Photo by Marvin O. Rydberg III

Our enemies in Iraq did not wear uniforms. This man was shot and killed outside the gate of our compound. He wore a soccer shirt on his back and sandals on his feet. He did not carry an ID card. We had no idea who most of these guys were or where they came from.
Photo by Roberto Carbonell

May 2005. IAVA executed the first trip by an Iraq veterans'
organization to Capitol Hill to discuss the war and veterans' issues. We met with Senator Hillary Clinton, Democrat from New York. Abbie, Herold, Perry, and I had a long
and interesting private discussion with Senator Clinton,
ranging from Army retention to female soldiers' issues.

During the D.C. trip, IAVA also met with Senator Chuck Hagel (center), a Vietnam
veteran and Republican from Nebraska. A vocal critic of the war, Hagel is the only
member of the U.S. Senate to have served as an enlisted man in combat.

CHAPTER NINE
JUST BECAUSE YOU'RE PARANOID DOESN'T MEAN THEY'RE *NOT* TRYING TO KILL YOU

A Paranoid is someone who knows a little of what's going on.

—William S. Burroughs

I got a letter from my old Platoon Sergeant, Mike O'Brien. Everyone called him O.B. A member of the NYPD ESU (Emergency Services Unit—the NYPD version of SWAT), he had saved a number of people at Ground Zero on 9/11, despite a dislocated shoulder and countless lacerations of his own. A former Force Recon Marine, he had been my number two in my New York Platoon. I wished I had him with me on the ground now—he was wise beyond his years and funny as hell. The letter read, "I'll keep a cold one waiting for you back at Ferrell's. Be careful over there. Trust your gut. Trust your instincts. Remember"—and here's the money shot— "just because you're paranoid doesn't mean they are *not* trying to kill you."

Paranoia comes hand in hand with a soldier's tour in Iraq. Insurgents and civilians are indistinguishable. We never knew who was friend and who was foe, and our minds reeled in a world that spoke a language we didn't understand. Is that kid holding an apple or a hand grenade? We felt like Custer's army deep inside Indian country. Every single day we were vastly outnumbered as conditions teetered on the verge of chaos. We felt like every time we left the compound there were bull's-eyes drawn on our asses. We tried to control crowds with limited tools, while avoiding civilian slaughters and international incidents.

One day, I had just gotten back from a patrol with Second Squad. We detained two men for breaking into the hospital. Doctors said they were part of a local gang that sold drugs. After we caught them, we had to carry them into the compound because they would not stop crying. Every time we detained a man in the early months of the war, he would become hysterical. Few things we said would calm him down. We finally learned the reason. When men were detained by the police or army under Saddam, they usually did not come back. When we took men into custody, they were sure we were going to execute them.

Despite repeated assurances from our interpreters, the two newest detainees wailed like newborns for hours from behind a cage of razor wire. They could be heard for blocks. A few guys expressed concern that their cries would incite a riot, or allow their fellow gang members to figure out where we had taken them. We duct-taped their mouths, and ate our lunches.

I was just starting lunch when Mac called me on the radio and told me to come up to the roof to check something out.

"Right there. You see the barrel?"

He was good. Directly across the river from our house was that small palace complex said to have once belonged to Saddam's wife. These elaborate mini-palaces were scattered throughout Baghdad like exotic summer homes. I peered through Mac's sight and saw why he had interrupted my fine dining feast. Just beneath a marble overhang was the barrel of a heavy machine gun, pointed directly at our compound. Three guards roamed the grounds. Mac had been watching them for an hour. For over a week, we had taken fire from the opposite side of the river and could not pin down the source. The fire was sporadic, and we faced dozens of buildings with hundreds of windows. It was like trying to spot a single face in the windows of a skyscraper. We would return sniper fire carefully, but were extremely concerned about hitting any of the civilians who swarmed the area. The river side of our building was all glass, and extremely vulnerable. An RPG hit would be devastating. But we were repeatedly denied permission to cross sector lines and hunt the suckers down. Now we had a bead on the source.

I ran downstairs to brief the Commander and request permission to take my Platoon across the river to eliminate the threat. But he was gone. He had traveled up to Battalion for his daily briefing. My earlier requests had been denied, but now we had new information—we conclusively had the location of the enemy. Waiting hours for the CO to return could cost the lives of my men. I knew if I asked Battalion for permission they'd deny me.

I made the decision to move.

I quickly laid out a standard five-paragraph operations order with two of my Squad Leaders, and briefed Andy. He confirmed the plan, and would stand by with two Squads in case we got into trouble. My Platoon Sergeant would maintain command of the Platoon in the rear. We rushed out of the compound with two Squads and three vehicles, skidding up to the iron-gated driveway, weapons raised. As we approached, a guard ducked behind the gate and ran back inside. I knew we had the right spot. A ramming with the first vehicle popped the gate, and we burst inside a circular driveway. An unmanned machine gun was in a guard shack pointed at the entrance. Two Iraqi men slowly emerged from the palace building with AKs by their sides.

We surrounded them, screaming for them to put the weapons down and get on the ground. They shuffled and stalled, refusing to lay their weapons on the ground, holding up a piece of paper. Finally one of my soldiers stepped forward and slammed one of the men in the head with the back of his rifle. The man went down and the other dropped his weapon. They were lucky we hadn't shot them. We were on top of them and had them zip cuffed in seconds. We put hoods on them and loaded them onto the trucks.

The detainees looked helpless, like we were taking them out for a firing squad. It's a scene that has now been shown on CNN a million times. Hooding detainees are commonly misunderstood by civilians back home to be some kind of horrible and brutal tactic. That is simply incorrect. We put hoods on them for a very sound tactical reason. It prevents the detainees from knowing where they're going. Does it scare them? Sure. But it also keeps them from calculating distances within our compound for mortar teams, and from viewing the inner workings of our defenses. It is not cruel and definitely not unusual. It helps us stay safe.

The detainees shook. One guy cried. They thought their lives were over for sure.

One of our men was watching us through a sight from our compound back across the river, and called to me over the radio. "Blue 6, there is still one more inside. I repeat, one Haji still inside the palace!"

"Go, Third! Get in there," I yelled.

The palace building was two stories of marble, and circular, like the Pantheon in Rome. Third Squad's Alpha team followed our plan to the letter. They stormed inside, followed by Bravo team. I trailed with the remainder of First Squad.

As we cleared the first floor, I heard screaming above me. I bolted up the grand staircase to where the guys had another Iraqi facedown in a doorway. We had caught him completely by surprise and not a shot had been fired.

"Bingo! Here it is. Hey, L.T! Get in here!"

Mac found a bathroom with the door bolted shut. The third

Iraqi had been guarding it. After a few good kicks, we removed the door, revealing an opulent bathroom with a rocket hole overlooking the river. A blanket covered an old rusted bathtub. Mac pulled it back to reveal a .50-caliber Dashisha Russian heavy machine gun, two AKs, an SKS sniper rifle, and enough .50-cal ammo to fuel a very healthy assault.

"This fucker woulda made Swiss cheese out of our house across the river, L.T."

"You got that right."

Outside, we also found an antiaircraft gun and some tanks of material that Sergeant Gipson was ridiculously sure were chemical weapons of some kind.

I felt vindicated as we loaded up the Iraqis and the weapons and headed back across the river. As soon as we entered the lobby, guys smiled and cheered. It instantly improved morale for them to know we wouldn't have to worry about getting blown up in our sleep by the mysterious gunner.

We were all shocked by the extent of the firepower. First the Iraqi men denied knowledge of the existence of the weapons. Then they presented a crumpled piece of paper that had the name of an American they said was with the CIA. They said he authorized them to have weapons because they helped support him before the invasion. Possible? Sure. Likely? No. Anyway, I was sure this mysterious agent—if he existed—didn't authorize them to shoot at our fucking compound.

Iraqis are very good at bullshitting, especially with authority figures of any kind. We actually grew to admire the skill. They'd make great poker players. Caught red-handed, they would repeatedly deny their obvious involvement.

After the initial interrogation of the detainees, our spirits were high. My men had performed brilliantly. We moved quickly to get the Iraqi team and their weapons up to Battalion Headquarters so they could be more thoroughly interrogated by psyops and intelligence personnel.

We pulled into the dirt parking lot of our Battalion Headquarters, housed in the opulent former Republican Guard officers' building near the Ministry of Labor, east of Medical City. Three of the more useless Captains from the TOC were waiting outside. As I briefed these three representatives of the group my soldiers called "the Battalion All-Stars," my men proudly unloaded the men and weapons, like returning deer hunters.

I was halfway through my debriefing when I heard someone scream, "Where's Rieckhoff?"

The XO (Executive Officer) came storming down from the side stairs of the building with the BC in tow. As I ran over, I could see the XO's face begin to twist violently. My stomach started to turn as I realized, to my amazement, that he was furious. Before I could even get into recapping the raid, he laid into me. I stood at parade rest, with my hands behind my back, and fully expected him to try to hit me. My men stopped unloading the EPWs and stared in awe.

"You don't even know who the fuck these men are! You don't even know what they were doing over there! You went out of sector! You're out of control!"

I thought his head was going to spin around 360 degrees.

"But, sir, these are the guys who've been shooting at our—"

"I don't give a fuck! How do you know they aren't working for the CIA? How am I going to explain this to the Brigade Commander?"

The antiaircraft gun, the stockpile of weapons, none of it mattered. In an instant, it became clear to me and my men that the TOC All-Stars were men whose primary concern was themselves, not their men. We had all feared that it was true, but now we were seeing it for sure. The XO and the rest of the Battalion All-Stars thought the war was over. To them, it may have actually seemed that way. They rarely left the compound, slept in air-conditioning, and never got shot at.

Through an interpreter, the Battalion Commander apologized to the detainees for inconveniencing them. All he cared about was who exactly at the CIA had contacted them. The BC and his crew didn't leave the compound often enough to realize that the men and their story were totally bogus. They didn't want to see the .50-cal and crates of ammo. They didn't want to hear from my NCOs. The petty concerns of enlisted soldiers were beneath them. My men stared, shaking their heads, sucking their teeth, and walked away in disgust to smoke.

Then the Executive Officer called to me, so all my men could hear him.

"Rieckhoff! Get your ass over here. If these guys have a story that checks out, you are fucked! You understand? You are totally fucked! I'll relieve you of command and send your ass back to New York. You hear me?"

I could feel my men watching from behind me.

"Yes, sir."

He turned dismissively and walked away. Then, so only I could hear him, he muttered, "If not, then good job. I guess."

It was wonderful to have such conditional support from my higher command to bolster the confidence of my men.

I never heard anything more about the incident, so I can only deduce that the Iraqis were not working for the CIA.

It felt like the fate of the city was precariously balanced on the edge of a knife. Our patrols were met with fewer smiles and more rocks each day. Intel reports warned of a mass coordinated uprising from the Shia to our east in Sadr City. Sadr City was formerly called Saddam City, but had been recently renamed in memory of a local leader and his martyred father. It was the poorest, most dilapidated part of town by far. Its massive, slummy residential buildings jammed with hot and angry people resembled the worst urban housing projects in the United States. Every time one of our patrols went through the zone, shots were fired at the vehicles from multiple directions. It felt like a scene from the streets of Somalia in *Black Hawk Down*. In Sadr City, there was a degree of boldness and disregard for personal safety that did not exist in the Sunni areas. Nightly intel briefings repeatedly mentioned the rise of a young influential cleric from the area who was inciting attacks on the U.S. forces. The bold ecclesiastic was the namesake of a grand ayatollah executed by Saddam in 1999, a thirty-year-old rabble-rouser named Muqtada al-Sadr.

One night Third Platoon was deployed to establish a blocking position on the eastern edge of our sector, bordering Sadr City. We rolled out with every vehicle we had and were told to expect large, angry, potentially armed crowds. Our job was to keep them away from Medical City and detain anyone with weapons.

Someone pay grades above me—probably in Washington— had finally made the decision to arrest al-Sadr. An aggressive plan to snatch him up in the night was laid out. Riots from the locals in response were inevitable.

I figured the takedown of al-Sadr was long overdue. This guy was a problem that needed to be dealt with sooner or later. He was a diplomatic, military, and political thorn in our side that was not going away. The way I saw it, we might as well nip the problem in the bud before it got any larger. For American forces to play political patty-cake with him would only allow his legend to grow larger among the people and create more problems. I thought the United States would take him out with a CIA poisoning mission or some kind of satellite-guided missile strike. We had come this far to take out Saddam, and I didn't think we would hesitate to eliminate a small-timer like Sadr.

We spent most of the night searching cars at a traffic circle and listening to the radio traffic from around the sector. Staring into a small crowd of angry Iraqi men who had been ordered off of a bus by my men, Rydberg murmured to me through his dip, "L.T., if the Iraqis ever get their shit together, we are in some serious deep shit."

I thought the same thing daily. We didn't realize at the time how right we were.

The snatch mission of al-Sadr never happened. But it should have. I don't know who made the call to cancel the capture, but I am pretty sure it wasn't somebody wearing a military uniform. We rolled back into the compound. I filled out my mission paperwork and hit the weights to relieve some frustrations. The Joes fired up the PlayStation for a game or two. Two years later, al-Sadr would grow to be a leader of the insurgency, commanding bands of coordinated attacks against Americans in cities around Iraq.

Toward the end of May a family with two kids was assassinated just south of our sector. They had just given us information on a weapons cache two days before. The killings sent intimidating shock waves throughout the neighborhood and left us feeling horrible and guilty. We demanded intelligence from Iraqis, but could not guarantee them any degree of protection in exchange. Giving us info became the kiss of death. We had incredible power, but not enough of the right kind.

We had destroyed Iraq's political and social infrastructure and failed to provide its people with another one to replace it. There were few police and still not enough American troops. The power was still out in Baghdad most of the time. With no garbage pickup or working sewage system, people just threw all their trash and refuse out the windows, to pile up stinking and rancid in the narrow streets. We couldn't even keep them safe from each other. In the absence of any other type of social institutions, the mosques and clerics assumed the dominant role among the people. As we retreated into compounds that were growing more formidable, they disappeared into mosques that became increasingly mysterious.

Both sides were frustrated. But in today's Iraq, just as under Saddam, might made right. This was democracy at the barrel of an M16. The most powerful person in Iraq was often a nineteen-year-old machine gunner from Florida. Or Kansas. Or California. His officers held the power of gods. I wrote in a letter to Bama that I would never again have this much unadulterated power in my life.

I could detain, harass, question, and beat anyone I liked, at any time. It felt good. And I felt guilty that it felt good.

We were taking out our anger, frustration, and fear on the very people we had come to help. Every time a detainee wept and wailed, soldiers sneered. "Fucking Hajis."

Things were unraveling on the home front as well. The guys had been away from their wives and children, their girlfriends, their jobs—their lives—for five months, and the strain began to show in some of their relationships.

Gunner, the guy with the tattoo on his torso—his girlfriend sent him back the engagement ring in the mail. He was wrecked. One of the older and wiser NCOs tried to lift his spirits by telling him a story he once heard. A Ranger was on a long overseas deployment fighting for freedom when his girlfriend sent him a Dear John letter. The Ranger was initially devastated. But Rangers don't stay down. He pulled together all the guys in his Platoon. He asked each of them for a picture of his wife or girlfriend. He put all the pictures of the different women together in one envelope, and sent it back to his girl with a note that read, "No problem. But which one is you?"

One of my soldiers got a letter from his wife telling him that she was leaving him. A nervous type who spoke in a soft Southern accent, he was already unpopular among the platoon, and felt isolated and depressed. But this shot drove him over the edge. He was smoking ferociously and his hands shook. On guard duty he fired his weapon repeatedly at what he said was an Iraqi with an AK, but the man next to him could not substantiate the story. Two NCOs told me that they did not want him out on patrol with their guys. He was unstable and unreliable. He might have been playing it up to get home, but he was a risk to himself and to the Platoon. I referred him to the chaplain and begged the CO to let me take him off the line. The chaplain did nothing. The Battalion surgeon did nothing. The system failed me and my soldier. There was no mechanism in place to deal with a soldier cracking under the pressures of combat and a divorce. He was a zombie. I feared he would hurt himself or someone else.

The next night we were sitting in the CP for a Company meeting when we heard a bang.

"What the hell was that?"

"Sounded like a gunshot."

"Nah, that wasn't a gunshot."

Then we heard screaming. A soldier ran into the room and said, "Come quick! Hurry!"

I ran around the corner and met Doc Spettel, the Bravo Company doc, in the hall. The door to the supply room was closed and something inside was blocking it. We shoved it open and saw one of my soldiers facedown in a pool of blood, his desert camouflage pants and the carpet dark and wet with it. An Iraqi pistol lay beside him.

My soldier had shot himself, and for an instant I thought he was dead. In that instant I wished I was dead too. I knew this was coming. I had tried to tell everyone. I had tried to stop it. And now I had lost him. I had failed him.

Doc and I rolled him over. He was alive. The bleeding was concentrated in his lower body, and was intense—but I was relieved to see he hadn't shot himself in the head. Doc pressed down hard on the bleeding thigh. If he had hit his femoral artery, he might still bleed to death.

"He missed the artery!" Doc announced.

We alerted Battalion and they had a patrol vehicle outside in minutes. The wounded soldier came to and tried to sit up.

"Relax, man," Doc ordered.

"Aw, shit," he moaned. "What happened?"

We pushed him back down as one of the guys tried to put him at ease with a classic line that we'd repeat for months later.

"You got bit by a spider. A really big spider. Don't worry, dude. You're gonna be fine."

He wouldn't be fine. The soldier was medevaced and out of Baghdad soon after. He had put one round in his leg. He said it was an accident, but nobody believed him. He said the old Iraqi pistol had jammed and he was trying to clear it, leaning hard into it on his leg when it went off. But that round was perfectly placed to miss the artery. He'd known where to shoot to get himself home without dying. He wanted to go home at any cost, and now he'd get his wish.

One of my NCOs also got some devastating news from home. He was a former Marine with great military bearing, highly respected by the men. A stocky guy who looked like a grown-up Spanky, he must have sweated off fifty pounds in Iraq. All the guys felt for him when he learned that his ex-wife was trying to take custody of his two little girls away from him. He was a wreck. He tried to focus on his job, but he was dying inside. His daughters were his world, and he had full guardianship of them by law, but his ex was taking advantage of the fact that he was deployed and incommunicado. She filed the paperwork and appeared at the court date. We didn't even have access to a phone. When he failed to show for the hearing, his ex was granted the kids. She was careful not to mention to the judge that the father of the girls was defending freedom in the name of America halfway around the globe. The judge probably just thought he was a deadbeat dad. I arranged for him to get a ride to a phone at the palace, but it didn't do much good. Trapped in Baghdad, the NCO couldn't even defend himself.

In an Infantry Platoon, pain is shared. Family pain was no exception. Seeing one of my best NCOs deal with family issues back home that I could not help him remedy was agonizing. It was maddening for him to think about the precarious safety of his children back home, I knew that. He was just trying to be a good father. I tried to keep him focused.

"Look, Sergeant. You can't fix it right now. I'm not telling you to give up. I know you're worried about your little girls, but if you don't get your head in the game here, you're going to get yourself killed and leave your girls without a dad forever. And you have eight children *here* to worry about. You have eight boys with mothers and girlfriends and wives waiting for them back home. You have a job to do, and that's keeping them alive. If you can't do that, let me know now, and I'll take you off the line and replace you."

"I'm all right, sir."

"Focus on the five-meter target, Sergeant." The expression came from the shooting range, where the targets are 5, 25, 100, and 250 meters away. You can't let the 250-meter target distract you when you've got that 5-meter one right in your face. That's the one that will kill you first.

He shoved his pain deep down inside for a few hours every day when he walked outside that wire. In the meantime, I battled with the Battalion S-1 personnel officer about his situation. The S-1 was not an Infantry officer. He had been attached from another unit, finance or something. He had no comprehension of what it was like to deal with soldiers. In his opinion, everyone just had to deal. I made his case, and he replied, "You know, Lieutenant, I have a wife at home too, and I can't just go home." It was always about him. An S-1 who doesn't care about soldiers is like a teacher who hates kids. I despised him.

That NCO was a damn good soldier who loved his men and couldn't bear watching another man lead his Squad any more than he could watch another man raise his daughters. The best thing I could do, the only thing I could do, was make him focus on the things he could control.

America will never appreciate the sacrifices that men like him make in situations like these. His is the type of heroism that the Army doesn't give medals for. But it should.

CHAPTER TEN
RIPPLES OF HOPE

It is from numberless diverse acts of courage and belief that human history is shaped. Each time a person stands up for an ideal, or acts to improve the lot of others, or strikes out against injustice, he sends forth a tiny ripple of hope. That ripple builds others. Those ripples—crossing each other from a million different centers of energy—build a current that can sweep down the mightiest walls of oppression and injustice.
—Robert F. Kennedy

Even as the general situation deteriorated,

our one bright spot was still the Iraqi kids. We loved those kids. Every soldier in the unit was determined to do everything he could to give them a shot at a better life.

A local man had tipped us off that Saddam loyalists and local Mafia would find rooftops near the closest elementary school and wait for class to start—then shoot. AK-47 bullets rained down on children and teachers to send a message: school is not in session.

We planned to change that.

The lone street that led to the school was narrow, with open sewage running on both sides. Skinny chickens poked and pecked

133

in muddy corners. At the end of this dead-end road was the precariously situated and gutted elementary school. The street was only wide enough for one vehicle at a time. With tall buildings around us in three directions, it was a perfect spot for us to be ambushed. My guys called the area Little Mogadishu, another reference to *Black Hawk Down.*

But the defiant teachers kept the school open. Only about a third of the parents kept their kids home. The terrified teachers taught as best they could, while their students faced abominable conditions. No electricity. No books. No running water.

We stopped the Humvees and walked up to the school. I pushed through a broken green metal gate. Two female teachers greeted us timidly at the entrance. The headmistress was just about five feet tall, and slouched inside her black burka. She hurried us inside. Esam, Rydberg, and I followed her as the rest of the guys stood watch from the trucks. The single-story building was a square of small classrooms with a tennis-court-sized courtyard carved out of the middle. On the wall of the entranceway was a six-foot mural of an Iraqi soldier and a child raising the Iraqi flag up a flagpole, both wearing huge cartoon smiles.

As we entered the courtyard, we could hear the children bustling and chatting excitedly. They sat overflowing in tiny classrooms, sneaking stares, waves, and smiles as their teachers tried to contain them. The kids in Baghdad still treated us like superheroes. Everywhere we went, they wanted to talk. They would ask us about our weapons, our sunglasses, our boots, chanting, "Good Bush! Good Bush!" But the teachers had these kids very well disciplined. Two boys about eight years old ran to the courtyard to see us, and were quickly pursued by an angry female teacher whipping their asses with a switch.

Esam rounded the corner ahead of me as the headmistress led us into her tiny office. She showed us bullet holes in the wall where people had driven by and shot up the place. A bent fan dangled from the ceiling, a broken clock hung from the back wall.

With metal-gated windows and no glass, it felt more like a jail cell than the principal's office.

I entered, while Rydberg stood guard at the door. The headmistress averted her eyes nervously. She shifted behind a broken desk, clearly freaked out about something. She spoke so rapidly Esam had to calm her sternly. She looked like she had ants in her burka. I assumed she was worked up about the bastards firing at the building, but that wasn't it. I poked my head out into the courtyard and scanned the surrounding rooftops, listening for incoming vehicles, but nothing seemed abnormal.

"Ahhhhh," Esam declared loudly. He turned away from the headmistress and pulled me aside. "Lieutenant, come here, please." We stepped outside the office. Rydberg leaned in to listen.

"Sir Rieckhoff, this woman thinks that you can see her bare body."

"What? What the hell are you talking about, Esam?"

"Your glasses. She thinks they can see through her clothes, and she is very ashamed."

Rydberg nearly fell down laughing.

Apparently the word on the street was that our dark wraparound sunglasses were in fact X-ray glasses. I took them off and handed them to Esam to show her.

She grinned and nodded gratefully, but was still visibly uncomfortable. She whispered to Esam that she was very afraid the bad people would see her talking to us and have her killed. I asked her to tell me where they were, but she refused. Yet very subtly, she motioned with her head and eyes to the big apartment building that loomed about fifteen stories high just overhead to the east. I got it. And I was pissed. I nodded sternly and told Esam to tell her to keep the school open.

I told her we would work to improve its conditions immediately. I told her that from now on, my men would be patrolling during school hours every day. And when we weren't patrolling, we'd be watching. I gave her my word.

She exhaled a bit, but was still nervous. She asked me if I would talk to the classes to calm the children. She said my presence was important and would make them feel safe. I agreed.

"Hey, Rydberg, time to play Mister Rodgers."

"Cool, sir."

Rydberg, Esam, and I followed the headmistress, who walked briskly, close to the wall, to stay out of sight of the bad guys' building. She turned into a doorway, and I followed. The second I stepped into the room, forty pairs of wide, dark eyes were locked on me, and an overflowing classroom of nine-year-olds in white-collared uniforms all moaned in unison, "Ahhhhhhhhhhhhhhhhhh-hhhhhhhhhhhhhh."

Wow. They were all just a few years older than my nephew Sean back home. I was shocked that after the last couple months of war and destruction, these kids still looked fantastic. Rydberg and I were two of the tallest soldiers in the Platoon. And with M16s and chests full of gear, we must have looked fairly formidable to a roomful of little people. They could barely sit still, wiggling and stretching to get a look at us. We were probably the first American soldiers they had ever seen this close. They leaned forward, smiling radiantly.

I thought they might tackle me. I tried to figure out what the hell to say to this riveted audience. I cleared my throat, and the room went silent, except for a chuckle from Rydberg.

"Hello!" I bellowed. The room was smaller than I realized and my voice boomed.

Instantly, and in perfect echo, like forty little parrots, they thundered back, *"Hello!"*

"As-Salaam-Alaikum," I said, reducing my volume.

Their eyes popped open even wider as they heard me greet them in Arabic. It means "Peace be with you," and it was about the only Arabic I knew.

"Alaikum-As-Salaam!" they roared back, bouncing in their chairs. I wished I could get my Platoon to listen to me like that.

Esam interpreted as I introduced us. I told them I was very happy to be in their school. That my men and I were here to help them, their families, and their teachers. I told them that they were all very brave, and that we would stop the Ali Babas from shooting at their school, and allow them to focus on their very important studies.

They were fascinated, and so was I. I could tell they had a million questions, and I wanted to answer every single one of them. I had about a million for them too, but we had to get back on patrol. So I told them I could answer only three. Then we'd have to be on our way back to work.

Forty hands shot simultaneously into the air like bottle rockets. I picked a little girl in the third row with long, wavy hair.

She stood perfectly, pushed back her hair, and said softly, "How . . . old . . . are . . . you?"

Holy shit. I was stunned. I wasn't expecting the questions to be in English. She sounded like she was from Cleveland. Rydberg was equally stunned. Esam smirked proudly, as if he'd expected it all along.

"I am twenty-eight years old. Twenty-eight."

They all repeated, "Twennteeeee-eiiiight . . . ."

This was fun.

"Question number two." I pointed to a little boy in the back with a crisp white shirt and big buck teeth. He kneeled high on his chair, boosting his short body by pushing on the shoulder of the kid next to him.

"What . . . is . . . your . . . name?"

"My name is Paul Rieckhoff."

They all repeated, "Pooooool Reeekaaaaa."

Rydberg laughed. I felt like the ambassador from Mars.

"Next. You, in the back." I pointed to another boy with a striped shirt and thick eyebrows.

"Where are . . . you . . . from?" he yelled.

"New York," I said proudly.

"Ahhhhhhhhh." They nodded. "Nooooooo Yooooork."

Good thing I wasn't from Tallahassee.

"Okay. One extra one, in the interest of education. You."

A little girl, half the size of the others, smiled shyly and took her time before bursting out with, "How are yoo?"

"I am *great!*" I exclaimed, and laughed.

And I was. As we climbed back into the Humvees, Rydberg and I were as giddy as two kids who had just been sneaking bong hits behind the school. Talking to that class was without a doubt one of the most exhilarating experiences of my life. That was why I came to Iraq: to help little kids keep their schools safe.

And maybe to kill a few bad guys along the way.

A few hours later, Sergeant Mac was up high in a water tower near the school with his scope. I also mentioned the school's situation to an SF team leader who stopped by the auditorium to pick up an SUV. He had a sniper team with thermal sights looking for work. Three days and a few raids later, the shooting stopped.

For the children in Sector 17, we were the only protection. Bechtel and Halliburton were nowhere in sight. That school would become Third Platoon's school. And nobody would mess with us . . . or them. The children in that school, and throughout Baghdad, were often our only real joy.

Being around the Iraqi children was like placing myself in an alcove away from the war. Every soldier in our Company was jaded by all the carnage and sadness around us. I had thickened my heart to protect it from being broken. It was like pieces of me dying inside without the light. But with the children in that school, I realized that my hardness was not pure, and that I was still a human being to them.

During our visit to the school, we learned that the teachers hadn't been paid in four months. If they didn't get paid this week, they could no longer afford to come to work. I put word up to Battalion, who had nothing for me. But keeping that school open had become a mission vital to us all on a personal level. One of the

NCOs pulled the guys together to provide relief. We pooled money out of our own pockets and collected over $300 to pay the teachers.

In letters home, we told friends and family to keep the candy and baby wipes. Instead, we asked them to go to Wal-Mart and Staples and buy school supplies. Pat, a wonderful secretary from my time at JPMorgan, collected enough office supplies from the Equity Capital Markets desk to fill thirty-five boxes. Kids from the Horace Mann School in New York City sent me pens, pencils, and drawings, all for our kids in Baghdad. When we arrived to deliver the stuff, we almost started a riot. It was like Christmas and we were Santa Claus. In addition to all the materials, we left the lone security guard with some hardware—an AK-47. A powerful statement about the state of affairs. It put things in perspective for me. We gave a school an assault rifle to try to keep it safe from people outside the school. In America, you sometimes need an assault rifle to keep the kids safe from danger inside the school. Despite the challenges, we were making a difference.

CHAPTER ELEVEN
I SAW A HOLY MAN
DIE TONIGHT

> All say, "How hard it is that we have to die"—a strange complaint to come from the mouths of people who have had to live.
>
> —Mark Twain

In early June, 3rd ID pulled out of Baghdad,

and the First Armored Division (1st AD) came in to take its place. Bravo Company stayed, and was reassigned from 3rd ID to 1st AD. Units of 1st AD took over responsibility for security at the Medical Center, while Bravo Company consolidated at the Ministry of Labor, a huge, Y-shaped office building to the northeast of Medical City.

But my Platoon still provided some security at the ER late at night, to help the doctors keep it open, a "friendship gesture" the staff had begged of me. It was on one of those nights that I watched a holy man die.

We were standing outside the entrance with Esam, explaining to some locals that, contrary to popular rumor, our combat boots could not detect and defuse land mines, when a pickup full of men came barreling up. A ragged bus full of people scrambled behind the truck.

Four men climbed out of the back of the truck, carrying the

corners of a bloody sheet in which a small, thin man lay. His wounded head was swollen to the size of a watermelon. What looked like gallons of blood streamed off the sheet as they rushed it past. The men placed the body gently on a rusty gurney, while dozens of frantic people swarmed around, women in long black veils screaming and slapping at the doctors.

My men rushed over and pushed them outside the operating room, pleading with them to give the doctors room to work. I shoved through the crowd to assess the wounded man's status, leaning in over the sweaty shoulders of two young doctors.

The wounded man had a small bloodless entry hole above each nipple and one between his eyes. Those eyes were swollen with terror, and scanned helplessly, but without tears. They panned the doctors tearing into his chest with a scalpel, and locked with mine. I felt him begging for me to do something to calm his fear. I never felt so powerless in all my life. He knew he was going to die. I couldn't believe how enormously the injury had swollen his head.

By this point, about three dozen people, mostly middle-aged, mostly men, were kneeling and praying loudly on the dirty floor of the ER. My men formed a line to keep them away from the operating doctors. The Iraqis whimpered and whispered for over a half hour while the doctors worked on the man behind a shower curtain guarded by my guys. Blood was everywhere. One of the doctors stepped from behind the curtain and lit a cigarette with his red, gloveless hands.

Iraqis ran in and out of the hospital in waves from across the gloomy street. They were going to the blood bank and back. The only way to get blood for a wounded person from the blood bank was to run over and donate it yourself. There were no reserves. So family members rushed over and carried their own blood back in to give to the docs for immediate transfusion. The hospital didn't have the money or capacity to screen for disease.

Esam spoke with some of the men and found out that the victim had been shot on the street. He was an extremely respected and influential imam at a local Shia mosque. The crowd was made up of his followers. They told Esam that the hit had been an assassination attempt.

As the chaos continued behind the curtain, Esam and I stepped outside to discuss what to do next, and to wait for the man to die. Esam lit a Gauloise cigarette and offered me one, as Iraqis automatically do. I sucked the cheap chocolaty French tobacco with my sweaty lips, and I asked him to help me understand the differences between Sunni and Shia. He was Sunni, and said that Shia are notably more dramatic, more exaggerated, more superstitious. I asked him what he thought happens after death.

"When you die . . . you die," he said, and smiled, blowing out his smoke. "You know, Lieutenant, there's an old Iraqi saying—cigarettes shorten everything. Time, money, life."

We finished our cigarettes and returned to check on the surgery inside. The holy man had finally died. We were relieved for him, but not for ourselves. The terrified doctors were debating how to tell the news to the cleric's followers. He had "died" three times in the last half hour. This time was apparently for real.

Esam and I huddled with the two head doctors and discussed how to get the body out of the ER without creating a riot. The uneducated and upset followers might try to kill the doctors for failing to save their leader. Through Esam, the doctors asked me to make the announcement of the cleric's death to the crowd. They felt the threat of my authority (and my six men with guns) would prevent a rampage. No one taught me how to deal with this shit in Officer Candidate School.

I reluctantly agreed, just as one of the followers burst in to see the covered body. He leapt from behind the curtain bawling and screaming, his grief making the announcement for me.

The followers all freaked out in unison, beating themselves.

"What the fuck are they doing?" a soldier chirped.

Five, maybe six old ladies all smacked their faces violently. A hysterical old woman in a full black robe wailed. Esam shouted to me over the wailing that she was calling out to the man who died—her brother. She knelt, smacking her face on the dirty tile floor. Blurry, black-lined tattoos crawled on her chin and eyebrows. With every other tooth missing, she looked like a dark witch.

A fat man with a beard arrived to hear the news, and promptly fainted. People lay writhing everywhere in agony, as though they had just been gassed. Saddened and shocked, my guys and I stood there motionless, with Iraqis screeching all around us. We stood there frozen, embarrassed, as dozens of people were violently mourning all around us.

Standing silently, so out of place, so foreign, we American soldiers could only stay back and observe.

Sergeant James teared up to my right. My heart ached for these poor people as they flailed and kicked. They restrained each other so we didn't have to. We stood there watching. Useless. Absorbing.

A teenage girl in a green T-shirt clutched an old woman who howled and screamed at the ceiling. Far away from my mind, I heard the radio chirp on Rydberg's back. The moment had trapped us like a spell.

Another man ran in from the blood bank, blood in hand, and out of breath, to hear the devastating news. Without hesitation, he ran to the wall to my left and slammed his head solidly against it.

Clunk.

Then again, even harder this time.

Clunk!

And he fell in a heap, crumpling to the floor.

Tow Truck said to me in amazement, "Shit, sir! That guy just knocked himself out cold."

And we both huffed uncomfortably. Too fucking unreal—yet disturbingly funny to us. We had become cold to it. The guys would tell the story of the man knocking himself out for days, laughing numbly at the absurdity of it. At that moment, I worried about how much this shit would really get to my boys later. Years later. How would I describe this moment to my future son one day? I felt like I was violating these people's privacy—but in a twisted way, I was thankful for the exposure to this foreign world.

"Lieutenant! Lieutenant!"

Esam shook my shoulder and my eyes refocused. I looked down to see the cigarette in my hand had burned almost to my knuckles.

The head doctor and Esam had conferred. Esam was infinitely wise and strangely cool in this type of situation. There were only seven Americans in the room, and about sixty followers of the cleric. Esam suggested that we find the head of the family, express our sympathies, and ask for guidance on how to move the body out of the ER to break up the crowd. I agreed. It made more sense than anything else I could think of.

The leader of the group was an ancient, emaciated man with a scraggly gray beard. He wore a long white shirt that extended past his knees—what American soldiers usually referred to as a man-dress. I braced myself for the worst and slid my M16 from the side to the front of my body as he approached me, flanked by two hefty younger men wearing soccer jerseys. He glanced at the four soldiers next to me, and then at my rifle, and smiled softly, un-afraid. "Are you serious?" his look said to me. Embarrassed by my unnecessary caution, I pushed the rifle back to my side and heeded the old man's lesson in diplomacy.

He took a deep breath and pulled a tattered pack of Miami cig-arettes from his front pocket in no particular rush. He offered me one, and I accepted. He savored the smoke as the screams rattled chaotically around us. He was sad, but calm, reverent and peace-ful. He put me at ease too. I sensed no anger in him whatsoever.

Esam relayed to him our condolences. The old man nodded gently. He took another slow drag from his cigarette, and told me that he was used to death—he had served for years in the war against Iran and had seen his share. He told me that Saddam had put him in prison for two years. Then, in English, he said firmly, "No Saddam. Good Bush. Good Bush."

The men next to him nodded in agreement without prompting. That hit me hard.

He made no request for money, and asked for no retribution. He explained that he needed only one thing from me: a note. He needed a letter of authority from an American officer so that his group could pass through the U.S. checkpoints around the city, established to enforce the 2330 curfew. No note, no passage. He liked Americans very much, and did not want to break the law, he told me. His people just needed to get home safely and quickly so that they could care for the body of their cleric in the proper Islamic way. This old man's leader had just been assassinated in a city that my Army could not secure, and he was so humble that all he wanted from me was a hall pass. I felt ashamed.

Hostility was quickly building within the crowd around us. Esam, the old man, and I collectively decided that we should roll the cleric's body out of the operating room and to the bus as soon as possible. Before the crowd had time to regain their composure and attack the doctors, or us. I didn't want to create a nightmare scenario that would be repeated on CNN or Al Jazeera for weeks.

I gave the signal, and two of my men hurled open the curtain like magicians. The old man's two bodyguards burst out from behind at top speed, pushing the body on the gurney. Two of my soldiers ran alongside it with their weapons raised like Secret Service agents guarding the president's car. The family members and followers still standing in the lobby saw the funeral express and dropped to their knees at the sight, weeping even louder as the gurney rushed through the crowd and out the door in a blur.

Elvis had left the building. Exhale.

Cigarettes for all. Another death experienced. Another feeling of helplessness. Another hall pass. Another night in Baghdad.

It was time for us to continue our patrol. A flurry of machine-gun fire popped two blocks away toward the river. A green flare streamed above the river. The CP called over the radio: an American unit had just been hit down the road and we should get moving to check it out. More firing. The guys were ready to go. Rydberg reported it to higher on the SINCGAR.

Just as we started to leave, a Humvee flew up to the ER. It backed up to the doors with two bodies in the rear stacked like bloody slabs of meat fresh from a butcher shop. Blood streamed off the corners of the tailgate in streams. The soldiers manning the Humvee were from a unit that had just gotten to Baghdad a few nights before, and was rapidly establishing its reputation for being quick on the draw. Every newly arrived unit was pissed off that it had missed the fighting on the way up, and wanted to make up for lost time.

The NCO in charge told me that these dead Iraqis shot at them from a rooftop. The Americans shot back. The Iraqis generally didn't do too well in these situations. We could see at night. And we had magic boots.

can unit had just been hit down the road and we should get moving to check it out. More firing. The guys were ready to go. Ryd-
berry reported it to higher on the SINCGAR.

Just as we started to leave, a Humvee flew up to the EB, P
backed up to the doors with two bodies in the rear stacked like
bloody slabs of meat fresh from a butcher shop. Blood streamed
off the corners of the tailgate in streams. The soldiers manning the
Humvee were from a unit that had just gotten to Baghdad a few
nights before, and was rapidly establishing its reputation for being
quick on the draw. Every newly arrived unit was pissed off that it
had missed the fighting on the way up and wanted to make up for
lost time.

The NCO in charge told me that these dead Iraqis shot at them
from a rooftop. The Americans shot back. The Iraqis generally
didn't do too well in these situations. We could see at night. And
we had magic books.

CHAPTER TWELVE
GOD BULLETS HURT

But what you've done here
Is put yourself between a bullet and a target
And it won't be long before
You're pulling yourself away.
—Citizen Cope, "Bullet and a Target"

In June 2003, the flaws in "post-war" planning became increasingly apparent.

Fuel shortages were rampant. In an attempt to regulate supplies properly, the gas stations became government (that is U.S. Army) controlled. We leveled a heavy hand to attempt to ensure some semblance of fairness. Output was limited, and delivery trucks were frequently attacked by insurgents. Iraqis waited for days in their cars on lines that stretched for over a mile. Sleeping behind their steering wheels, pushing their cars when they ran out of gas, they waited for delivery trucks to arrive at the pumps. Management was unreliable and corruption was rampant. We had to detain numerous gas station managers for lying, cheating, extortion, favoritism, and a host of other violations. Police did not have their own gas stations, so we also had to force people to allow police vehicles to the front of the lines. Then police would often abuse the system, and try to get gas for their civilian vehicles on off days. (Baghdad police were like corrupt Keystone Kops. For thirty years they had kept order through violence, intimidation, and bribery. They didn't like to park their patrol cars on the street for fear they'd be shot up or stolen.) Tempers were high. So were the incidents of violence. It seemed like every day a station was being attacked.

A standard patrol for our guys included the ridiculous task of checking and chronicling fuel levels with a long measuring stick at every gas pump in the sector—not exactly something they teach at the Infantry school at Fort Benning. Then the next patrol out would check the level again, to ensure that the operators weren't skimming off the top for their own profit.

I had just returned from one of these patrols with Third Squad. We rolled through the gate at the Ministry of Labor and called in. "Wolfpack Main, this is Blue 3 returning to compound, over."

"Blue 3, Blue 3. This is Wolfpack Main. We need you to go back out and proceed immediately south. Repeat. Proceed south toward gas station Charlie. A friendly unit has been hit. Get over there and check it out. Be careful, over."

"Wolfpack Main, this is Blue 3. Roger that. We're en route, over."

Fatty did a 180, turned the Humvee around, hit the gas, and we were flying down the four-lane street toward the gas station we had just left. As we rounded the corner, we could see traffic backed up. Our Humvee jumped the curb with a thud as we drove on the median and scanned for shooters.

"Shit. Somebody got fucked up!" the soldier in the turret yelled down to us.

Up ahead we could see thick black smoke pouring upward, the kind that only came from explosions. First thing we saw was a burning produce truck. The cab was blasted and the back of it was filled with boxes of burned vegetables. Glass and smoke were everywhere. A small shack of a store stood alone on the right side of the road, its entrance all shattered glass. The inevitable crowd was forming.

"Oh, God," I heard Phil growl behind me.

I looked ahead and my stomach dropped.

A command Humvee was burning in the middle of the street. I was sure it was our unit's vehicle. It was just blown to hell, sparking and twisted. Judging by the degree of devastation, I was pretty sure we had just suffered our unit's first combat loss. It would have been very difficult to survive that.

There is no more sickening feeling in the world than seeing your guys hit. For an American soldier in Iraq, seeing an American Humvee damaged is like watching your home burn to the ground and not knowing if your family made it out alive or not.

We faced our Humvees in opposite directions and set up a perimeter. I got on the radio as Chesty's guys fanned out. A few of us ran up to the vehicle to see if there was anybody inside, anything salvageable. It looked empty. Somebody yelled to look out for ammo that might cook off and explode. If there were any grenades or 203 rounds left inside, our bad day would get much worse. The wheel rims were molten, the melted steel cascading down like condensation. The skeletal shell of the vehicle glowed red in a pool of bubbling orange fluid, bright and thick, like neon honey. Phil picked up a smoldering Kevlar helmet lying in the debris. It was red-hot. He dropped it. It bounced pathetically as Phil scrambled to pick it up again.

"What do you got, Phil?" Chesty screamed at him.

The Iraqi crowd was building, well over fifty now.

Phil finally got the NVG bracket off the front of the helmet and read the name tape. He didn't recognize the name. Wolfpack Main called to tell us that all personnel had jumped into the lead vehicle and were free from the kill zone. We pushed out the perimeter as the crowd grew and units started rolling in from other sectors of the city.

That blown-up Humvee was a close call. We all knew it. It was at the spot where there was a bottleneck in the road by the gas station. We had passed by the same spot not five minutes before and nothing had happened to us.

Turns out it was a patrol from some command that was on its way to ORHA (the Office of Reconstruction and Humanitarian Assistance) for business. A few days later, one soldier died of wounds sustained in that ambush. If any day over there rattled me, it was that day. Why weren't we attacked? Did we have adequate security set, making the bad guys think us too risky a target? Did something in the explosive device malfunction the moment we passed? I will never know how many times I was a second away from dying.

The press was there within minutes, reporters pushing out in front of the crowd and demanding access. A British newspaper took Li'l Mac's picture for its front page. And in the midst of all the confusion of reporters and other units' QRF showing up, Chesty was walking across the median in the road when he planted his foot in a chuckhole and tumbled ass over end, right in front of a BBC camera crew. The guys roared with laughter and ribbed him for hours. A few days later, during a phone call home, he discovered his wife had seen the footage on FOX News. He was pissed. Not because his wife saw him stop, drop, and roll, but because until this point, he had her convinced he was working a desk at the Baghdad International Airport.

The quality of military intelligence drives all counterinsurgency operations. In June 2003, Lieutenant General McKiernan, head of the U.S. military land component, was ordered to move himself and his entire headquarters out of Iraq and back to Florida. Within days, hundreds of intelligence officers had left with him. That month, I saw a considerable drop in the quality and volume of intelligence we received in our nightly reports from higher. And an increase in violence. The removal of these key intelligence assets was one of the biggest errors in the battle against the fledgling insurgency.

On the night of June 16, just outside our sector, a sniper shot and killed a First Brigade soldier riding in a Humvee. The calm was cracking, and we became increasingly concerned, especially about the threat of snipers. In a city with a million rooftops and windows, a sniper shot could come from anywhere at any time. And you'd only know you were in his sights when you were hit.

As the temperature rose in the city, so did the violence. Tracers overhead seemed to get more frequent every night. Thursday nights were especially intense. The men all called Thursdays "Wedding Night." It was the only night of the week on which people got married in Baghdad. The weddings were beautiful to see, with people dancing in the street and singing, cheering us as we patrolled past them. To me, the weddings looked like a cross between a rave, a block party, and a Greek wedding. The celebratory fire from AKs filled the sky like lightning bugs.

Iraqis fire their guns in the air to celebrate everything from weddings to soccer victories. They ignore the fact that those rounds eventually come back down. We called them God bullets. Sometimes they fell into children and exploded their little skulls.

Ibrahim, our janitor, showed up late one morning. He was a slim, polite man who looked about fifty years old, which in Iraq means he was actually about forty. He was perpetually smiling, and incredibly reverent. With a cigarette in his lips, through Mohamed or Esam, he often told us about violence and mutilation from his time in the Iraqi army fighting the Iranians. And about what it is like to have sex with a camel in the desert. He was the most dedicated laborer I had ever seen in my life.

When I got to the front gate that morning, Ibrahim was hunched over, another man gently pulling him along by the shirt. He could barely speak; his eyes winced in pain as he walked closer to the building. I could tell he was not well. His eyes welled up and he started to cry, apologizing profusely for being late to work. The man with him was his cousin. Ibrahim said he could not work that day but had brought his cousin to work in his place.

Ibrahim had a bullet lodged deep in his neck. Dark, congealed blood stained the skin behind his hair. As he was walking home from work late the night before, a bullet had fallen from the sky and slammed into his body. It knocked him to the ground and nearly stopped his heart. It even knocked the cigarette from his mouth.

Whispering prayers to Allah, Ibrahim thought he was going to die. Somehow, his main concern was that he would be letting us down by missing work. He assured me that his cousin was strong and a very good worker. He had a fucking bullet in his neck and he was worried about who would clean our toilets for the day. This man just walked clear across Baghdad, to sweep our floors, with a bullet lodged just millimeters from his spinal cord. He made five dollars a week.

We called Battalion to request the surgeon. Every step was torture for him. The boys were gingerly loading Ibrahim into the Humvee when we found out that our request was denied. The Colonel ruled that American surgeons would only operate on Americans and Iraqis shot by Americans. Since Ibrahim was shot by another Iraqi, he was "shit out of luck," according to Battalion.

We were pissed. "Fit to be tied," as Sergeant Willie kept saying. Sergeant James cried in frustration. Once again, we were handcuffed by the idiocy of officers in the rear who experienced our daily fights through the radio and pushed paper in defense of freedom.

We laid Ibrahim on a cot in the back room. I never saw a man in so much pain. Everything he did hurt. He could barely even drink water. I held his hand and tried to help him drink, holding the cup to his mouth. It is hard to reassure someone without speaking the same language. Imagine the confusion of facing your own death. Now imagine someone explaining it to you in a language you don't understand.

The bullet was too deep inside for Doc Spettel, the Bravo Company medic, to get it. We needed to get Ibrahim to a surgeon—he didn't have long. The boys collected a few hundred bucks to pay for the surgery. We took him to the hospital we once guarded and paid for our friend's life. Business in Baghdad.

Back home in the land of *Desperate Housewives* and Starbucks, Americans rarely hear about Iraqi civilian casualties. They barely hear about American casualties. The worlds of American civilians and Iraqi civilians are detached from each other. For most Americans, the war in Iraq is an issue rather than an experience. But I saw how the fates of Iraqi civilians and American soldiers were intimately intertwined.

Ten days later, "Bullet Neck" cruised back through our front gate. From then on, he kissed each of us every day before he went home, and prayed fiercely to Allah for us whenever we went outside the wire.

CHAPTER THIRTEEN
COLLATERAL DAMAGE

> I hate war as only a soldier who has lived it can, only as
> one who has seen its brutality, its futility, its stupidity.
> —Dwight D. Eisenhower

By July of 2003, violence was on the rise.

It was hard for us to tell if it was temporary or signaled the growth of a larger movement. But we knew things were more dangerous. More soldiers were dying, and every time we left the gate on patrol, fewer Iraqis were giving us thumbs-up and waving. Things were starting to turn.

I had just gotten back from a patrol when I got some mail from home and started to have an idea about why things were changing. In addition to a few letters and a two-month-old *Maxim*, I got some ESPN.com and CNN.com news printouts. My friends all knew I was a sports, news, and politics junky, and that I wanted to keep informed as much as possible.

One CNN.com story flabbergasted me. It was dated July 3, 2003, and was titled: "Bush warns militants who attack U.S. troops in Iraq." It described a macho speech by the president in which he stated: "There are some who feel like the conditions are such that they can attack us there. My answer is, bring 'em on."

Bring 'em on? What the hell was he thinking? My soldiers and I were searching for car bombs in Medical City and scanning rooftops for snipers, and our president was in Washington taunting our enemies and encouraging them to attack us. Who the hell did he think he was? He had finally taken the cowboy act too far. Iraq was not a movie, and he was not Clint Eastwood. The armchair bravado and arrogance of our commander in chief affected our lives directly and immediately. If I had seen this news story, so had the Iraqis. I just could not fathom what would motivate him to say such a thing. Iraq was in a very fragile state, and we needed our president to be a statesman, not a bully.

The enemy was already "bringing it on" all over Baghdad. Three U.S. troops had been killed in separate attacks around the city in a thirteen-hour period just a few days earlier, including a soldier from our Regiment. Twenty-two-year-old Specialist Jeffrey Wershow was from our sister Battalion, the Second of the 124th. He was stationed out at the convention center in another part of Baghdad with an OCS classmate of mine from New York who was a Platoon Leader in the unit. Wershow and three other soldiers were providing security for U.S. officials visiting Baghdad University, once run by Uday Hussein, the son of Saddam Hussein. My soldiers used to covet patrol assignments to the university because it gave them a chance to catch a view of the young and often attractive female students. The local men knew that, and weren't exactly pleased with the American soldiers ogling their women. Nothing pisses a man off more than the threat of another man coveting his women. That's true in every culture.

Witnesses said Wershow was standing in line to buy a Coke when an Iraqi walked up behind him and shot him at the base of his skull, just below his Kevlar helmet. The gunman fled into the crowd, and wasn't pursued by other U.S. soldiers on the scene. Instead, two soldiers attempted to provide first aid to Wershow, while the other stood guard against another attack. They did the right thing and took care of their friend, who died a few hours later. Collins knew Wershow from his days in the 82nd, and was devastated when he heard the news.

The Commander in charge of security in the area, Lt. Col. Peter Jones, described the incident in the press as "an aberration."

Aberration, my ass. It was the same tactic used the day before in the killing of a British cameraman outside the Baghdad Museum. The close-quarters sneak attacks in crowded areas were terribly menacing. Maybe not for Lieutenant Colonels who never walked patrols, but for my enlisted grunts, who walked the streets every day trying to win Iraqi hearts and minds, it was scary as hell. Any man shaking your right hand could shoot you in the face with the gun in his left. The tactic was incredibly difficult to guard against, because we were so often in close quarters with Iraqis. Most of them had friendly intentions, but everywhere we went, there were Iraqi crowds, and now we were looking for pistols. Tempers were high. Any time Iraqis tried to get close to us we'd shove them away. Each attack drove a larger wedge between us and them. We just couldn't afford to take any chances by letting them in too close.

We were all on edge. On a dismounted night patrol with first squad, we stopped a suspicious car that turned out to be a drunk driver. We sent him on his way, but he became belligerent and got into a wrestling tussle with Sergeant Tank. We all found Tank struggling with the old man funny—until they fell to the ground and the man grabbed for Sergeant Tank's M-16. Without hesitation, I kicked the man solidly in the head with the full force of my boot. I kicked him so hard it sounded like I had punted a football. He went still, and I thought I had killed him. The Squad fell silent. I held my breath, and could hear rounds snap across the city. Then the old man began to moan. He was fine (except for a headache). My nerves were not. The constant threat of violence made me dangerously violent.

Violence had become commonplace. We faced RPGs, car

bombs, mortar attacks, snipers, and now Jack Ruby–wannabe as-
sassins. But even they became unremarkable. They were just
memorable incidents by which we could mark time. In conversation, an event didn't happen on "Tuesday" or "Friday." It occurred "the day after the mortar landed in the parking lot" or "the
same night that little girl came into the ER with her foot blown
off." Weeks became just another irrelevant civilian mark of days
going by. They all bled together hazily. Our sleeping was short
and in irregular patterns. We worked constantly in the daylight
and in the dark. And rest was never restful. So much occurred in
every twenty-four-hour period that a new day just seemed like
an extension of the last one. It was a universally shared feeling
that guys referred to as "*Groundhog Day* Syndrome." Most of the
time, I didn't know what day it was. The concept of "days off,"
"workweeks," and "weekends" was as alien to me as the surface
of the sun.

Even in this setting, things still happened occasionally that
were so absurd that we had to laugh. I was on Battle Captain duty
when Battalion called and instructed us to send a Squad out to investigate a situation reported on the main street near our compound. A dead horse was lying in a traffic circle. The horse had
been there for days, and dead animals on the side of the road were
not exactly unusual in Iraq. But lately there had been a string of
IED attacks in Baghdad where the explosive device was hidden in
the carcass of a dead dog or horse.

The CO dispatched Andy and a Squad to investigate. He called
back a few minutes later to report that yes, in fact, there was a
dead horse in the traffic circle. He told me the rest of the story
later that night after he returned.

The horse was nasty, bloated, and covered with flies. He
checked it for wires and booby traps, and the carcass was deemed
clear. But the horse would remain a threat to passing patrols unless it was removed. A horse weighs at least a thousand pounds,
and is far too heavy to lift. Since it was already so badly decom-

posed, dragging it with a Humvee would have pulled it to shreds. Andy decided to deal with the situation.

He walked to one of the Humvees and grabbed a can of fuel from the back. He had chosen cremation. He doused the horse with the gas and lit a match. Didn't work. A soldier mentioned to Andy that diesel fuel burned at a much higher temperature than regular gasoline.

Hmmmmm. Next he asked a soldier for a lighter. That didn't work either. But he was determined. By now a crowd of Iraqis had gathered to watch the young American officer deal with the body of Mr. Ed. Andy was barely twenty-one years old, but full of initiative. A crowd was watching, and he was not about to be done in by a dead horse. He demanded that one of his 203 gunners hand over his weapon, along with a 203 flare round. Andy was really going to set this sucker ablaze.

He ordered everyone to stand back, and fired the round. It made its distinctive *whoomp* and flew out of the barrel. Like the ignition temperature of diesel fuel, Andy had vastly underestimated the flight pattern of the 203 round. It flew like a rocket, glanced off the horse carcass, and bounced hard in the air. Uh-oh. All eyes were locked on the flight path of the round as it flew through the air and crashed directly through the window of a nearby house. It was like hitting a baseball through your neighbor's window, but much, much worse. Shit.

The carcass did not catch fire, but the house did. An old lady ran out screaming bloody murder, and the place was ablaze in seconds. Andy stood speechless in the middle of the traffic circle with the 203 in his hands.

The episode illustrated for Andy, and for us all, that collateral damage can happen in any number of ways.

Third Platoon had been told from the start that we'd be heading home by July Fourth. Mission accomplished and all that. We all got excited and antsy as the day approached. Everyone walked just a little more carefully on patrol and scanned that much harder for IEDs. No one wanted to take a hit the day before we all shipped out. All the guys wrote letters to their loved ones like the ones I wrote to Bama, telling her how excited I was that I was going to be holding her soon. Asking her to pick a romantic spot anywhere in the world, preferably with a white beach and tall cocktails, to celebrate our reunion. Thanking her a million times over for her love and friendship and support through the previous six months. Every day at least one of my guys would ask me, "Hey, L.T. You get any word yet?" It was like Kuwait, only worse.

We all knew that the mission was nowhere near accomplished in Baghdad. By most measures, things were getting worse, not better. Still, we hoped.

July 1, 2, 3 passed with no word. On July Fourth it came: our tour was extended through September. Three more months in hell. Three more months away from girlfriends, families, jobs.

Tour extensions are the National Guardsman's nightmare. You're not like regular Army. Soldiering is not your full-time occupation. You've got another job. You are what some people pejoratively call a "weekend warrior." You're ready to serve at any time your governor or the president calls on you. You never know when or for how long that's going to be.

My guys had served six months at this point, and served brilliantly and courageously. That's a hell of a way from being a weekend warrior. And now they'd serve another three months.

For guys whose marriages or relationships were already strained, the news was devastating. Every mailbag carried a new Dear John letter.

Tour extensions are also a nightmare for any combat personnel whose contracted term of duty is coming to an end. The military has a policy called "stop-loss," by which it can prevent troops from leaving the armed forces after their contracts have expired. Stop-loss is a fine-print loophole in the contract that allows the Department of Defense to force servicemen and -women who are normally scheduled to retire or leave the military to remain on duty. These are people who have volunteered to serve their country, and honorably completed their commitments, who are now being forced to continue to serve, like conscripts. That's why stop-loss policies have been called a "backdoor draft."

With recruitment down and not enough standing troops, stop-loss is a way for the Pentagon to make up for the shortage of soldiers needed in Iraq and Afghanistan. The military first used stop-loss during the Gulf War, and has used it at an unprecedented level in Iraq, where troop strength has always been stretched to the breaking point. It's been estimated that without stop-loss, troop strength would be down as much as 25 percent.

So that's how Third Platoon celebrated Independence Day 2003—holding the hand of another fledgling democracy as it struggled for its own independence. With AK tracer trails flying overhead instead of fireworks, and patrols instead of picnics, and MREs instead of hot dogs.

CHAPTER FOURTEEN
THE GREMLINS THEORY

> It is important to emphasize that guerrilla warfare is a war of the masses, a war of the people. The guerrilla band is an armed nucleus, the fighting vanguard of the people. It draws its great force from the mass of the people themselves. The guerrilla band is not to be considered inferior to the army against which it fights simply because it is inferior in firepower. Guerrilla warfare is used by the side which is supported by a majority but which possesses a much smaller number of arms for use in defense against oppression.... the guerrilla fighter is a social reformer, that he takes up arms responding to the angry protest of the people against their oppressors, and that he fights in order to change the social system that keeps all his unarmed brothers in ignominy and misery.
>
> —Che Guevara, *Guerrilla Warfare*

"L.T., we're too busy mopping the floor to turn off the faucet," One of my sergeants said one day.

He was right. In Iraq, America is making more enemies than it is killing.

The Bush Doctrine is a flawed foreign policy that fails to understand the basics of human nature. Preemptive military strikes

165

and democracy at the point of a gun cannot create instant democracy like geopolitical Cup-a-Soup—just add water.

Both the American and Iraqi people have been sold a bill of goods. Our tactics for fighting the insurgency are failing, and Third Platoon found that out the hard way. Underestimating the desperation, anger, and sheer numbers of "bad guys" was a mammoth mistake.

The insurgency is not made up of just Iraqis. It is bigger than that. Syrians, Iranians, Egyptians—we saw them all poised against us. Without enough coalition troops to properly handle the occupation, Iraq's borders were like Swiss cheese, and the bad guys flowed in.

And the insurgents had no trouble recruiting new warriors. The Iraqis are not so different from the rest of the world. The bottom line is that people simply do not like to be occupied. Nobody likes to have a tank parked in their front yard. Iraq will not be stable before suffering incredible losses and struggling through decades of development. The Bush timetable is ridiculous—Iraq will not develop into a functioning democracy until the entire adult generation dies and a whole new generation comes to power. The living generation of Iraqis suffers from serious mental trauma caused by decades of violence, abuse, and torture. They are damaged goods.

Think of it this way: Iraq is like an entire country with battered woman syndrome. U.S. forces are like cops responding to a domestic violence case. We have removed the abusive husband, but the wife and children are not "all better" the day their oppressor gets locked up. The family has deep mental and physical wounds that will not disappear overnight. They desperately need care, treatment, and time to heal properly. And to compound the problem, the cops have eaten from the fridge, busted the TV, and left the front door open with a broken lock.

The civilian war planners in Washington seem to believe that there are a finite number of bad guys. They think that if you kill enough insurgents, you will vanquish and be rid of them. They fail to understand that every day in Iraq we are creating more insurgents who want to kill Americans. Bill O'Reilly can scoff all he wants when the insurgents call themselves freedom fighters, but that is how they see themselves, and as Sun Tzu said, "Know your enemy." To a huge population of angry young Muslims all over the Middle East, we are the bad guys. We are an army of occupation. If I were an impoverished, idealistic Muslim teenager in Pakistan, I might want to go to Iraq to fight the good fight and kill Americans, too. For the insurgents, combating the Americans is as noble a cause as going to Spain to fight Franco was for the idealistic young Americans of Ernest Hemingway's generation during the Spanish Civil War.

Right now we are making more enemies than we are killing in Iraq. It is like we're pouring water on Gizmo from the 1984 movie *Gremlins*. In the film, when water accidentally spills on a mysterious and exotic pet, a Mogwai named Gizmo, it causes him to multiply and produce an army of mischievous little brothers. Among these offspring is the exceptionally nasty-tempered Stripe. And just like Stripe, a Muqtada al-Sadr or al-Zaquari leads a coordinated uprising that unleashes massive violence and destruction on the local population.

Every time American troops accidentally kill someone in Iraq, we create new recruits for the insurgency. Countless young Osama bin Laden wannabes are plotting attacks on the United States at this moment. President Bush tells us that the occupation of Iraq will make us safer at home. It won't. The brother of someone we killed in Baghdad is plotting right now to blow up the 6 train in New York, the Staples Center in LA, your local mall. One major difference between Iraq and Vietnam: this war will follow us home.

We conducted countless raids in Baghdad. To experience these raids is to understand why America cannot win in Iraq without dramatically changing its course. A lot depends on how American troops conduct themselves after a search is completed—how they react when they are wrong. Unfortunately, procedures are mostly improvised on the spot, and raids too often leave families, neighborhoods, seething with anti-American rage.

It was 0300 hours in a run-down section of Sector 17. My Platoon was looking for weapons in an Iraqi home. We had been told there were RPGs and roadside bomb-making materials in this house. The intelligence looked solid, and our Commanders were sure it was actionable.

So we executed a "cordon and search," surrounding the neighborhood with imposing M1A1 Abrams tanks, Bradley Armored Personnel Carriers, .50-caliber guns mounted on Humvees, and concertina wire. Apache and Kiowa helicopters circled overhead. It was dark, hot beyond belief, and deafeningly loud. We had the target tight in our grasp. Time to squeeze.

My soldiers and I stacked up outside a thick gate to the house. Four Squads, each with eight men, curled outside the front doors of four houses on the same block. Nineteen-year-olds, barely out of high school, and thirty-year-old vets of the first Gulf War lined up together on the ancient walls. They spit tobacco juice, wiped sweat from their eyes, and thought about their girlfriends, their kids, and their futures. They had no idea what was behind that damn door. They never knew until the second it opened. This was nothing new. They had been here before—on dozens of nights, at dozens of doors. They squinted intensely through the shady green tunnels of their night vision goggles, weighed down with water, bulking gadgets, and weapons. They waited for the "go" from me.

The radio squawked in my ear. "Blue 6! Blue 6! Pensacola! Pensacola! Go! Go!"

"Roger that!" I snapped back.

Time to earn our money. *"Go, guys! Go! Go! Go!"*

Boom! Hinges burst and metal groaned. The door bowed, pieces flew, eyes scanned, and feet shuffled forward in one strong and violent motion. We had done this hundreds of times in training. In the Army they say, "Slow is smooth and smooth is fast." Don't rush, take your time, proceed carefully.

The family who lived inside was sleeping on the roof—it was much cooler up there—and couldn't get dressed in time to answer the door. They screamed and yelled in Arabic. We screamed and yelled in English—sweat pouring, babies wailing, muzzles swinging, and hearts pounding. We huddled them into the far corner so we could cuff them, control them, and search the house. The women cried uncontrollably, the men were angry and proud— always glaring. And the children just watched intently. Often, they were surprisingly calm, curious, and attentive.

We occupied their home, invaded their personal space. This Squad came without an interpreter, because we only had one for every four Squads. We stormed into their house like the Gestapo. We saw how they lived, the tea left in tiny cups, the bed mats on the floor, the pictures of their grandparents on the walls. We looked under the rugs, in the closets, beneath the clothes they were wearing. No weapons anywhere. Not so much as a fucking slingshot.

Now what?

What do you do when you're wrong?

The bad units would leave without a word. They would never call in the L.T. They'd just move on to wreck another house.

The good units understood that we were more than just soldiers. We were global citizens, diplomats, and the personification of America. Every single thing we did represented our nation— precisely what the soldiers at Abu Ghraib forgot. For decades, this one family of Iraqis would have a view of America and Americans based largely on these soldiers on this day. Forever, this family would remember the day America came knocking on their door. We had to make absolutely sure to get things right.

When we got it right, it didn't just happen. We had thought ahead, we had a plan. We took our time to get it right. We were patient and attentive. We fixed things in this house before we moved on to the next one. We respected the people of this house and understood that they were not the same as the family in the next home. We respected their culture. We recognized that we needed to tend to the family's needs, in spite of our deadline. We took off our dark sunglasses so they could see our eyes—let them see that we were real human people, just like them. We smiled and showed them that we were not infidel cyborgs from another world. We tried to understand them and their lifestyles. We stepped out of our comfort area, shared the risk a bit.

The good soldiers had studied a bit about Iraqi history. We tried a greeting or two in Arabic. We shared the two-cheek kiss, did not show the bottoms of our feet, offered up a cigarette.

On this occasion we called and let the CO know that we got this one wrong. We were honest with our boss. He arrived and called in Esam, to communicate with the family that we were very sorry to have disrupted them.

We apologized. Mea culpa. Whoops.

We admitted that the intel was faulty. We admitted we were wrong.

All over the world, the Bush administration's hubris and arrogance have pissed people off. The whole world watches what we do in Iraq. Every morning kids in Nigeria and Argentina turn on the TV and see us executing Bush's foreign policy, and think that's America. Generations of servicemen and -women did not make the sacrifices they did so that President Bush could make Americans look like assholes around the world.

So it was critical that we showed remorse and humility. My men made every effort to repair the stereotypical image of the ugly American that so many people around the globe have grown to despise.

We explained to the Iraqis that we did not hate them. We offered to pay for the door. We gave them paperwork for them to submit to Bremer's desk jockeys at the OCPA (Office of the Coalition Provisional Authority) for loss compensation. (The forms were written in Arabic, because we were not arrogant enough to assume they read and wrote English.) We put everything back where we found it. If we looked under the bed and pushed the covers to the floor, we replaced them. We made sure our boots didn't track sand all over the house. We took pictures to document the facts. We had nothing to hide. That way, if anyone from outside came to investigate the incident, we had proper documentation.

Next we provided them with security. Bremer's office did not work quickly, and it would be a while before this family got the money to fix the door. So we brought padlocks with us to keep the thieves away when we were gone. We did not want to leave a soldier to watch the door for them, because nobody likes to feel occupied, but we provided them with a way to protect their house when we were gone. And we did want to be gone, just as they wanted us to be gone.

Finally, always, before we left any house, we focused on the kids. We never left a house without handing candy to the kids. It was always about the kids. "We lose the kids, we lose the war," I told my guys. In Third Platoon, an essential part of every soldier's combat load was one cargo pocket filled with candy: these kids were the future of Iraq and the future of Iraqi-American relations. The candy was a small gesture of reconciliation and kindness that might reverberate for years. Or maybe it was just putting a Band-Aid on a tumor.

My Platoon did things right most of the time. Even if my president did not. Sometimes it was easier than others. It wasn't our choice to come here and wage this war, but we chose how we would be remembered. By the end of our time in Iraq, we had made friends and done all we could to fix what we had broken. After our first cordon and search every one of my soldiers "got it." Maybe some folks in Washington should go to Iraq. They could pick up a rifle, kick a door in, and see what it's like. Then maybe they'd get it.

Still, no matter how careful you were, how hard you tried to get it right, something could always go terribly wrong.

One night an NCO was leading a squad from Second Platoon on a house-to-house raid. The NCO was a solid soldier and a good Squad Leader. He and his men lined up in front of a house and approached the door. As they did, he looked in a window beside the door and saw a man inside holding a pistol, apparently pointing it at them. The NCO did what he was trained to do—he shot through the window, and the man went down.

Our guys burst through the door. The man lay on the floor in a pool of blood. The pistol was near his limp hand. The NCO's heart sank when he saw that it was a toy.

Members of the dead man's family huddled in the doorway to a back room. They looked strangely calm. With Mohamed interpreting, they explained that the man had been extremely retarded. He slept in a cage. They didn't seem to blame the Americans for killing him. They seemed almost relieved.

On July 22, I was sitting in the Ministry of Labor CP when I heard the distinctive *rat-tat-tat-tat-tat-tat* from an AK-47. This fire was close—really close. At first, I thought it was a firefight going on at the gate. Then I heard more gunfire, and from different caliber weapons. Maybe our guys on the roof? Then pistols, and then a burst from a machine gun. Getting heavier.

The shooting went on for five minutes. The sound of fire bounced around the block like a Ping-Pong ball. It sounded like birds calling to and answering each other.

The fire got louder and heavier. It started to sound like we were under attack. But none of our guys were returning fire. We radioed our guys on the roof.

"What's going on out there?"

"Don't know. Maybe another soccer match, sir. But it's coming from all over the city. And it's getting worse."

Another celebration. Just step outside your house and start

shooting. The famous image of Saddam shooting the shotgun from his hip. I thought of Ibrahim. It's all fun and games until someone loses an eye—or their kid. It made me wonder if they ever taught Iraqis about gravity in school.

I worried about it all the time. Iraqis could shoot up in the air next to a jittery Iraqi security guard, or one of my Joes. We could return fire, and kill a gang of civilians who were just doing what is, in their culture, the equivalent of screaming "Yippee!"

Then again, my guys were used to hearing gunfire. Thousands of bullets soaring into the air, and no one got excited about it.

Until the entire city seemed to erupt. And First Platoon was outside, with some foreign reporters. When I called to them, all I could hear was gunfire, and my heart dropped.

One of the guys ran down from the second-floor TV room. We'd had Mohamed get a local electrician to jerry-rig a Haji satellite dish. Usually all we got was Iraqi news and some bizarre Danish music video station. Sometimes we got Al Jazeera and CNN.

"Hey, sir, it's on TV," he reported. "We got Uday and Qusay! The 101st killed 'em up north. That's why the Iraqis are freaking out. We got the motherfuckers. Maybe even Saddam."

We ordered our guys inside. Bullets were falling like heavy rain. Nobody wanted to write a letter home to a wife whose husband was killed by a God bullet. I could see outside that the city was lit up like the Fourth of July.

A few minutes later, First Platoon returned. I could tell from their faces something was wrong. Nobody was hurt, but everyone was shaken. There was a reporter for the Associated Press with them, and he was crying. He sat on the front step and lit a cigarette with shaky hands.

The guys had been a few blocks down the street on a routine patrol. They were walking down a narrow alley, as they had done a thousand times before. Out of nowhere, the block erupted with gunfire. It seemed to come from everywhere. The guys all took cover and spread out. At the end of the street they clearly saw a muzzle flash. Someone in the dark firing an AK. The Squad Leader at the front of the line returned fire, along with a few other guys. The rounds flew in the direction of the muzzle blasts, and the AK fire stopped.

And then they heard screaming. A scream of unimaginable anguish. The pain of a parent.

The man firing the AK had been hit twice in the chest. His young daughter had been standing next to him. She was also hit. The bullets tore into her head. They said she was about nine years old. The doc was trying to save her when the men were ordered to return to the base. The family threw her into a car to rush her off to the hospital, but she was already gone.

There was no way the Squad Leader could have known she was there. It was nobody's fault but the stupid father's. Didn't he realize there were American soldiers patrolling the area? That man went from the joy of liberation to the total terror of loss as fast as bullets fly.

It was dark, and our guys were in a very bad area. You're waiting for the shooting to come every day. And when it finally does, it's not like it is in the movies. You can't always tell precisely where fire is coming from. There's only a small difference between the sound of someone a hundred meters from you shooting up in the air and someone shooting right at you. If you take the time to tell the difference, you're probably dead. The Squad Leader was a good soldier, and he was looking out for his men. He wanted to live to see his children back home. The war had put him in a place with no good solution.

He and the men around him were devastated. We tried to console him, but it did no good. There was no way to describe the feeling of loss in his face. He knew he couldn't ever fix it. He couldn't take it back, no matter how many times he'd try for the rest of his life. But it was not his fault.

The full story ran on the Associated Press wire the next day. It was headlined "Deep distrust festers in Iraq," with the subhead

"Major combat over, but U.S. occupiers facing uphill battle." The reporter noted that, as this child had died, so did "the goodwill that this company of Florida National Guard had worked for more than two months to build. . . . Now those same neighbors who waved at the patrolling soldiers are vowing revenge against them, and the events of that July 22 night have become a lesson in the murderous unpredictability of soldiering in Iraq."

The article went on to say that "Iraqis who expected the invading superpower to hand them the American dream are becoming bitter that their hopes, though clearly inflated, haven't been realized. . . . While happy to see Saddam Hussein ousted, many now see the occupiers as barbarians bent only on stealing their oil."

A middle-aged Baghdad man told the reporter, "People are getting angry, and believe me, you won't like the Iraqi people when they're angry." And a twenty-seven-year-old "said he was considering joining the new Iraqi army the United States is organizing, but was keeping his options open. 'I can always join another army, an army against them,' he said. 'If they stay in Iraq, I will.'"

I hated the war. I hated the Iraqi father. I hated the AP reporter for being there to see it. And I hated him for writing about it. He wasn't sticking around to write a story about the school supplies we were delivering the next day.

I hated that the president sent us into a situation like this. And my hatred was growing. I was obviously not the only one.

CHAPTER FIFTEEN
BAGHDAD ISLAND

If you're hunting sometimes . . . you can feel as if you're not hunting, but—being hunted, as if something's behind you all the time in the jungle.

—William Golding, *Lord of the Flies*

Baghdad Island, on the Tigris River just north of the city, a former amusement park with roller

coasters and merry-go-rounds, stood in the middle of a war zone. It was like Coney Island on crack. Covered with dust and grit, the rides were skeletons from a once-fun place that had seen fierce fighting during the invasion. A huge space-needle tower shaped like a turkey thermometer jutted up to the sky, offering a commanding view of the area. Units stationed there had contests to see how fast soldiers could climb the hundreds of stairs to the top. The island sat just outside of Baghdad proper, surrounded by date fields and farmland as far as the eye could see. The muddy Tigris River wound narrowly from the north, twisted like a piece of yarn. In some spots, it was narrow enough to throw a rock from one side to the other.

We were sent north to Baghdad Island to hunt down the "Mad Mortar Men," an undetermined number of insurgents who hid in the date fields and lobbed mortars onto the unit headquartered on the island. The rounds had been getting more frequent and increasingly accurate. One landed directly on the roof of a head-quarters building, but did not detonate. The unit didn't want to wait for a shell to land in the mess hall, but the rules of engagement prevented the Army from firing back with artillery near populated areas. Finally, some officer there had had it, and we were brought in to find and kill the nuisance. As one of only two Light Infantry units in the city, we were like the hit men or ex-terminators of Baghdad—other people called us in to do their dirty work.

It was a shitty assignment. On the island, we lived in an old cafeteria with no AC, forced to deal with the conventions of an-other unit's nitpicky chain of command, which rode us about mi-nor crap like headgear and clean uniforms. We were humping in the woods all day long to the point of exhaustion, and didn't have the luxury of time to wash and press their DCUs. My Platoon spent its downtime watching DVD movies and playing the new Madden NFL 2003 on PlayStation2. It was the only thing sent in a care package that got more attention than the newest issue of *Playboy*. The whole Platoon got in on a tournament. One day the generator kicked out in the middle of a major showdown between Willie and Rydberg. The crowd, a dozen deep, groaned. Just then, the Mad Mortar Men started to lob shells at us. The guys were more pissed that the generator had gone out and interrupted the game than about getting shelled.

For over a week, my men and I slogged through hundreds of acres of elephant grass and irrigation ditches, looking for three guys with a mortar tube. Palm trees stood thick in perfect rows that were laid generations ago. They created a thick overhead canopy that looked more like the jungles of Vietnam than Iraq.

It was Infantry work at its core, patrolling straight out of FM (Field Manual) 7-8 or the Ranger Handbook. Constant day and night ambushes. The typical ambush in Iraq was much less exciting than it might sound. For hours, we lay still in the weeds, sweating, devoured by mammoth insects, waiting for an enemy who never revealed himself.

We tried to get intel from the locals, but that was useless, as usual. The only thing we got was that the bad guys fired the rounds from the back of a pickup truck. Mortar rounds are relatively easy to fire, especially inaccurately. It was conceivable that these guys just stopped the truck, lobbed a few rounds in the vicinity of the buildings on the island, and hauled ass.

During one patrol we were miles deep into some date fields, far from the main road, when we stepped into a clearing and saw a tiny house—a hut, really, alone up a trail. As we approached, three figures dressed like ninjas ran from behind the hut and disappeared into the palm trees. They were covered head to toe in black, except for their eyes. A fire team gave chase.

"*Qif! Qif!*" we yelled, Arabic for "Stop!"

A paunchy middle-aged man with a doughy grin came out from behind the building with his hands raised and eyes wide. The guys raised their weapons, but nobody fired. He smiled hesitantly, and called in Arabic to the ninjas, who slowly crept toward us like wounded dogs. He attempted to talk directly to me in Arabic, which was unusual. He nodded when Mohamed explained to him that I didn't speak Arabic, but he still looked confused. The ninjas crept closer, and I could see they were not men. They were small, like teenagers, and carried wicker baskets for date gathering. Their clothes initially made us very cautious, because they wore the same type of outfit as the fedayeen. But they were not fedayeen. They were women. The build and the eyes gave it away. All three were clearly petrified.

Through Mohamed I asked the man why the women had run. He replied that we were the first Americans he and these women, who all worked for him, had ever seen. He yelled nastily at them, commanding them closer.

We must have looked even more bizarre and frightening to these people than they did to us. It was like we had just landed from

Mars. Mohamed explained that these were isolated farming people. The women were essentially slaves, and the man worked them like dogs. Very fat and clearly lazy, he commanded them aggressively to move around and pick things up. The three women were all thin. Big, tired eyes, hard from the sun, were all that showed through the black outfits except for their dirty, hard hands. Mohamed explained that their master, and their religion, prohibited them from showing any more skin. As I sweated, I thought about how brutally oppressive the outfits must be in the heat.

The man explained that since the war began months ago, the only Americans he and the women had seen in person were the ones who hung out of the doors of the helicopters that flew overhead. He was fascinated by my radio when it chirped. It felt like we were in a time warp. With no electricity or running water, the man and these women lived on dates and chickens in their tiny mud hut. The women stood nervously while Rydberg took pictures with his digital camera. Mohamed tried to explain the device to the man, who was visibly disturbed and scared of it. It was like going back in time and explaining a car to someone in the 1300s.

They told us they had heard the mortar fire but had no idea who was responsible. I realized that although we were the first, we might also be the last Americans these four people would ever see. My men and I represented their view of America and all 300 million Americans forever. They would tell their children about America based on a twenty-minute experience with us. After a gift of a pack of cigarettes and a few MREs, we left the Land of the Lost. Rydberg told Mohamed to instruct the man not to eat the chemical heating envelopes in the MRE. Instructions on the bag were all in English. Eating the heater wouldn't kill you, but it was not recommended. More than a few Iraqis learned that lesson the hard way.

A few days later, we got a tip. A local man came to the gate of the island compound with intel that the Mortar Men had been firing the night before from an area about a kilometer north of the island. We went out and found a few scraggly trails through a date field that might have been perfect for someone waiting to pull in with a pickup and pop off a few rounds. We saw tire tracks, and the locals seemed uneasy. That was enough for me. It was as good a lead as any.

I took Third Squad; we crept our way through the farms, skirting the road. About fifty meters into the date field, we set up as the night deepened. We emplaced machine guns, determined sectors of fire, and concealed ourselves. Rydberg sat next to me and got comfortable as I pulled an eight-digit grid coordinate out of my GPS and read him our exact location to relay to the island. The device was incredibly reliable, easy to use, and about a fourth of the size of the Army-issue GPS, or "Plugger" (Precision Lightweight GPS Receiver, or PLGR). The latter was a 1994 beast that weighed about three pounds and gave only text display of coordinates, time, and velocity. My civilian, store-bought Garmin Rino had set me back almost $300, but was far superior. It was the size of a cell phone, had map-based GPS, a better night setting, and used batteries I could actually find in Baghdad.

When the island had our grid, we could call in illumination or mortars—provided the JAG (Judge Advocate General) approved. Every fire mission had to be approved by a military lawyer. No shit. This ensured that fire missions in residential areas were in accordance with the Geneva Convention or some shit. As a result, fire missions required so many levels of approval that by the time you got your answer (which was usually no), the enemy was gone. From Generals in Fallujah to Lieutenants on Baghdad Island, every soldier in Iraq was forced to hold back combat operations to play a game of Mother May I with a lawyer of some kind or another.

We set in and waited. No cigarettes. No talking. Radio silence. Totally tactical and disciplined. I examined the kill zone from top to bottom, until I had memorized where every tree was. It was just us and the mutant insects of Iraq. Maybe it was the weapons of mass destruction that Saddam hid beneath the soil somewhere that made the bugs grow so insanely large. The nasty suckers looked like little helicopters.

Two hours in, a pair of Black Hawks gently slid across the skyline. I hoped they wouldn't mistake us for bad guys setting an IED ambush. By the third hour, I had started to count the rocks in the road to keep my brain occupied. Guys battled to stay awake. The flies and heat were relentless, and we were primed like a cork, ready to pop. Countless times before, the enemy had melted away. We wanted someone to shoot so fucking badly. And this was the perfect spot. We longed for the satisfaction of a conventional kill, a clean kill. We wanted to pull the trigger and release all our bottled-up anxiety and frustration on someone who deserved it.

Soldiers are trained to be very good at being uncomfortable. It is one of the things we are best at. We lay there motionless for four hours. Listening and waiting to kill.

Then I heard something. The guys heard it too. Everyone held their breath. Something had disturbed the rhythm of the land. The crackle of insect noises slowed. Something crawled near my left ear and I let it. The hair rose on the back of my wet neck. No moving except for my eyes and my finger. Weapon selector switches had been clicked from safe to semi hours ago (so as not to tip the ambush for the enemy by clicking a safety off loudly). I peered into my optic with both eyes open and stared through the tiny red light to the kill zone as I gently slid my index finger down the pistol grip to the trigger and curled it at the second joint. The signal to the men to initiate the ambush was simple. Once you saw my tracers, let it fly.

A sound from behind panicked me. Fuck! Had the enemy outflanked us?

Then a weird howling burst out from the bush. We were surrounded. It was so piercing and otherworldly we all jumped out of our skins. A wordless, animal cry, as though we were surrounded by coyotes. In the trees, everywhere.

"What the fuck?" someone shouted to my right.

And we all burst out laughing, that kind of too-loud, shaky laughter that comes with the sudden release of fear and tension.

It must have been a pack of the feral dogs that roamed all over Baghdad. Maybe in heat. It was a miracle we didn't shoot the hell out of all of them. And each other. Whatever they were, our uncontrollable laughing scared them off. We couldn't stop. It felt almost as good as a kill.

"I actually got a fucking hard-on, man!" one of the guys shouted.

Our position was totally compromised. The village two clicks up could probably hear us now. Nothing to do now but wipe the laugh-tears from our eyes, pack up, and go home. I'd just gotten the new Black Eyed Peas CD in the mail anyway.

That was as close as we ever got to the Mad Mortar Men of Baghdad Island.

And we all burst out laughing, that kind of too-loud, shaky laughter that comes with the sudden release of fear and tension. It must have been a pack of the feral dogs that roamed all over Baghdad. Maybe in heat. It was a miracle we didn't shoot the hell out of all of them. And each other. Whatever they were, our uncontrollable laughing scared them off. We couldn't stop. It felt almost as good as a kill.

"I actually got a fucking hard-on, man!" one of the guys shouted.

Our position was totally compromised. The village two clicks up could probably hear us now. Nothing to do now but wipe the laugh tears from our eyes, pack up, and go home. I'd just gotten the new Black Eyed Peas CD in the mail anyway.

That was as close as we ever got to the Mad Mortar Men of Baghdad Island.

CHAPTER SIXTEEN
HOPE IS NOT A COURSE OF ACTION

I am prepared for the worst, but hope for the best.
—Benjamin Disraeli

We had just returned one afternoon from an "ambush" mission off the island when the CO told me to get my guys ready to go back out. We were returning to the city to augment the Spartan Brigade on a huge cordon-and-search mission. A shortage of Light Infantry was always a problem, and we often "tasked out" to other units for some added muscle.

We returned to the city and spent the next seven hours knocking on, and knocking in, doors around Baghdad. Up stairs, over walls, and into courtyards looking for weapons that mostly never materialized. Although we really did want to flush out some illegal weapons, we also wanted to show the Iraqis that we were watching them and that we were in charge. We could burst into their houses without notice and disrupt their lives. The idea was that this would keep the enemy off guard. The usual result was that the weapons searches pissed off a few hundred Iraqis who hadn't been pissed off before.

After a full night of playing Gestapo games, we were exhausted. My men were literally sleepwalking. I gathered them on a curb for an attaboy and told them to drink water and have a smoke. Then the radio chirped and Rydberg waved me over.

It was the CO, instructing me to find him in the street immediately. The guys knew the night wasn't over, and moaned as I left them on the street. I ran over to an armored Humvee on the median, my uniform soaked in sweat, dragging Rydberg in tow.

The CO introduced me to a serious and intense Colonel. His eyes were wide, maybe even a bit crazy. "Listen here, son," he said. "I need a Platoon, and you're it. You're going to go down into Sadr City right now and deal with a situation. There's a gang of Hajis holed up in a building and we need some guys to go in there and kill them. The MPs have 'em boxed in now. They are nasty and cornered. And they will fight to the death!"

Rydberg stifled a laugh. This guy thought he was Patton or something. He talked with a false intensity that only a Field-Grade officer who didn't kick in doors could muster. Like playing it up for nonexistent cameras. He seemed so cranked up we could barely take him seriously. Rigid, I nodded reverently.

"Do you understand me? They will fight every one of you to the death! Load your men up in the trucks and get the fuck down there and kill 'em!"

"Yes, sir."

As we ran back to the Platoon, Rydberg looked over and gave me a very clear "What the fuck?" look. I shrugged. Business as usual. Whether it was the president or a Colonel, there seemed to be lots of guys cranked up for a fight that others then waged. It is much easier to talk shit when you don't have any skin in the game.

The guys were already loaded up on the back of the trucks. They had probably searched fifty houses in the last few hours. Breaking doors, scaling walls, climbing stairs, and detaining people in the brutal heat. And we had been operating one Squad short. Chesty and Third Squad had been sent to Baghdad Airport for duty as a Brigade aircraft QRF squad. If any Brigade aircraft went down anywhere, Chesty's Squad would scramble into two

Black Hawk helicopters and secure the crash site. Good change of pace for them, but I really could've used another Squad of soldiers right then. Yet the president was telling folks back home that we had plenty of troops in Iraq. After all, there was an election coming up. It's hard to say you have a handle on things and ask for more help at the same time. And an increase in troop numbers probably wouldn't help his approval rating.

I pulled myself up into the truck and told the guys to listen up.

"This is no bullshit. The Colonel is sending us down to Sadr City. We're going to follow that Bradley and take a building with bad guys in it. He says they have already shot up some MPs and are dug in. The MPs now have the place surrounded, and we're going in to finish the job. NCOs, check your Squads and ammo. We're rolling out in one minute."

Everyone looked worried as hell. Except Phil, who'd fallen asleep. Li'l Mac and the Fat Boys (our two machine gunners, Coleman and Curry) with their big guns did not believe anything was going down. Guys were pissed. And I couldn't blame them. They had been jerked around every day for months. Shit, they had been jerked around all year. Ninety-five percent of our missions had turned up nothing. They were tired of hunting down invisible enemies and kicking in doors over bad intel. They were tired of searching for weapons of mass destruction that nobody could find. They were tired of Colonels screaming about terrible monsters that never appeared. Tired of disrupting families in the middle of the night. Tired of being the bad guys. I had to get them focused. My football coach in high school used to tell me, "You can't take a play off. Not one. That'll be the play we get burned on." He was right then, and it rang true in Baghdad. Taking your eye off the five-meter target could jeopardize the lives of every man in the Platoon.

Rydberg told the men that this one looked real, but they had been through a hundred false alarms. He repeated the Colonel's speech with total sincerity, saying, "They are going to fight to the death." The men's expressions ranged from fear to disgusted skepticism.

We jogged across the street to link up with a Captain from another Battalion who would serve as our guide to the attack site.

"Sir, I'm Lieutenant Rieckhoff. Third Platoon, Bravo Company. I was told to report to you."

He was about my age. Thin with blue eyes. He looked more like a surfer than a soldier.

"Good. You and your men ready to go?"

"Yes, sir. Can you show me on the map where we're going?"

"I really have no fucking idea, man. I have the general area, but no grid or anything. I got the order about one minute before you did. You get one of my Squads attached to you. They're very solid. They'll ride in the Bradley and link up with you when we get there. I'm planning on going full-bore until my GPS guides me to the building or the fuckers start shooting. Have your vehicle follow behind my Bradley."

"Is there any sort of plan, sir?"

"Not really. Let's just get there and see what we see."

"Sir, can we get a quick pause behind your Brad before we hit that block to recon the site and check the scene?"

"Sure. Why not? Let's get moving. Supposedly our guys are pinned down."

Great. Five minutes later we were flying through blacked-out Baghdad in the back of a deuce-and-a-half with the headlights off. It was a shady night with no moonlight at all. NVGs were down on everyone who had them, including the drivers. Problem was, only about five guys could actually use them without taking their hands off their weapons.

Officially, "Leaders and soldiers are properly wearing NVGs on head/helmet harness and properly mounting night sights on weapon systems during limited visibility operations. This greatly facilitates movement and security at night. Additionally, soldiers are using their AN/PAQ-4s in conjunction with their NVDs during night engagements to assist in target acquisition."

That's great for doctrine. Reality in Baghdad was dramatically different. Head mounts broke all the time, and supply couldn't get my guys replacements. These small metal brackets, which cost about fifty cents, attached NVGs to the guys' helmets so they could see in the dark, hands-free. Half the guys had to hold their NVGs in one hand and their weapons in the other. Some just went without night vision.

The Army loves to say that we "own the night." But only a few of us had tactical lights, "tac lights," and we had bought those ourselves. I had been asking Battalion for lights for months. NVGs are great when they work, but they're useless without ambient light. In a dark house or tunnel, you can't see a thing with NVGs.

It takes about two minutes for your eyes to completely adapt to the dark after you remove NVGs. Flashlights worked much more effectively. But we didn't have those either. I had a Mini Maglite I had bought back home in the Post Exchange (PX). It was the same kind you can buy at Wal-Mart, strapped onto the handgrips on my M16 with electrical tape. (My dad had sent a case of electrical tape from back home.) We were all pretty nervous doing this mission with this shitty equipment. We knew what we were doing, but the preventable equipment deficiencies made us more vulnerable than we had to be.

Whizzing through a trashed city with no power is bizarre. My NVGs bathed everything in a ghostly green haze. I could see tiny taillights on the back of the Bradley in front of us. I told my guys to prepare for the worst. We knew we were going into a bad area, and everyone tightened up. Helmets got cinched down as dips of Cope were shoved into cheeks. The usual jokes and grab-assing stopped. The guys were all focused and contemplative. Despite the rattling of the engine, I could hear everyone else breathe. It got darker as we drove deeper into the city. So many holes, alleys, windows, and crevasses. No ambient light broke through the canopy of wires drooping from tattered buildings.

I scanned doorways and rooftops as the blocks grew more dilapidated and abandoned. IR (infrared) lasers from the weapons of the entire Platoon waved across the buildings and windows like a show at the planetarium. When we didn't see people hanging out on the streets to stay cool, we knew we were in a bad area. We were also in the back of a deuce-and-a-half that could be heard coming from a mile away. With no armor, and no shielding of any kind, we were totally exposed. Our vehicle was like an elephant wandering past the lions' den, holding the tail of the Bradley in front of it. An IED would kill us all. Every time I rode in the back of a truck with my men to an insertion point, I was waiting for it. I expected our luck to run out eventually. My mind was constantly racing and planning. I looked for the spots where we'd drag the casualties and return fire. I wasn't sure if it was good planning or paranoia.

The truck growled and gears ground as we bounced into the air and back down hard every time we hit a hole. We had to be doing sixty miles an hour flying behind one lone Bradley barreling into what felt like a black hole. We had long since passed the point of no return. It felt like we were jumping off a cliff.

Up ahead we saw an MP Humvee stopped at an intersection with two soldiers crouched behind it. Our truck downshifted hard as we rolled closer. MPs were distinguishable by the brassard on their shoulders that read "MP" in English and in Arabic. They had clearly been taking fire and were excited to see us.

The brakes whined as the truck jerked to a halt. The driver ran around to drop the rear gate, which clanged loudly enough for people in Damascus to hear it. So much for tactical silence. He was a tall, skinny Private with deep eyes that were scared and darting. It was clear he hadn't done many of these missions before. He had a look on his face that we saw pretty often. It was what one soldier called the "Thank God I am not an Infantry sucker like you" look. An expression that said, "Better you than me!" He paced behind the truck with his weapon raised loosely in one hand like a gangster in *Menace to Society*. One of my NCOs slammed the barrel down hard.

"Hey, fuckhead! Watch where you point that shit!"

"Sorry, Sergeant."

"Fucking pogues," another soldier grumbled at him as my boys climbed down.

The men fanned out in a semicircle and took cover and a knee. Two more MP vehicles sat motionless up the block with nervous MPs crouched behind them. I found the setup kind of funny. It looked like a hostage negotiation scene from a cop movie. I expected a fat cop with a donut in his hand to emerge with a bullhorn and shout, "Okay, Haji! Come out with your hands up!" The deuce-and-a-half was like a two-ton bull's-eye for RPG rounds, so we moved away from it, into the protection of the sidewalk shops' shadows.

Behind me a soldier mumbled, "Nice that these fucking chickenshits call us in to do the killing and dying for them." It was clear that the MPs wanted no part of whatever was down that street. Extremely encouraging for me and my men.

"You couldn't spell wimp without MP!" another one of my guys said loudly as he strode past them crouched behind the hood of a Humvee. Rydberg and I ran up to the side of the Bradley to get the deal from the surfer Captain.

He climbed down and introduced me to his Squad Leader. I noticed the NVGs firmly bracketed on the Sergeant's helmet and a fully tricked-out M4 in his hands. Wiping a string of dip spit from his chin, the Captain said, "They're in a building right around that corner. There's an Apache overhead tracking them on the roof. I have comms with the bird. They'll be our eyes in the sky. See that intersection? They're holed up about a block down on the left. You ready?"

"What? No, sir. If they've been there this long, they're probably not going anywhere. Can we do a recon?"

The Captain shrugged. "Sure, Lieutenant. What do you want to do?"

I didn't know whether to be impressed or worried by this dude's casual attitude.

"Well, sir. You have this great big Bradley. No sense in us flying in naked if we don't have to. I'd love to be able to use it for protection and fire support."

He shrugged again. "Makes sense to me. Let's do it."

He signaled to the driver, and a few seconds later the Bradley crept around the corner. Me, the Captain, Rydberg, Willie, and the Spartan Squad Leader crouched behind the tracks and poked our heads out just enough to get a look at the target. It was a curved street with shops on all sides. The target building was three stories high and about a hundred and fifty meters away. It looked like some kind of a garage. I craned my head around the other side of the crusted track of the Bradley to see where I could position a gun team for fire support. A street intersected this one directly across from the objective. A gun team could go there.

But there was still the approach. The roof of the building had excellent command of the surrounding streets. There was no telling how many bad guys were up there, how many might be inside, or what kind of firepower they possessed. If my men and I just ran down the street to burst in the front door, we could well be chewed up before we ever got there. The John Wayne shit only works in the movies.

You plan for two variations in a combat operation. You plan for the MLECOA, the Most Likely Enemy Course of Action, and for the MDECOA, the Most Dangerous Enemy Course of Action. In the former you make your plans based on guesswork and intel (which is usually unreliable), and hope to hell the enemy acts the way you expect him to. Pretty much the way our leaders had planned the invasion and liberation of Iraq. In my opinion, hope is not a course of action, so I usually planned for the MDECOA, the worst-possible scenario. That way, if the enemy surprised you, it'd be a good surprise.

So I fully expected us to need lead umbrellas once we made our move. There were awnings over most of the shops that would provide shadow and cover as we approached. Parking the Bradley by their front door would intimidate the hell out of them, and it could provide excellent fire support with its 25mm cannon. The Apache circling above was also available for fire support. In fact, I didn't understand why the Bradley and helo couldn't just level the place and save me and my men the trouble. The Captain said, "Collateral damage must be minimized. You don't want to piss off the locals."

I hated that shit. It was a standard answer. What about collateral damage to my guys? What about the pissed-off mother back home who would be getting a folded American flag? Higher command always seemed more worried about Iraqi property than American asses.

But the Captain had an idea. "I can bring the bird down on top of the building as you guys hit it. That'll kick up the dust on the ones on the roof and give you guys some cover."

"Sir," I replied, "it will also disorient the hell out of my guys. If the bad guys can't see, neither can we."

"Just give it a shot. It'll work."

Give it a shot? Easy for him to say. He'd be behind ten tons of armor during this little adventure as my guys looked down their barrels in the dark.

There was another problem. Since we were combining different units, our radios were out of sync—again. Inside, we could scream and use hand and arm signals, while Rydberg would have to call all the way back to Spartan Main on the other side of Baghdad to relay back down to the street and talk to the Captain in the Bradley fifty feet away from us. The Bradley was also our commo link to the Apache. Fan-fucking-tastic. We were getting ready to storm a building full of assholes ready to "fight to the death," and if I needed help I had to play the telephone game. And every kindergartner knows how that usually turns out.

We regrouped in front of an abandoned butcher shop. A stain of dried chicken blood had seeped out under the wood door. I quickly briefed the guys on the details of my Op Order (Operations Order) and had them repeat it back to me. The guys from Spartan had never trained with my guys, but we would have to make it work. I wasn't going to say no to eight more guns. You never had enough muscle for a fight. Tank would take First Squad around the next block and set up the 240 facing the front of the building. Sergeant Willie's Second Squad would be in the lead, and I would follow. Then the Squad from Spartan would trail behind me and take the ground floor. In a group of guys usually smiling and joking, the faces on my men were all deadly serious.

The responsibility of picking who will go first into a potential ambush is an extraordinary burden. I realized early on that being a proficient officer, especially at the Platoon level, is sometimes about choosing who will likely be the first to die if things go wrong. I picked Willie's Squad because it was crunch time, and I trusted them the most to perform. He insisted that he be the first guy in the stack. It was against protocol, but I let my NCOs run their own Squads. I told them to suck the egg. I didn't tell them how to suck it. And Willie was my best. For soldiers, being the best isn't always the best thing for your survivability. I firmly believe that is why some soldiers do their best to stay mediocre. Stay out of the spotlight. It's what guys give you as the best piece of advice in Basic Training.

"Shoot anything that gets in our way," I told them. "Don't fuck around, fellas. This is the real deal."

All their eyes locked more deeply on mine than ever before. I tried to remember what color eyes each guy had. I wanted to stockpile the info in case anyone died. I thought about which ones were married or had girlfriends; then I tried to remember every woman's name. All that was racing in my subconscious. Willie had two little redheaded daughters back home. I couldn't help but think about them as he lined up his guys and checked their gear. Willie knew his shit. There was nobody I'd rather have at the front of the stack hitting the door. He looked me dead in the eye and said, "We're ready, sir."

The Bradley rumbled down the street, the turbine engine whirring, as we ran past bolted and empty shops, slaloming through garbage and pushcarts. Time slowed a bit and the hypersensitivity kicked in. I saw a tattered Coca-Cola poster inside a dark window. My hands were wet with sweat, and I could feel my heartbeat in my eardrums. Rydberg was right on my hip. My eyes pinned on the windows of the target and my weapon raised, I was looking for any sign of movement and fully expected fire to rain down any second. Slow is smooth, smooth is fast. That's how they teach it, but it didn't apply on that night. We hauled ass to get out of the open and under the overhang near the door, to surprise them before they could hit us.

The Apache descended over the rooftop, and suddenly it was like being inside a tornado. I tried to force my eyes open, but couldn't get them to crack. I reached out for the back of the soldier's vest in front of me as I felt Rydberg's hand on mine, just like our training had conditioned us to do. I screamed at Rydberg over my shoulder, "Get the bird up! Tell them to pull up! We can't see anything!"

"Spartan Main, this is Blue 6! Spartan Main, this is Blue 6! Get the bird out of here! I repeat, pull the bird away!"

If we were getting shot at, I didn't know it. All I could hear was the deafening rotor wash. Ten of us were shoved into a ball at the metal door, with nothing to do but wait for Willie to crash through it. We were blind and vulnerable. Out in the open.

"Go, Willie! Go!" I screamed, and pushed the man in front of me like the sled at football practice. It was so loud I couldn't even hear myself.

Willie finally broke it open and we all slid into the echoing darkness of a hallway. "Watch for booby traps, Willie!" I shouted into my headset. Our entry was perfectly quick and violent. My eyes darted into dark corners and searched for wires and cords. I followed Willie and Second Squad up the sinister stairs with my weapon pointed down and to my right, to the garage area below. The Squad from Spartan fanned out, tac light beams waving like light sabers through the dust clouds and darkness.

The building was three stories high, with the bottom two the open garage. Rydberg was getting info from the chopper from over the SINCGAR and yelled from behind me, "They're on the roof! On the roof!"

"Willie, keep going up! They're on the roof!" I echoed.

Up the stairs. Feet shuffling, blood pumping. The emotion I felt was definitely not what I would call fear. It was an almost uncomfortable rush of being super-alive, my senses amped up like I was one big nerve. I held my breath, praying that I wouldn't hear any of my men scream.

I hated this part of being an officer. My job was to hang in the rear and let the Squad Leader hit the target first. My men had to go before me, and it killed me. I wanted to be out in front hitting the doors, but that was not my job. The thought that I might be rushing forward onto the bloody bodies of my men, to reach the dead body of the father of two little girls, rushed into my mind and made me gasp. I shoved it down and kept moving upward. In my earpiece, Willie huffed, "The floor is clear!" I couldn't see a thing. It was like pushing through a haunted house at the carnival. I kept waiting for someone or something to pop out and do something unexpected.

We swept out through a metal door onto the rooftop. The helicopter was still too damn low and I couldn't hear anything but rotors. The guys fanned out to the corners of the rooftop, which was about the size of two tennis courts.

"Clear!"

"Clear!"

"Clear!"

I rushed to a corner and took a knee, out of breath. Rydberg slid next to me as the guys scanned the neighboring rooftops.

Nothing.

"Find out where they are!" I screamed at Rydberg.

He relayed the request to Spartan Main, who relayed it to the Apache, who relayed their response back to Spartan Main, who relayed it back to us:

"Gone, sir."

"What?"

"Gone, sir. Gone. The pilot says they're gone."

"What the fuck? Willie! You guys got anything?"

Willie jogged over to my corner. His entire Squad was tight, on knees, with sectors of fire chopped up evenly like slices of pizza.

"Nothin', sir. There ain't nothin' here."

"Fan out and check the surrounding rooftops. I'm sure they're on the run, but couldn't have gotten far. Maybe we'll get lucky."

"Roger that, sir," and he was off. Willie never yelled at his guys. His team leaders respected him and were ready to be instructed. He leaned in and calmly ordered them, and they got moving.

"That was a rush," one guy said. "That was the craziest thing we've done since we got here."

We were simultaneously disappointed and relieved. Some 7.62 shell casings were scattered around the roof. Somebody had been here shooting AK rounds. We were just too late. It always seemed like we were just too late. My guys were always itching for the textbook engagement that never seemed to come. Some of us were glad it hadn't. Others were incensed.

But it was frustrating for me as a leader. It was hard to keep telling my guys to get ready for a threat that never materialized. Rydberg had created a list of new acronyms for our Platoon, which was always responding to crises that didn't materialize. He scrawled them in Magic Marker on the wall of the Platoon room:

FARF—False Alarm Reactionary Force

FARP—False Alarm Reactionary Platoon

FART—False Alarm Reactionary Team

I felt like the L.T. who cried wolf. We kept getting cranked up again and again for an enemy that struck us swiftly and melted into the dark. It always felt like we were chasing ghosts.

The Captain climbed out of the Bradley and joined us on the roof. He seemed as amazed as we were by the disappearance of our ruthless enemy. Willie and his Squad broke down some more doors and kicked in some walls. Some surely out of frustration. The mechanic who owned the building we were destroying wouldn't be too happy when he came to work the next morning.

The rest of us spent the next hour climbing gutters and fire escapes like Spider-Man in sixty pounds of gear. Searching in rooftop chicken coops. At one point my leg disappeared through a decrepit roof up to my hip. A splintering wood beam was the only thing that stopped me from planting my face on the concrete three stories below.

One of the soldiers chuckled. "Haji rooftops weren't built to hold your big Yankee ass, sir!"

We linked up with the weapons squad and mounted the truck for the long ride home. Weapons squad told us that they had watched ready, with fingers on triggers, as we hit the house. They said they were nervous as hell for us and felt helpless. All they could see was flashes of lights, dust, and shadows. They also told us that the Colonel who sent us on the mission, the "till the death" guy, showed up soon after we hit the house. He sat in a Humvee across the street and drank coffee from a travel cup. One soldier said it looked like he was watching a football game on TV.

CHAPTER SEVENTEEN
ALI BABA

> ARCHIE GATES: What's the most important thing in life?
>
> TROY BARLOW: Respect.
>
> ARCHIE GATES: Too dependent on other people.
>
> CONRAD VIG: What, love?
>
> ARCHIE GATES: A little Disneyland, isn't it?
>
> CHIEF ELGIN: God's will.
>
> ARCHIE GATES: Close.
>
> TROY BARLOW: What is it then?
>
> ARCHIE GATES: Necessity.
>
> TROY BARLOW: As in?
>
> ARCHIE GATES: As in people do what is most necessary to them at any given moment.
>
> —*Three Kings*

Some soldiers are corrupted by war. They wield incredible, life-and-death power—the power of superheroes. And in a place like Baghdad, they are surrounded by temptation—gold-plated AKs, Rolexes, boxes of cash, hot vehicles. It can lead a frustrated, overworked, and underpaid country boy down a dangerous path.

One night I came out of a leadership meeting and a Sergeant not from my Platoon tugged me on the arm.

"Hey, Lieutenant. I need to talk to you. You got a minute?"

"Of course."

We stepped into the makeshift ammo room. The Sergeant was a good man. Extremely well-read and intellectual. He was thoughtful, constantly discussing the impact of our operations on the hearts and minds of the Iraqis. He usually had a smile on his face—but not this time. His brown T-shirt was pitted with sweat and his eyes darted nervously.

"If I tell you something, will you give me your word that you will not let anyone know it came from me?"

"Sure. What's going on?"

"You have to swear, sir. I mean it. This is serious. I have kids. I don't want to end up with a round in the back of my head on our next patrol."

"You got it, Sergeant. Tell me."

He turned to look over both of his shoulders and pulled the door closed.

"Here goes. . . . Your guys are stealing money."

I could feel my blood pressure rising. "What?"

"It's true. Only a few guys in the Company know about it, and one of them confided in me last night. He's all torn up about it, and he trusted in me because we're friends. He told me guys have been skimming off the top at the checkpoints and after raids. I don't know who the guys are behind it, but I know they're in your Platoon, and I bet you a month of my salary that shady Thomas is involved."

I felt sick.

Thomas was always wheeling and dealing. It was great to have an industrious NCO like him who could "find" things for the Platoon, but that was a fine line to walk. It was his job to inventory any and all confiscated items, from boxes of cash to police motorcycles. The job gave him incredible oversight power. He loved to try to keep me out of the daily dealings of the Platoon.

"Shit, sir," he'd say. "Don't you worry about that! That's NCO business. I'll take care of it."

Initially, I deferred to his experience. He had been with Third Platoon for years. He knew the men, the system, and the inner politics of the Battalion, and I was just a cherry Lieutenant from another state. The worst thing I could have done as a new Platoon Leader was to rock a well-run boat.

According to the Sergeant who tipped me off, he had become drunk with that power and led some of my men in a complex and diabolical heist.

I called one of my most honest and trusted young soldiers off guard duty and told him to follow me up to the rooftop. We watched the sun set above the milky Tigris and shared a cigarette. I told him to be straight with me about all that he knew. His hands shook as he confirmed what my source had told me.

I was in a quandary I never could have predicted. I didn't know who in my Platoon was involved and who was not. I didn't know who knew about the crime and who did not. I was torn about how to act. It would have been great to be able to keep this in the family, but I didn't have any idea how far-reaching the involvement was. Maybe the First Sergeant and CO were involved? Maybe Andy? Thomas had betrayed me; who was to say they hadn't also?

The good guys had become the bad guys, and I had to move quickly. If I waited, I'd tip my hand and the culprits would have time to plan a response.

I pulled the CO and First Sergeant into a chem-lit bathroom and told them what I had heard: Thomas had taken about $30,000 and split it with a few of the guys in the Platoon. Both were cool, calm, and firm—a surprising change of pace, but a testament to their true characters. We sat on the tile floor of the bathroom and formulated a plan to trick those who had betrayed us, the Iraqis, and the United States.

We were angry, but not too surprised. We all knew our men.

Some of them were just not that bright. Some were too bright for their own good. None of them was wealthy. Take a gang of poor guys, expose them to tons of cash, limitless power, and fluctuating rules, and some of them will fuck up in some way. Not all of them, but some of them. The weak ones. The ones who are easily influenced. The young ones. The arrogant ones.

We told not one additional soldier in the Company about the situation. It made all three of us very sad. Then the sadness turned to anger and cunning.

A few minutes later, the Commander and I made a run up to Battalion to brief the Battalion Commander. It was the middle of the night, and the Colonel had been sleeping. It was the first and only time I would ever be in the BC's personal space. It was like being in the president's bedroom. He had more area to himself than any of the other five hundred men in the Battalion. A captured life-size bronze statue of a lion dominated the room with ridiculous opulence.

I sat in the dimly lit room with my CO, the BC, and a few of his senior staff officers. I felt very uncomfortable sitting with these Battalion officers in their luxury and safety. They didn't walk patrol or stand guard duty. I doubted if any of them had been shot at since coming to Iraq. I knew these officers were judging me and my men as I explained the scandal. I knew they didn't understand how my men could have succumbed to temptation. And I imagined that they were not happy that I was telling them about it. Now they had to do something. Now they had to do the paperwork, call in CID for an investigation, air our dirty laundry for all to see. It would make us all look bad.

But I had to do it. For the guys who had done the right thing. And for the Iraqis we were supposedly here to protect. I remembered a quote from Adam Smith, who wrote, "Mercy to the guilty is cruelty to the innocent." I felt the same way.

I didn't sleep that night.

First thing in the morning, I gathered my Platoon together at 0930 to load trucks.

"Don't pack up," I told them. "Grab your gear and your weapon and let's go. We gotta move!"

No time for them to prep, plan, or hide. With the CO and First Sergeant screaming to hurry up and the guys bitching and moaning, we loaded the two deuce-and-a-halfs. Engines running. But Thomas was missing. He and another soldier named O'Connor. I worried that somebody had tipped them off, and told the First Sergeant so. We couldn't give them a chance to plan or to destroy evidence. The First Sergeant ran through the building screaming for Thomas to get his ass on the trucks. Flustered and sweating, Thomas came jogging out with O'Connor suspiciously in tow, and the trucks rolled forward. Thomas thought something was up, but wasn't sure. His eyes were fearful, but doubtful. He thought he was smarter than me, but he wasn't positive. He thought he could beat the officers. He thought he could beat me. His arrogance and selfishness would be his downfall.

I felt his eyes searching my face. He was looking for clues; he got my poker face, and I was sitting on aces. I smoked a cigarette calmly, gazed at the cloudy Tigris River, and positioned myself on the other side of the truck so I wouldn't have to talk to him.

The trap was set. This was the most complex and difficult ambush I had ever crafted, and it was for my own men. I felt like I was leading pigs to the slaughter.

Gears mashed and brakes screeched hard as we rounded corners. Then the truck made a hard right and entered the Battalion compound at the former Republican Guard officers' building.

"Hey, sir! Where we goin'?" Thomas asked nervously.

I took a pull from my cigarette and pretended not to hear him.

The open parking lot came into sight with the Sergeant Major and BC waiting, arms crossed, like two parents in the living room as a high school kid returned home hours after curfew. The men were confused. The Sergeant Major marched over to the truck. "Sergeant Thomas, get your men off the truck. Let's go! Get 'em off the trucks. I want a formation now."

"Waz goin' on, Sar'ent Maja?" He smiled.

"Get 'em off the fucking truck *now*, Sergeant Thomas. No fucking questions."

I stepped away from the truck and stood at the back of the assembling formation in my usual spot. A few guys tried to talk to me, but I didn't respond.

The Sergeant Major continued, "Form up in Platoon formation! Let's go!"

Then the Battalion S-3 (operations officer) stepped forward. He was a short, politician-looking, pretty-boy Major universally disliked by the men.

"Drop your gear!"

The men grumbled, confused and looking for an explanation.

"*Do it!* Then clear and stack all weapons! Sergeant Thomas, make it happen! All knives and weapons are to be left in place. You understand me? Empty everything you have and keep only one canteen of water."

The men scrambled to follow the orders like Privates facing an angry Drill Sergeant at Basic Training.

"Hurry up!"

They laid down their gear, ensuring that everything was properly in line.

"Now listen up! Your Platoon is being investigated for alleged criminal activity."

I could see them tightening stomachs and fists.

The Major continued. "A health and wellness inspection is being conducted right now of all your stuff back at the Bravo Company CP. I am now giving you a direct order not to speak to each other until further notice. Violators will be punished by courts-martial under the UCMJ (Uniform Code of Military Justice). And punishment will be severe."

They were spooked. By now a few Battalion pogues had appeared on the flanks of the formation, and were carrying their weapons and long faces. The heat was really rising.

"You will be moved to the building behind me immediately. There will be one man per room. You will be given one MRE and one bottle of water. You will be under armed guard. This is no joke. Inform the guard if you have to utilize the latrine. You will stay in the rooms until further notice. No talking. Sergeant Major, move 'em out."

"Right face!"

Every man was ushered into his own ransacked room, one by one. The building was a shit hole and the rooms were like jail cells.

"Lieutenant Rieckhoff! Fall out and see the BC!"

The S-2 (intelligence officer) and Battalion military intel liaison were waiting for me, just as we had planned it the night before. We met in a conference room and I told the whole story again. I could see that they didn't trust me. They thought I was in on the whole thing. I had come to them with the story, and now I was a suspect. Typical. They would revel in any opportunity to rattle a line officer.

Over an hour later, I was in my isolation room, sitting on an old couch with my mind racing. I couldn't stop wondering what the hell the guys were thinking. I was trying to figure out how many of them were involved. How could I not have known what they were doing? I guessed there were maybe four or five culprits. Sergeant Thomas seemed to be the kingpin. He had taken a disproportionate amount of money—much more than the others got. They saw him sending big brown envelopes home to his wife and realized they had been screwed. That was how I found out about the whole deal. I guess there really can be honor among thieves.

I scribbled a letter to Bama like I was Martin Luther King writing "Letter from Birmingham Jail." I had no cigarettes and no chew. I felt like biting the buttons off my DCU top. *Stars and Stripes* advertised that back home there were fantastic vacation deals waiting for returning soldiers. Disney World was offering free admission. That sounded good. Lieutenant Rieckhoff, you've just spent the last year getting shot at and mortared, what are you gonna do? I'm going to Disney World! I was living in a fantasy land anyway, might not be that much of a change. Seven-day cruise packages were only $600 per couple. Seeing water would be nice.

The Major popped in after a few hours and said they had found $1,100 U.S. on Thomas. He had some of it in his wallet. The rest was shoved into the ceiling of the room they had him in. All $100 bills.

Crooked bastard.

I hoped not too many of the young guys were involved. It was tough knowing that my men, most of whom were great soldiers, were being put through this ringer. Something new every day. Embezzlement was a risk at my old job on Wall Street, not in the Army. Maybe I was naïve, but this was the last thing I expected to happen when I went to war.

They started interviewing my Platoon at 1000. The hours crawled. At 1700 hours, I was still stuck in the same fucking room. On patrol the day before, I had picked a flower from the grounds of the Lebanese embassy. I found it shoved deep in the bottom of my right cargo pocket. My girlfriend would appreciate a flower from Iraq, even if it was dried up and crinkled and came from a jail cell. I put it in an envelope and hoped it would make her smile.

Two soldiers from CID (Criminal Investigation Division), the Army's version of Internal Affairs, interviewed me. Fat guys from a Pennsylvania Reserve unit, they didn't wear rank and I was supposed to refer to them both as "Mister." CID soldiers did not disclose rank so as not to have too much or too little influence over their interrogation subjects.

I learned CID would be stopping all our mail and checking it for any cash my Platoon might have tried to send home. I found it unlikely that they could track down everybody's mail and check it—half our mail was missing somewhere between Baghdad and Savannah anyway. But the CID guys said they even had the power to question mail recipients. Sergeant Thomas's wife, for example, would be getting a phone call or a knock at the door. She might actually be relieved when she saw it was a search warrant and not a death notification.

Thankfully, it turned out that most of the men in the Platoon were not involved. In total, CID implicated ten of my thirty-eight guys. It found money or got admissions from nine of them. In their gear and personal belongings, the Sergeant Major found some of the money and three stolen pistols. One of them actually tried to hide the money from CID during the interrogations by shoving it up his ass. UCMJ charges ranged from larceny to violating a direct order. The entire heist was indeed spearheaded by Sergeant Thomas. Sergeant O'Connor was the second-highest-ranking NCO involved. I like to think they were the only ones, but I'll probably never know.

Thomas was removed from his position immediately. For days, CID kept him alone in a room as they questioned him over and over again. He had no idea who had cracked and who had not. The guys told me his behavior got really weird. He started writing on the walls of his room in black pen, listing every accomplishment he and the Platoon had been responsible for since we were activated: numbers of patrols, enemy detained and killed, weapons confiscated. It became like the diary of a madman. He spent the rest of the war in isolation at Battalion, sweeping floors and doing random chores while awaiting his court-martial trial, which would not be completed until months after we redeployed. For months, the guys would pass him inside the compound pathetically trying to work back-alley deals and plead his case as they came in from patrols. Justice in Iraq was anything but swift.

Eventually, Thomas would do some jail time, lose rank, and be demoted to E-4. The CO, First Sergeant, and I all gave sworn statements for use in his trial. I was amazed that he was not kicked out of the Army. The Company leadership all lobbied for his never again having the privilege of wearing the uniform, but somehow he was able to stay in. Recruiting numbers must have really been down. At least I could be sure he'd never be a leader of men again.

The investigation also turned up rumors that he and his wife had been involved in various efforts to defraud the government for years. Soldiers told me that they had collected money for off-post housing while living on post. And to top it all off, rumors flew back home with stories about Thomas's wife stealing money from the Family Support group that was intended to go to things like flowers for funerals. Thomas's own behavior was beyond disgusting and violated every single element of the NCO creed. He tried to enrich himself through his position and violated the trust of those he led.

The implicated soldiers were removed from my Platoon and lived at the Battalion compound, while the rest of the Platoon moved in at the Ministry of Labor. The NCOs all went down. I thought they should be thrown out of the Army entirely. That didn't happen, but they each took lumps from the UCMJ.

Some of them were just not in the right frame of mind. I think that after a week or so in Baghdad we all started to feel that we were above the law. A lot of guys probably felt that they were entitled to certain things. Pistols, Iraqi dinar, air conditioners stolen from Saddam's palace. For the ones who planned the scam and took advantage of their subordinates, I had no sympathy, and neither did the BC.

But for the others, the ones Thomas and the NCOs had led astray, I lobbied for leniency. One was only nineteen. Another was twenty years older than that. I tried to put myself in their shoes. I imagined how hard it must have been for them when faced with the terrible temptation of thousands of dollars in U.S. cash, while mortgage payments, credit card statements, and doctor bills were piling up back home for the wife and kids. They were otherwise good soldiers who had made a very bad decision. I felt that they should pay for that decision, but not be ruined forever by it. I wanted my men back. Not Thomas and the NCOs, but the others. They deserved a second chance, and the Platoon as a whole wanted them to have that chance. They had lost rank and some money via an Article 15, but the Platoon would be better off with them than without them. Not to mention that I'd have to function severely undermanned with a twenty-eight-soldier Platoon.

Initially, the rest of the Platoon was a collective emotional wreck. Many of them probably hated me. I wouldn't have been at all surprised if I'd caught a 5.56 round to the back of my head on patrol. Others were relieved to have the crooks gone. We were unsettled for days, but we found a way to make it work.

It turned out that Thomas had hatched the scheme maybe only a few days after we arrived in Baghdad. Money was all over the city. We did busts nightly that reaped thousands of dollars. For weeks he tried to convince me to hit the building just behind the school.

"Hey, sir. That building is the one. That building is trouble. We need to check it out. We need to take it down."

It made sense at the time. It was the place from which the shooting at the school originated. We took potshots from there all the time. We all knew that building was trouble, but only in retrospect could I see that he had an unusual preoccupation with it.

Thomas finally convinced me. I lobbied the CO and got approval to make the raid. I still don't know all of what happened that day, but here it is as best as I can deduce.

We hit the place with the entire Platoon in the middle of the day. The buildings were more likely to be empty at that time. We had heard that two brothers were the centerpieces of all the recent criminal activity in the southern region of Sector 17. Mohamed knew the guys. He said he'd heard they were bad dudes, that they had been robbing banks in the area during the invasion and in the weeks that followed. And because he knew them personally, he didn't want to come on this mission. He grew up down the street from these guys. His parents knew their parents. It was very awkward for him. He was afraid of retaliation. But I was not going to go on any mission based on info from him and have him sit somewhere safe while we got ambushed. Informants always came along for the ride in my Platoon. I wanted to make sure he had some skin in the game, and I told him if he didn't come along I'd fire him or lock him up. It was hard being buddies with an Iraqi.

We didn't know which apartment the brothers lived in, so we'd hit them all. At the time, it seemed like housecleaning for all the right reasons.

The tower was six stories tall, with a stairway running up the middle. Each floor housed four one-bedroom apartments. A small security element from Weapons Squad and Sergeant Thomas would remain at the truck to collect weapons, hold EPWs (Enemy Prisoners of War—properly referred to as "detainees"), and maintain a CCP (Casualty Collection Point), where we'd take any of our guys who got hit. I took two Squads and we started on the top floor, making our way downward.

Raids and searches were nasty business. Anybody who enjoyed them was sick. Sometimes I felt like I was a member of the Brown Shirts in Nazi Germany. There is nothing more invasive than demanding entry into the house of someone who has a 95 percent chance of being innocent of all wrongdoing. But the other 5 percent was enough to justify it at the time.

We knocked once. If the occupants came to the door, they were met by a bouquet of M16 muzzles and aggressive shouting in a foreign tongue. If nobody answered, we broke the door down. We carried sledgehammers and axes, but on most Iraqi apartments a few hard kicks did the trick. We entered all four apartments on a floor simultaneously. Searching under every bed, in every closet, behind every door. O'Connor kept Wolfpack Main updated on our progress, and I commanded from the middle of the hall as the Squads searched inside. Most of the apartments were so small that the whole Squad barely fit inside.

After the guys were done searching, I came in to check out each place, and apologize to and thank the residents for their cooperation. I tried to be as respectful as possible. But I felt like my apologies were empty. There was so much to be sorry for. Every family was impoverished. People were almost always crying and begging. For the most part, they couldn't understand us and we couldn't understand them. All of us learned to block it out. We just tuned out the screams and focused on our jobs. Many of the family were filled with squatters—people who probably didn't live there before the invasion. The homes were poor and dilapidated, the occupants overwhelmingly unhappy to see us. I often thought about how Americans would react if soldiers started searching homes and disrupting families in housing projects in East Harlem or trailer parks in Arkansas. It seemed so strange that our government had sent thousands of poor guys halfway around the world to search the homes of thousands of poor people.

We didn't find anything until we got to an apartment on the ground floor. Two men were in there, surrounded by tons of stereo equipment, ceiling fans, air conditioners, CD players, a huge TV . . . a regular bachelor pad. Inside a shit-hole building filled with squatters. Very fishy. It would be like a dude in the South Bronx driving a $250,000 Bentley—you knew he had done something wrong to get it. The men were in their mid-thirties and full of bad attitude. I didn't like them from the moment I saw them.

The rules passed down were always changing, but generally, we allowed one weapon per household for self-defense. I had Mohamed ask them if there were any weapons in the apartment. They said no. In the next-door apartment an old woman was screaming bloody murder. I asked them again. They said no. Then one of my guys found an AK.

"Well, what the fuck is that?" I asked.

Their eyes went to the floor. Then the usual game of lies began. I asked one of them if there were any more guns. He said no. I told him not to lie to me again. He insisted there were no weapons.

"Is he sure, Mo?"

"Yes, L.T. He says he is sure."

One of my soldiers yelled from the back of the apartment, "Fuck him, L.T.! Look what I found!"

Another weapon. We detained both of them. By this time the old woman in the other apartment was going completely crazy. I walked over to assess the situation. I heard the guys yelling at her to sit down. Everybody was stressed.

"Sit the fuck down, lady! I said, sit down!" Sergeant Johnson was livid, pointing at the couch, where another woman and two little girls were crying. "I don't want your damn shit!"

Johnson met me at the door while the guys went through the bedroom and a back closet behind him.

"Oh. Hey, sir. We got this covered."

"What's up, Sergeant J?"

"They got money, sir. Tons of money. They got lots of jewelry too. All kinds of shit. A box of money like I've never seen before. Sergeant Thomas is in the back there now counting it up and taking an inventory."

"How much do they have?"

"Not sure. Looks like thousands. Stacks of hundred-dollar bills. All brand-new."

The money was probably from the bank robbery. Most law-abiding Iraqi families did not have tens of thousands of U.S. dollars in a box. Especially not if they lived in a shit-hole apartment.

Second Squad continued its search while the old woman howled. I couldn't understand anything she was saying. As I stepped outside to call up a report on the radio, she pulled on my vest, pleading with me. I pulled her hands off my gear and pointed at her to sit down. I'm sure I screamed and cursed a few times. I was hot, tired, and sick of people crying, screaming, and lying. And I really hated anyone putting hands on me. The last thing I needed was the old woman accidentally yanking on my rifle trigger or pulling the pin on a smoke grenade.

Through her wailing and my guys shouting, I yelled to Mohamed to come over and interpret for me. He hated being put in the middle like this, especially because he knew the family, but he was very good at it. An interpreter's job was mediating as much as translating.

"What the hell is she saying, Mo?"

"She say that you soldiers steal her money. She saying you are Ali Baba. Blah blah blah."

She nodded furiously. *"ALI BABA! ALI BABA!"*

"What? Hell, no. We are not Ali Fucking Baba, bitch!" Johnson yelled at her.

"At ease, Sergeant J!"

We heard this all the time. Every time we confiscated anything, people accused us of being thieves. That was what they were used to under Saddam. This woman had no idea that we processed everything for distribution to the Iraqi police or new army. All she knew was that I was taking it away from her. I was also detaining her two sons, but she was more worried about the box of money.

"Tell her we don't want to steal her things. We are confiscating the money. Tell her that her sons lied to me, and are being detained. Tell her to try to calm down. If she tries to put her hands on my soldiers again, I am going to detain her too. Tell her that if their stories check out, her sons will be back in a few days. If not, they are going to jail."

I called the report up to higher, as one of the soldiers walked inside from the parking lot. "Hey, sir, you should see this."

I followed him to a side garage under the building that revealed two gorgeous, shining Harley-Davidson police motorcycles. They certainly didn't pick those up on eBay.

"Wild. Do they start?"

"The guys are working on that now, sir."

They also had a bus that they couldn't provide any paperwork for. Like just about everyone else in Baghdad engaged in dodgy dealings, the two guys, when I asked what they did for work, claimed to be "businessmen." Right. And I'm a peacekeeper.

Two motorcycles, boxes of money, some weapons that supposedly didn't exist, a hysterical old woman, and lots of yelling and screaming. I was tired of this shit. War was not all it was cracked up to be. I wished I were home drinking a cold beer on my couch and watching *The Daily Show*. But that wouldn't happen for a very long time.

The heist had happened right under my nose. I was accountable. I am responsible for everything my Platoon does, or fails to do. The buck always stops with me. I should have kept a closer eye on them. I should have kept Thomas on a tighter leash. It took place in my Platoon—under my watch. While I was in the hallway, the other room, and talking on the radio, my men were taking money from the Iraqis. They filled their cargo pockets, whispered and conspired.

The old Iraqi woman was right. We were Ali Baba.

The money was in a metal chest about the size of a mini-fridge. It took four guys to get it off the ground and load it onto the truck. We took the weapons, and some other evidence, and two soldiers had the privilege of riding the motorcycles back to the CP. The BC rushed down to our compound about an hour later. He never moved that fast. He didn't come to praise my soldiers for a job well done, but because he wanted to play Hell's Angel in camouflage in Baghdad and personally ride the bikes around town and back to Battalion.

When we detained people we treated them well. They got food. They got water. They even got cigarettes. We tried to give them shade from the sun. We didn't beat them up or kill them. My men were under a watchful eye, and behaved as well as they could under the circumstances. We usually only kept detainees for a few days. Long enough for the Battalion intelligence officer to interrogate them. After that, we either let them go or passed them up to higher for processing at Brigade. From there, they went to a jail somewhere in the desert.

That's what happened to the two brothers—off to jail. Someplace I had never heard of. A place called Abu Ghraib.

CHAPTER EIGHTEEN
FIGHTING THE MEDIA WAR

Times have not become more violent. They have just become more televised.

—Marilyn Manson

We struggled constantly to deal with the meddlesome and judgmental press. They infested Baghdad like roaches. We almost universally despised them. As far as I was concerned, any journalist who agreed to be embedded with the military surrendered all claims to professional impartiality. There's a good reason people called them "in-bedded" journalists. How could they possibly report freely and accurately when we guarded their asses? They were mobbed up. As the violence escalated and independent reporting became more dangerous, reporters were entirely dependent upon the Pentagon for access to the war—and to the story. They saw only what the military brass let them see. Their every step was guided by military chaperones. They depended on the military to protect their skins if a situation ever got dicey. And we grunts were not allowed to speak freely to them. Our Commanders censored and monitored us constantly. Speaking out, complaining, telling the truth could get a soldier into a whole world of trouble with his superiors. It was no wonder so much of the coverage I saw of the war, on the Internet or in articles my friends mailed me from home, was so weak and inaccurate.

They never got the other side. The Iraqi side. When was the last time you saw Colonel Ollie North interviewing an *Iraqi* about Operation Kickass or whatever clever name the Army came up with? It would be the equivalent of a reporter covering the story of a white cop shooting a black man in an American inner city, and only interviewing the cops, not the family and neighbors to get their take on the event. You'd only get 50 percent of the story. And a very slanted 50 percent.

Most of the press sat in the protected palace enclave sharing the same sources and calling themselves investigative journalists. If reporters wanted to get the real story, they would have to go and walk the streets of Iraq without military protection. They might get their heads cut off, but it'd be a hell of a story.

War reporting should not be about balance. It should be about accuracy. There's never a perfect equilibrium of good and bad news stories in any situation. People always complain that the news doesn't show enough good stories coming out of Iraq. That's because it is a war zone. The news is already bad. Imagine how much worse the reports would be without all the Pentagon spin. If you want good news stories, go to Disneyland.

For grunts, having a reporter or a TV crew around was mainly just a pain in the ass. Most of them were what we called "jock-sniffers." Many just wanted to do their time in the war zone so they could earn their combat-reporting stripes and get the hell home. Some guys tolerated the press better than others. I'll never forget the day one of my Squad Leaders radioed from the gas station to say there were people there who demanded to speak to me.

"Who, Willie?"

A bit sheepishly, he replied that a couple of French reporters had been making nuisances of themselves and refusing to heed his orders, so he'd handcuffed them to a lamppost.

"Doggone Frenchies wouldn't listen to me, L.T.!" he barked. "I done told 'em! But they didn't listen to me. So I tied 'em up like doggone hogs to a pole! Now they gonna listen."

Then there was the radio reporter we were ordered to show around. He was an impossibly chipper British dude, and he showed up at our CP wearing the cleanest, shiniest dark blue body armor we'd ever seen. Real Darth Vader shit, including a shiny helmet with a big, bright network logo printed on the front.

Rydberg sidled up to him. "Nice outfit," he said laconically. "Haji snipers love those helmets. They get extra points for putting a bullet right through that logo."

"R-really?" The reporter grinned nervously.

I told Chesty to take the guy out on patrol with him. Chesty hated dealing with reporters even more than most.

"Sir, do I have ta fuckin' take 'im?" he growled.

"Sorry, Chesty."

Chesty scratched his jaw.

"Well, kin we fuck with his head a little?"

"Knock yourself out. Show him a good time." I shrugged.

Chesty and his squad squeezed themselves into a Humvee. In the back, two guys sat on benches on either side, one guy stood in the middle manning the gun, and they made the reporter twit sit on the floor in the middle, where he couldn't see anything but the gunner's ass and crotch.

As they drove around the dark streets, he tried to do some reporting anyway. He broke out his tape recorder and mic.

"I'm sitting in the back of an American troop vehicle, patrolling the streets of—"

"Shhh!" Chesty hissed. "We're coming into a bad area here." All the guys suddenly looked very serious. They doused the headlights and spoke in tense whispers.

The reporter grinned and nodded excitedly, his shiny helmet

bobbing. *"I'm sitting in the back of an American troop vehicle . . . ,"* he whispered into his mic.

Suddenly Chesty yelled, "Omaha! Omaha! Get down! Incoming!"

The vehicle screamed into a hard turn. Overhead, the gunner started banging away deafeningly. The guys shoved the reporter's face to the floor. The Hummer veered and banked, left and right, as the gunner kept firing and everyone screamed.

Up in the front, Chesty wore a satisfied grin. They were totally faking it. They were careening around a deserted area of the city, the gunner roaring away at nothing.

The reporter wobbled out of the Humvee when they brought him back in to the post. His helmet was crooked. A terrified grin was plastered on his shiny face.

"You all right?" I asked him.

"S-splendid!" he said. "T-terribly exciting!"

Below his shiny black chest armor, I could see that he had pissed himself. I never did hear his report.

In September, CBS's *60 Minutes* came to cover the story of Sgt. Sean Blackwell. Blackwell was the leader of the Mortar Squad and a good ol' boy as country as fried chicken 'n' grits. He and his Squad were assigned to security duty in front of the Baghdad Ministry of Health building. They swept incoming cars for bombs, checked IDs. He had struck up a friendship with a beautiful Iraqi doctor named Ehda'a who regularly passed through the checkpoint. They chatted a little longer every day, and pretty soon they became friends.

The CO didn't mind. He had a thing for pretty women, and despite the reservations of the First Sergeant, he let it happen. So the woman and a pretty friend would stop by the compound to sit with Blackwell and a grizzled, quiet soldier from Second Platoon named Corporal Dagen in the common areas. As long as they were checked for weapons and they weren't left alone, it was allowed.

In a few weeks, Blackwell claimed he was in love. Dagen did too. Andy and I were now dealing with two of our soldiers double-dating in a war zone.

There was no law in the UCMJ addressing fraternization with local women. Ehda'a was smart and gorgeous, with big eyes and a pretty smile. She had captivated Blackwell and our Commander. With no one waiting for him back in the States, Blackwell was open-minded (or naïve) enough to give it a shot. It was easy for her to overcome his redneck trailer park background for a ticket out of Baghdad, where all a smart and pretty female doctor could look forward to was the threat of death or kidnapping. Blackwell was a good, solid man, but Ehda'a was way out of his league. And he said so. The whole romance was entirely improbable. I cautioned him at length, and kept him on a tight leash. But the CO was all right with it, so I was too. We were all skeptical, but love can emerge in the strangest of circumstances.

A few weeks later, Blackwell announced that he intended to marry Ehda'a. There was no precedent. To our knowledge, no American soldier in the war had yet married an Iraqi civilian. But intermingling between occupiers and the occupied had been a part of warfare since the days of Troy, and it was certainly not something new to the U.S. Army. Every American base is filled with Korean and German Army wives.

The CO gave his blessing. Blackwell announced he would convert to Islam and hoped he could marry his muse inside our compound at the Ministry of Labor. It would be a Muslim ceremony, with a local imam doing the honors. It did not interfere with our daily operations one bit, and after the money scandal, Bravo Company needed some good news.

Now, all Blackwell knew about Islam was what little Esam and Mo had told him, plus what he'd read from a book Bama had sent me, *Nine Parts of Desire*, by the *Wall Street Journal* Middle East correspondent Geraldine Brooks—sort of an *Idiot's Guide to Islam*. It was a crash course, but it provided Blackwell with a lot more cultural training than the Army ever gave any of us. The date was set, Mohamed would bring some traditional food, and with the CO's permission, the wedding plans rolled along.

Then the Battalion Commander changed his mind and killed it. "Absolutely not," he told the CO. And the CO, as usual, caved in and failed to fight for his soldiers. The company Sergeant Major was furious with Blackwell and Dagen. In his office he screamed, "Mooslums and Christians just don't fuckin' jive! What about the food they eat? The clothes they wear? They don't even believe in Jesus Christ!" Blackwell and Dagen were prohibited from seeing the girls, who were banned from the compound. But Blackwell was adamant.

For weeks the CO had allowed the romance to continue, and now he was changing his course. Forbidden love is all the more intense. Blackwell felt betrayed, and he was driven. "Fuck 'em," he growled. "I love her and I'm gonna marry her."

I pulled him aside. "Blackwell," I said, "whatever you're thinking, don't do it. I know the CO jerked you hard on this one, but if you do something stupid and violate a direct order, I won't be able to help you."

I ordered every man in the Platoon not to help Blackwell and Dagen to violate the order in any way. It didn't matter if they condoned the romance, the BC had laid down the law. The only communication Baghdad's Romeo and Juliet had was through letters passed back and forth through our interpreters.

But Blackwell did it anyway. On August 17, he and Dagen talked a Squad in Second Platoon into helping them make it happen. They took the two out on a routine patrol for a secret rendezvous. Our interpreter Sid was waiting in a tiny garden behind an al-Wasiriyah restaurant with the two girls, an Iraqi judge, and a reporter from Cox News Service. Blackwell was wrong. He had divulged the time and location of the patrol and endangered every man in the patrol. He was a good soldier, but he had made a conscious decision to put himself before his soldiers. As the Squad stood watch out front, Blackwell and Dagen married the two Iraqi women.

The next day the AP ran the story worldwide. So did *People* magazine.

Somebody at the Pentagon contacted the BC, who came down on Blackwell and Dagen like a storm of anvils. Dagen caved in and cooperated fully, and was let off with a slap on the wrist. Blackwell fought it the whole way. He knew he had a powerful and valuable story. Book deals and an appearance on *Oprah* were probably waiting. He was sent to the rear, isolated, and eventually chaptered out, which enabled the Army to kick him out without court-martialing him and fueling the press attention. Blackwell was sent home while his new wife remained in Baghdad. Many of the locals were enraged, and Ehda'a was now at tremendous risk. And the whole world wanted to know about it.

A few days later, a *60 Minutes* producer flew to Baghdad to get the story. The S-1 sent him to see me. The producer pressed me hard for the inside scoop on Blackwell, but I wouldn't give him any info. I wasn't stupid. His brother had gone to school with me at Amherst, and he was amazed to find me in Iraq. Not too many Amherst grads joined the Army. He gave up on the Blackwell story and decided he wanted to show America what the press was missing in Iraq, and chose to follow my guys on patrol instead.

Walking out the front gate on patrol with a producer and two cameramen, we looked like a carnival troupe. CBS filmed us interacting with the locals and putting a helmet on a smiling Iraqi kid. The out-of-shape cameramen huffed under the awkward weight of their equipment in the midday heat and my guys chuckled. Violence was increasing in our area, and they filmed the spot where an IED had detonated the day before, just a few hundred meters from the gate. A few months later, a soldier would die in almost the same exact spot. At one point during the patrol, we scrambled in pursuit of gunfire in a nearby alley. Sounds crazy, but in Baghdad, we chased the gunfire. The men fanned out and I barked orders, cursing and completely forgetting the CBS microphone on my chest. "Keep your heads on a swivel!" I yelled. One of the cameramen leapfrogged in front of the Squad to get a better shot—and almost got shot himself.

"What the fuck am I going to do if I have to shoot at somebody and you're in between us, asshole?" one of my guys screamed.

"Sorry, I wasn't thinking," he muttered.

We rounded the corner and headed down a narrow street with our rifles raised—to find a crowd of smiling Iraqis. The shooting turned out to be celebratory fire from a wedding.

"It looks like fucking Carnaval," I snapped. Back in the States, it was broadcast as "It looks like *beeep* Carnaval."

A few weeks later, *60 Minutes* was back in our compound with correspondent Scott Pelley to do the interview section of the piece. We made them wait until the Giants' Monday night game (Tuesday morning in Baghdad) was over. We rarely got to watch a game live. The Giants blew it in the fourth quarter. I stood leaning against a Humvee as the reporter peppered me with questions. He tried to get me to rip into Bush, and talked about something he called "the Sunni Triangle." Captain Bagpipes stood behind the camera the entire time with his arms crossed and a "watch-what-you-say" scowl on his face. He eyed me intently as I was interviewed, leaning in on every word. He was there to make sure I stuck to the Army-approved script. He wouldn't let me talk about the Blackwell case specifically, so Pelley asked what I thought about the war in general. The camera's eye bored a hole in my forehead as I wrestled to find the words that would be true to my feelings without landing me behind bars or stripping me of my command.

"I think we've made incredible strides," I replied. "This is the hard part. This is the road nobody has gone down before and the U.S. is breaking some new ground here. It's going to be a difficult struggle. Germany wasn't repaired in four months. Japan wasn't repaired in four months. It's gonna take time to reestablish this entire government, this entire country. But I think it has enormous potential. And I think the sky's the limit for the people of Iraq."

What I said was true. But I felt like a POW recording a confession. I wanted to give a wink or signal to let people back home know that my words were carefully chosen. When it was over all I could think was, "Welcome to Media Spin 101. I am your host, Professor Rieckhoff."

A few weeks later, after the story ran, my e-mail in-box was full of notes from family and friends who had seen the piece. My men and I were locally famous. The BC congratulated me on my on-screen composure and eloquence. The best feedback came in a phone call from my mother. "It was good to see you. Everyone was so happy to see you and the men, okay and smiling. But next time you get on TV, could you try to watch your language, please?"

"Yes, Mom."

The end of the Blackwell story? In August 2004, *60 Minutes* got involved again. They couldn't resist Blackwell's tragically romantic story of love in wartime. He had been discharged from the Army and was living in Jordan. A producer with a camera crew brought him to the Jordan-Iraq border, and another producer secretly drove Ehda'a out of Iraq to meet him. It was Hollywood-level drama. She crossed into Jordan wearing a bulletproof vest, and they were reunited in a passionate hug. America watched on TV. And thought the media coverage was spontaneous.

The happy couple stayed in Jordan for a while, and then flew to the States to begin their new life. They got a book deal. Blackwell worked in a factory. Ehda'a could not qualify for an American medical license and got a job selling shoes in Sears. Welcome to America.

They now live in Baghdad. Baghdad, Florida.

Embeds weren't the only form of media that changed the way we connected with the world back home. There was also the Internet. We didn't have Internet access for the first four months we were in Iraq. Once we did, everything changed. A local Iraqi had set up an Internet café in the back of the Battalion building, where soldiers could get e-mail maybe once a week. We paid five dollars an hour for the opportunity to hop online. We prayed for good news, baby pictures, spam, ridiculous forwards, and porn clips from home. A large sign was posted on the wall: REMEMBER OPSEC. Maintaining operational security meant that Joes couldn't e-mail their wives the details of an upcoming mission that could be intercepted by the enemy.

Ten PCs were circled around a small TV that played an Egyptian music video channel. The bizarre video for the Darkness song "I Believe in a Thing Called Love" blared constantly. There was something especially weird about watching a retro eighties heavy metal singer with long hair and spandex pants while I sat in Iraq wearing camouflage waiting for the Hotmail home page to download at a snail's pace.

Guys brought ponchos to the Internet room for a bit of privacy. They'd get the wife or girlfriend to give them a special show through a webcam, and they didn't want the rest of the Squad watching. Some soldiers went onto dating Web sites and tried to convince strange women to get naked for them. The sad sob story of an undersexed, patriotic soldier away at war could really move mountains.

Our Internet access was totally unreliable and always in high demand. An errant mortar hitting the satellite dish, a sandstorm, or a local power outage could be counted on to interrupt service often.

The Army created a new, high-tech set of problems for itself by allowing soldiers access to the Internet. Imagine the wife or girlfriend on the other end of an instant message conversation when all of a sudden it goes dead. Staring at the computer with her newborn on her lap, she has no idea if her man has just been incinerated by a car bomb, called to an emergency mission, or if it was just another power failure.

When a soldier in any unit was killed, command prohibited

e-mail access for the entire unit pending notification of the next of kin. It made sense. The Army didn't want Joe in Baghdad e-mailing his wife with the news about the recent death of Sergeant Snuffy before Sergeant Snuffy's family was properly notified. A wife finding out her husband was killed via a forwarded e-mail or by overhearing a conversation on the checkout line at Wal-Mart was the last thing the Army needed. But the policy also meant that whenever e-mail went down for a few days, an entire Battalion's families were in a near panic, holding their breath, staring at the phone and praying that their soldiers hadn't been killed.

My girlfriend would wait anxiously by the computer for my hour on the Web. Through the webcam, I could see her smile, her latest hairstyle, her brave face. The apartment looked the same as when I had left, but I knew she was struggling to keep up a strong appearance.

The Internet allowed me to keep tabs on the latest news and sports scores. It was pretty crazy that I could come back from patrol, drop my gear, and surf the Web. I even followed the stock market. After my girl sent me an iPod for Christmas, I saw an opportunity. It was the most amazing invention I had seen in a long time. My old Wall Street instincts kicked in, and I saw value. I went into my Schwab online account and bought a few hundred shares of Apple stock for less than twenty bucks per share—and recommended that any guys in my Platoon who were interested do the same.

In the winter of 2003 I also began to search the Internet for Iraq war veterans groups—and found none. It was almost one year into the war, and not a single new group had popped up to represent the perspectives of those who had been on the ground. There was one Web site for OIF (Operation Iraqi Freedom) vets set up by some well-intentioned Vietnam vets, but not a single group created by the newest generation of Iraq vets. I was both surprised and disturbed.

The 2004 presidential race was heating up back home. The

press was calling it the most important presidential election in a generation. I agreed. Iraq had changed everything. I listened to the BBC on a tiny transistor radio and tried to keep up on the latest news from back home—and around Iraq. I tracked the presidential race on the Internet and through articles and magazines friends sent to me. I got the issue of *Time* with a new sensation named Howard Dean on the cover.

I sent some money online to General Wes Clark's campaign. He was the only man I felt had the military experience necessary to guide us out of the mess in Iraq. I didn't care if he ran as a Democrat, a Republican, or an Independent; he was a combat vet and the type of tested leader America needed at this pivotal time. The stakes were too high.

That September, we got word that rather than going home, our tour would be extended again, through November. This did not have a positive impact on morale. For American soldiers, Baghdad was becoming a more hostile environment every week. At the end of the summer, the insurgents had significantly ramped up their terrorist tactics, like detonating car bombs in front of buildings that housed anyone who cooperated with coalition forces. Our leaders devised an ingenious response: they placed American soldiers in front of potential target buildings as guards. We might as well have had signs hung around our necks that read KILL ME.

One potential target in Sector 17 was the Turkish embassy. After not cooperating with the invasion initially, the Turkish parliament did an about-face in the first week of October and voted to send troops to Iraq to help coalition peacekeeping efforts. This decision practically planted a bull's-eye on the embassy door.

The Army sent engineers to erect concrete barriers in front of the building, and Third Platoon was dispatched to stand there every day waiting to be blown up. Despite repeated requests, we couldn't get the same types of barriers for our barracks. Our own government had decided that Turkish civilians were more worthy of protection than American soldiers. We stood there for a week, expecting to die. Stopping cars and searching under hoods and inside coffins, we were the first line of defense.

Late on the afternoon of October 14, a couple hours after we had been relieved, a suicide bomber drove a carload of explosives straight into the barriers, detonating right where we had stood guard. We rushed back over to the site to assess the damage, help with the wounded, and gather intel.

The huge explosion had atomized the car, recognizable only by the engine, the drivetrain still attached, smoking next to a tremendous crater the bomb had gouged in the street. Palm trees all down the block burned like torches. One whole wall of the building was shattered, bits hanging off like pieces of a disassembled puzzle. Amazingly, no one but the driver had died, and only two embassy staffers were injured.

The swelling crowd of locals stood in the street and gawked, and we began to shake them down for information. Of course, no one had seen a thing. No one ever did. Hundreds of people standing around, and not one of them had any information. Typical.

As the crowd, crew, and press converged, a scruffy guy with a weird, half-crazed grin emerged from the crowd and approached us.

"I know who did it! I know who did it!" he exclaimed through Mohamed.

"Okay," we said skeptically. "Who did it?"

He cackled, reached behind him, and pulled out a dirty, wadded-up paper napkin.

"This man did it!" He grinned.

We thought he was going to show us a photograph or ID card of Ali or Akbar who lived down the block—some neighbor he had a beef with and wanted to get into trouble. It happened a lot.

Instead, he unfolded the napkin. On it lay the skin of half a man's face. With half a mustache.

Evidently the blast had blown the bomber's face clear off his skull, and this man had found half of it lying somewhere nearby, like a ripped mask.

Our jaws dropped. The man laughed uproariously.

And you know what? We did too. It was unbelievable. We even took a picture of it.

I have this belief that even, or maybe especially, in times of horror and unbearable psychological stress, humans have an innate need to relieve some of the constant pressure through humor. Anybody who's lived in a war zone or survived a concentration camp will tell you this. It's bizarre what strikes you as funny in these nightmarish environments. Like those soldiers who had laughed their asses off at Ka-Bob. And this guy with his grisly joke. He's probably still getting a kick out of telling that story and shocking the Americans.

It's not pretty. I'm not proud of it. I'm just telling you it happens.

CHAPTER NINETEEN
CHRISTMAS IN BAGHDAD

> Piggy and Ralph, under threat of the sky, found themselves
> eager to take a place in this demented but partly secure
> society. They were glad to touch the brown backs of the
> fence that hemmed in the terror and made it governable.
> —William Golding, *Lord of the Flies*

On November 12, 2003, an explosion rocked the compound. Our Battalion had just lost its first soldier. On Veterans Day.

I knew when I heard the blast that one of our guys had been hit. I don't know how, but I knew. Every time I heard a blast, I held my breath and said a prayer.

Specialist Robert Wise was killed only about a hundred meters south of the Battalion compound when an IED hit his convoy. It was just a few meters away from the spot of a previous attack, the place the *60 Minutes* crew had filmed. His Squad was on security detail for EOD—Explosive Ordnance Disposal. EOD escort duty rotated throughout the Battalion; my guys had done it just a few days earlier. Wise died as the result of shrapnel wounds to his head from a 155mm mortar round.

I didn't know Robert Wise. But I know he was a good soldier, and a good man. Everyone spoke of his infectious smile and good nature. Although he wasn't one of my soldiers, he was my blood. All the men felt the same. As the violence grew, it was us against them. Wise was assigned to our sister company, Alpha, and his death hit us all hard. It was a tremendous dose of reality and mortality. We had been at war over six months, but only when Wise was killed did it all really sink in. Everyone's eyes were more focused. Laughter was muted in the chow hall. It was the first time many of the guys realized they could actually be killed. Wise's death cracked the illusion of immortality in our Battalion—and in my Platoon.

I had never been to a military funeral. I had hoped the first one I attended would be my own. Wise's boots, rifle, and dog tags were posted in the center of the opulent marble hall of the Republican Guard officers' building. The same place where Saddam and his men once partied as their people suffered. The Alpha Company CO spoke about Wise fondly, as did one of his closest buddies.

Then the First Sergeant performed the traditional roll call. He called a few soldiers by name. One by one. He called their names and they answered, "Here, First Sergeant." Then he called the name of the fallen warrior three times: "Wise. Wise. Specialist Robert Wise." An assigned soldier stood and said, "First Sergeant, Specialist Wise is not present."

Then they played taps. And did a ten-gun salute. I had never seen a sadder thing in my entire life.

After Wise was killed my men were suddenly all scared of dying, especially the ones with children. They had had enough. One had already cracked. At home on leave, he had gone AWOL and never came back. During November, there were more IED attacks in our sector than in any other part of Iraq. The mortar attacks in our area were more frequent as well. More civilians were dying in our area. I felt Iraqis looking at me more nastily on patrol. The tide was beginning to turn.

We spent Thanksgiving Day waiting to use a phone to call our families and loved ones. The fucking Haji landline phones were useless, so we used cell phones. Problem was, in all of Bravo Company there were only two cells—one for the CO, the other for the rest of us. When you finally got your turn you had to make it short and sweet. Guys breathed down your neck.

One soldier's wife told him, "So President Bush was in town today."

"What town?" he asked.

"*Your* town. Baghdad."

We hadn't heard a thing about it. The president had flown into the FOB at BIAP, made one of his rah-rah speeches, and flown back out again. No way he was going to come into the city itself and rally my troops at Fort Apache.

Shortly after that we got extended. Again. They told us we'd be extended indefinitely. No going home for Christmas. But by this point, none of us believed anything we were told. General Dempsey, the Division Commander, arrived at our FOB to give us a pep talk. You knew things were bad when they sent the Division Commander. By December 2003, our Battalion had the dubious and undesirable distinction of being the only one from the invasion that was still in Iraq. And it showed.

General Dempsey spoke to the entire Battalion crammed into an old theater. He was likable, candid, and clear. Not too many officers make it all the way to General without a degree of mojo. Generals are all pretty good talkers. Dempsey could have been a senator or the CEO of a big corporation. He told us that he was proud of us. We had performed well beyond expectations. We had done everything everyone had asked of us and then some. But we weren't going home just yet. He told us to stay focused on our mission.

The rhetoric was fine. But every man in that auditorium could feel things in Baghdad getting tighter. Many were stop-lossed. The divorces were piling up. Tempers were short. Soldiers with small businesses back home were ruined. We knew there was a limit to how much we could stand. And how much the local Iraqis would tolerate. Both sides were tired of broken promises and unfulfilled expectations. We knew our luck was running out.

On December 13, troops of the Fourth Infantry Division dragged Saddam out of his hidey-hole in his hometown of Tikrit. The people of Baghdad went nuts. We were issued pictures of his capture to show to the locals. Images were powerful in a culture used to misinformation. The only thing they really trusted was what they saw with their own eyes. Millions of people danced and chanted in the streets to the deafening blare of car horns and AKs.

But not everybody in the city was celebrating. Many Iraqis were saddened by Saddam's capture. Good Iraqis. One of the food vendors left the compound in tears. And I couldn't understand why. I pulled Mohamed aside for an explanation.

"L.T., the Iraqis are humiliated. Saddam, this old man, this old crazy man, treated us so badly. When the Americans captured Saddam, he looked weak and old. We are embarrassed that you had to come all the way to Iraq to capture this old man for us. It is humiliating to have been held down by a man that seems so weak . . . so human. It is demeaning to have another country do for you what you should have done for yourself. It is like depending on another man to defend your wife. L.T., we feel like fools."

At least three bombs rocked the city that night, including one that exploded in front of the Palestine Hotel, a favorite target of the insurgents because it was the home base for most of the international press. It was just the start of an amped-up new wave of terrorist activities in the city.

As Christmas approached, the timetable for our departure was pushed back again. All they told us now was that we'd be leaving "sometime next year." Morale hit rock bottom.

And that's when our luck ran out.

On the night of December 23, Bravo Company was tasked with conducting a cordon and search to surround and capture or kill three wealthy Iraqi men who allegedly had been financing the building of IEDs throughout Iraq. The mission was dubbed Operation Paymaster.

I did not go out on this one. My role was to monitor events from base. We put out two Platoons of Light Infantrymen, about 80 men, armed to the teeth, supported by half a dozen tanks, ten Bradleys, two helicopter gunships overhead, three sniper teams, and another Company of Infantrymen on standby in case of a SNAFU (Situation Normal—All Fucked Up).

It was a big operation, and one that turned out to be what my soldiers would call Totally and Completely Fucked Up.

It was an extremely dark night with no moon. Two Squads, totaling about eighteen men, stacked themselves in a column at the corner of a high wall surrounding a big, beautiful house. They were ready to blow the front gate and enter the house on command from higher. Suddenly the sky rained tracer rounds and everybody took cover. High walls boxed them in on both sides— they were caught in a textbook ambush. Sergeant Dustin Tuller had just been transferred out of my Platoon over to Second. The officers had orchestrated a deal to trade him to Second in exchange for a problem NCO. Tuller, who was directing his new Squad from across the street, got caught out in the open. He was cut down as AK-47 rounds tore through his legs.

Sergeant Jason Crawford was at the head of the column. Crawford, J-Craw, as everyone called him, was one of the most likable guys in the Company. He was smart, fearless, and always smiling. A natural leader, he was always at the front of the stack, the first guy in every door. Just as he turned the corner to enter the driveway, he saw a muzzle flash from the courtyard. He took a knee and felt the back of his skull under his helmet—feeling for his brains, I guess. He thought he was dead. His Squad scooped him up and shoved him to the rear as they rushed into the courtyard. A second later the shooter lay dead, a .38-caliber pistol near his hand.

The bullet had entered Crawford's face just below his nose and lodged in his upper jaw, knocking out one front tooth clean. But that was all. He'd be fine. A few stitches and a lost tooth—a Baghdad Root Canal, he called it. He returned to patrol with his Squad three days later. He was Bravo Company's Christmas miracle.

Sergeant Tuller wasn't so lucky. He had lost a ton of blood, and the medevac chopper was slow to arrive. We all thought he was dead. His body armor SAPI plates had stopped at least three rounds that would have surely killed him, but his legs had been unprotected.

The next day, one of the first soldiers to donate blood for Tuller was forty-three-year-old Command Sergeant Major Eric Cooke. As the Brigade Sergeant Major, Cooke was the senior enlisted soldier among fifteen hundred men. He was probably the most loved and respected man in the Brigade, a legend and father figure to the younger guys. He went straight to the aid station and rolled up his sleeve. That was Cooke, always leading by example.

Tuller was flown to Germany, where they amputated his legs, saving his life so he could return to his wife and three children.

On the night of Christmas Eve I went out on another massive Brigade-level mission with the men. It was a weird one. The psychological operations officer had decided to use a powerful sound system to blast out Christmas carols through the neighborhood. I'm not sure what kind of effect he hoped that would have on our Muslim hosts, but it drove me crazy. Walking streets bathed in a green glow through my NODs with "Jingle Bells" and "Rudolph the Red-Nosed Reindeer" blaring was an Alice in Wonderland experience.

We were a few hundred meters away from our target block when PFC Bill Broach went down. The guys yelled from the rear, and I heard over my radio earpiece, "Broach is down! Broach is down!" Snipers were an increasing problem, and I feared the worst.

We stopped the Platoon and I ran back with Rydberg to investigate. Broach was fine. He had twisted his ankle stepping off a curb. We stopped so the doc could wrap it for him. Broach was a real character, one of the most country of all the country boys in the Platoon. He was Third Platoon's Forrest Gump, and he was one of the the few guys who actually gained weight in Iraq—he said MREs were the best chow he'd ever eaten, and he devoured them. He was also a klutz, always dropping equipment and falling down for no apparent reason. The men in First Squad cared for him as you would a child. We called him "Baby," as in "Who's taking care of Baby today?"

As we waited for the doc to take care of Broach, the men took a breath, mentally preparing themselves for the anticipated rush of hitting the target block. I called over the radio, "Let's go, guys. Move out."

I had taken about ten steps when we heard a massive explosion and the street shook. The blast was only about 150 meters up the road. It was a huge IED that sounded like an artillery strike. We all took a knee. A soldier to my right made the sign of the cross over his body armor.

Had Broach not tripped at that moment and slowed us down, we would have been right next to the IED when it went off. If not for Broach's clumsiness, my entire First Squad and I would have died that night.

We scrambled up to the blast, following a 113 ambulance vehicle. A Humvee was peppered and smoke was billowing.

"Up there! Up there! It came from up there!" The medics pointed to the adjacent building, and we hit it hard. A Colonel stood in the median and screamed, "Get 'em! Get those fucking savages! I want those fucking savages out here now!"

We had been on edge all week and the caged animal was unleashed. Rage is a powerful stimulant. For the next hour my Platoon and our entire Company tore the place apart, ramming doors and slamming civilians. Third Squad hit one side and Second Squad hit the other. Rydberg whizzed around a corner to find a soldier from Third Squad with eyes as big as saucers. "Man, I almost shot you," the soldier gulped.

"Yeah. Thanks, man."

There was no holiday spirit in Baghdad that Christmas Eve. And there was no mercy. Everyone was guilty. Lines of civilians were bound like cattle on curbs. We tossed an entire neighborhood, and anyone who even looked suspicious was detained.

Whoever had tried to blow us up that night had achieved his goal. One explosion had turned the Americans into monsters in the eyes of the locals. We could hand out candy for a year on that block and never regain their trust.

We found some RPGs, and a few mortars, but nothing major. Our tempers were short, our nerves frayed. We didn't get a chance to kill anyone. And we were intensely disappointed.

When we returned to post, exhausted, Platoon Sergeant Jensen and I acted on a plan we'd been hatching for days. As soon as we entered the FOB, we started tearing into the guys. Before they could even unload from the trucks and move to guard duty, we were on top of them. I yelled like a madman.

"Listen up! I want every single fucking man in Sergeant Jensen's room in ten minutes. Everybody. We're doing a Platoon AAR right now. No sleeping. No bullshit. Drop your gear and be up there in ten mikes (minutes)."

They were confused as all hell.

Sergeant Williford pulled me aside. "Hey, sir. My guys are shot and have to head up to guard duty now. Can we do the AAR (After Action Review) tomorrow?"

"No, Sergeant. We can't. Get your guys up there now."

I had never disregarded his input before at any point in our entire deployment, and he was stunned.

We crammed the entire Platoon of thirty-eight tired and sweaty soldiers into Sergeant Jensen's tiny room, the walls covered with family snapshots and his kids' crayon drawings.

"At ease!" Jensen bellowed. At ease means shut up.

He and I paused for effect, scanning the room of faces. Then we launched into a quick debriefing. We reviewed the tactics used during the raid, and laid out guard duty rotations for the night—typical AAR shit.

Then Jensen looked at me and winked. I gave him a nod. We smiled and announced, "Merry Christmas, boys."

Jensen opened a wall locker to reveal a stack of colorful gift bags. He gave each soldier a surprise package that his wife had sent from back home.

The Platoon hooted. Jensen's wife deserved a medal. Every single man got a DVD, some candy, and other goodies. They tore into the packages like kids. It was a nice piece of home that helped us forget where we were. I pulled out a wonderfully ridiculous Santa hat and perched it on my big head. My dad had sent a gleaming bottle of Chivas Regal that I had saved for months. We shared the whiskey as soldiers and as friends. Each man got only one swallow, but it was damn good. At barely nineteen, Webb was the youngest man in the Platoon. I ordered him to take the first swig. The oldest man in the Platoon, crusty old Chesty, was next. Alcohol was expressly prohibited in the Iraq theater of operations, but this was a family affair. And it was Christmas. I drank last. It was my first taste of liquor in almost ten months. I held it in my mouth and savored the warmth.

I imagined my family back home. It was probably snowing in New York. My mother at midnight mass, praying. My brother explaining to his son that I was not coming for Christmas this year because I was far away fighting bad guys. My dad anchored to the TV. My girlfriend crying.

We choked back tears, shared jokes, and tried to keep each other sane. We laughed and ribbed each other like only soldiers can do. It was locker-room bonding on another level. With our families seven thousand miles away, we were all we had. A bittersweet bond that only soldiers can truly understand.

Then the First Sergeant knocked on the door and pushed inside with his eyes wet. The laughing stopped abruptly. We all knew something was wrong.

"Sergeant Major Cooke is dead."

We were stunned. The IED that had exploded up ahead of us had killed him. This was the first we heard of it.

As the First Sergeant turned to walk out the door, he turned back around, eyes full of tears, and reminded us that not twelve hours earlier, Cooke had been giving blood for Sergeant Tuller.

Then he walked out. We sat in startled silence.

And that was Christmas in Baghdad.

CHAPTER TWENTY
A VIABLE EXIT STRATEGY

> There was only one catch, and that was Catch-22, which
> specified that a concern for one's safety in the face of
> dangers that were real and immediate was the process of
> the rational mind.
> —Joseph Heller, *Catch-22*

Cooke's death sent waves of shock and fear through all of us. If Cooke could die, we all could. As the Brigade Sergeant Major, he was viewed by the soldiers as indestructible. By killing Sergeant Cooke, the enemy had scored a direct hit on the top of our chain of command. It was the first time they had gotten one of the cards in *our* deck of fifty-two.

I couldn't stop thinking that if not for Broach's two left feet, I might be dead. And all of Third Squad thought the same thing. This is the type of analysis that soldiers do. We realize that our lives are often spared or taken by the smallest of events. Our lives had become a game of inches. And soldiers count those inches often. We save them up and wonder how many more we have. We laugh about them, we trade them. We love them and hate them. It's like the stories you hear about September 11, the guy who missed his usual train, or the lady who got a flat tire, and it ultimately saved their lives. Soldiers tend to think like that every day in combat. It makes you feel like you have some kind of control over whether or not you die, when you know you really don't.

At the start of January, we were told that we were really, finally going home soon. No specific date, but soon.

After that, we counted the days. Nobody wanted to do anything stupid to get himself or anyone else killed. Everyone got a little bit paranoid like Captain Yossarian in *Catch-22*. Morale was high, but fragile. I made a point of personally walking with almost every one of my patrols during those last few weeks. I wasn't going to send guys out to do something I wouldn't do myself. If my guys got caught in some shit in the last few days, I was going to be there with them, not playing video games back in the FOB.

The CO had made it clear that we would be sending out patrols until the very last day. That was smart. We couldn't afford to let our guard down in the eleventh hour. A fundamental aspect of a good defensive strategy is keeping the enemy off your gates. Keeping them guessing. And constant patrols did that. I stayed on top of them in the last few days. Every soldier walked a little faster, worked a little harder, looked a little closer. None of my soldiers was going to die because of short-timer's disease.

The guys determined among themselves a rotation to minimize the exposure of anyone with kids. It was an enlisted man's code that I had no place interfering with. Some of my soldiers told their buddies to stay behind while they went outside the wire, walking in their place. That's a level of love I had never seen before in my life.

But one guy refused to go out on patrol, a Sergeant and team leader who had served as a Marine in the first Gulf War. He was well decorated and respected, and one of the oldest. That gave him tremendous insight, but it also made him stubborn. He had been transferred to my Platoon after a falling-out with the First Platoon Leader. He fit in right away and took over for the fire team in Second Squad that Blackwell had led before getting into trouble.

The Sergeant and I got along well. I respected him, and he seemed to respect me. I didn't bother him with excessive bullshit. I trusted his technical expertise and judgment. He was like the grumpy, wise old owl of Third Platoon.

Maybe another Platoon Leader would have just court-martialed him, but I wanted to try diplomacy first. This was something we could keep in the family. Jensen and I had a sit-down with him. The Sergeant explained that he was done. He'd had it. He'd had enough of the bullshit and didn't want to risk his ass. We were leaving soon, and he thought the only purpose patrolling would serve would be to get people killed. He loved his guys, but he loved his family more. He had a wife and kids at home, and wasn't going to let them down forever by getting his ass killed in the final days of our deployment. I didn't have kids, and couldn't imagine facing the same responsibility.

I explained to him that his personal feelings could not dictate the operations of the Platoon. He had a job to do, and I needed him to do it. I depended on him. His men depended on him. Either he went out on patrol or I would move forward with court-martial action for cowardice.

The Sergeant relented and went back to his team. We never spoke of it again. I was proud of him.

On January 9, I celebrated my twenty-eighth birthday at the FOB. My A-bag packed, I was counting the minutes. And I got a surprising birthday gift from a very special friend.

As we trained the Iraqi Protection Security Force (IPSF), we made a number of great friends. The IPSF was designed to serve as a human barrier at government sites like the Ministries. Its recruits were to become the equivalent of the capital guards in D.C. The IPSF was the first crew of Iraqis we trained in Iraq—before the police and new Iraqi Army or ICDC (Iraqi Civil Defense Corps—the Iraqi National Guard).

Training the IPSF was sort of like coaching a Little League baseball team. The recruits were uncoordinated, communicated awkwardly, and lost attention quickly. During training, we used creative incentives like old CDs and DVDs. Without a doubt, the most inspiring incentive was *Maxim* magazine. In the sexually restrictive time of Saddam, the boys had never gotten to see much T and A. One magazine with Pamela Anderson on the cover would motivate training for hours and could nearly cause a riot.

The trainees came in all shapes and sizes. With their hand-me-down equipment, they quickly became known around the Company as the "Bad News Bears." IPSF soldiers would sit on guard duty with two Americans. The plan was to Iraqify the vital government sites around the city, one by one. As they stood up, we'd stand back. Conversations between Americans and Iraqis were difficult, but entertaining and incredibly educational. I was impressed with how quickly the trainees learned English, and my men learned Arabic.

The most colorful of the crew was a nearly seven-foot-tall giant that we called Big Foot. Big Foot just might have been the tallest man in all of Iraq—with monstrous feet. He was good-natured and a bit of a joker, with a permanent wide grin and a cigarette always in hand.

One day, outside the Ministry of Labor, a group of my soldiers shared stories and cigarettes with a few of the ISPF guys, Big Foot among them. As they chatted, I noticed Big Foot's toes hulking over the edge of his sandals, like Bill Bixby's after he turned into the Incredible Hulk on the old TV show. It looked terribly uncomfortable.

Through Mohamed, I asked Big Foot, "Don't you have shoes that fit your feet?"

He laughed deeply. "La. La. La." (Arabic for "no".)

He told me that it had been years since he had outgrown the largest shoes available in Iraq. He was poor, and especially during the years of sanctions, unusually large footwear was tough to get.

When I asked him what size he wore, he wasn't even sure. Mohamed and I guesstimated him to be about a size 19 U.S., about the same size as Shaquille O'Neal.

I had an idea. Using Mohamed's cell phone, I left my girlfriend a message, asking her to send an e-mail to all her friends to see if anyone knew how to get a pair of size 19 shoes. I figured with all her crafty friends, some who worked in fashion in New York, somebody might be able to come up with something.

It was important to me that we show Iraqis that dreams could come true—and that we could help them make that happen. I had to show them that working with the Americans and accepting the American way of life had rewards. I wanted to flex what author Joseph Nye called our "Soft Power."

And then, honestly, I forgot about the call entirely. About four weeks later, I got two care packages from home. In one I found sundries, magazines, a few CDs, baby wipes, and a wonderful letter from my girlfriend. The other was from my friend Dan Warnier in New York.

A few weeks before, he had sent me a three-foot-long salami from the legendary Katz's Deli on Houston Street in New York. Katz's is famous for its pastrami and corned beef; and for a slogan from World War Two: "Send a salami to your boy in the Army!" Some of the Southern boys in my Platoon had never even seen a salami. But they loved it. I set the meat in the middle of the CP on a table with a bayonet to cut slices, and it was gone in about an hour.

But this box was no salami. As I tore back the brown paper, and pulled open the black box, my mouth dropped. The guys started to laugh. Inside lay a brand-new pair of black Nike Air Jordan basketball sneakers. Size 19. They were gorgeous. And huge. Each one was bigger than my entire head. It must have taken five cows to make those suckers. The silver Michael Jordan logo shined like a jewel. Guys yanked out disposable cameras and took pictures of the shoes.

Now I just had to find Big Foot. Problem was, he had been fired from the IPSF the week before for lying to a female American soldier about being a CIA agent. He was trying to impress her, but the command was not impressed.

I carried the shoes in the back of our Humvee on patrol for a few days. Nobody seemed to know where Big Foot was. I found it hard to believe that nobody could locate a seven-foot-tall Iraqi, but Baghdad was a tough place to track people down. You couldn't just call them on their cell phones or send them e-mails.

As we were checking on a gas station one day, Mohamed called me over to tell me that one of the guys working there was the cousin of Big Foot. A small, shady-looking character in a tattered soccer jersey, he told me that he knew where Big Foot was and would be happy to make a delivery. I knew better than to just hand them off to this guy. I told him through Mohamed, "You had better get these shoes directly to Big Foot. He must get them today. You understand?"

He nodded and smiled. But I had no guarantee that he wouldn't sell the shoes for an AK or a few gallons of gas. I needed to reinforce my intentions.

"Listen to me. Look up in the sky," I told him. "We have satellites. Lots of them. And I can find out everywhere you go. I will be watching. And if you don't bring these shoes to Big Foot, I will know. And we will find you. And kill you."

The smile dropped from his face. He understood.

January 9, 2004. I was catching some sleep after a long night of patrolling when one of the guys woke me up.

"L.T., you're not gonna believe this! Big Foot just showed up at the front gate in a full suit and tie—with flowers! He heard it was your birthday and wanted to bring you a gift and this note. He had this bouquet of flowers for you! And it was the funniest thing, along with the suit, he was wearing the black Air Jordans. He got 'em."

I was happy and relieved that he actually got the shoes. By the time I got back to the gate, Big Foot was gone. His note had been dictated to an interpreter at the gate: *"Lieutenant Rieckhoff and the Third Platoon, thank you very much for the wonderful shoes. Happy Birthday and God bless you all."*

I never saw Big Foot again. But I am sure that wherever he is, he is still wearing those black Air Jordans. And smiling. One pair of shoes had done more than a hundred bullets could ever have to win that man to our side forever.

A few days later, the Battalion had crammed itself and all of its gear into some trucks and left Baghdad. We were going home.

Getting out of Iraq involved as much hurry up and wait as getting into it. A transportation company drove us out to the FOB at BIAP, but you couldn't just pile onto a C-130 and fly out of there. Nine months after the airport had first been taken, it still wasn't totally secure. Flights in and out took fire from AKs and other small arms and SAMs (Surface-to-Air Missiles). A French news network documented a DHL plane taking a hit. The brass were terrified that one missile might take out a C-130 full of soldiers. Most troops were convoyed down the long road to Kuwait to fly out from there.

At BIAP we clambered out of the trucks and mustered in a muddy parade ground. Everyone was nervous and giddy, yet somber and hypervigilant. Stomachs were tight. Nobody wanted a last-minute mistake to result in disaster. Companies were broken up into "chalks" of about fifty guys. I was the ranking man and therefore our chalk Commander.

On the fifth day we finally got the word to move. We would be among the first units to fly straight out of Iraq—but not from BIAP. Instead, we climbed into five-ton trucks for the one-hour ride to the more secure Balad Air Base, a former Iraqi air force facility north of Baghdad. Bradleys and Apaches escorted our column for the ride. BIAP and the rest of our Battalion were pelted with a mortar attack right after we drove out. There were no casualties.

We dawdled at Balad for the next few days. The place was really built up. It didn't look much different from a military base in Germany. The soldiers stationed at Balad had a dramatically different experience of the war than we had. There were 150,000 U.S. troops in the country, but a large number of them never really got much closer to the war than they would have watching it on TV back in Arizona or Florida. The only Iraqi some of them ever saw was the guy mopping the floor of their office. They sat in air-conditioning and pushed paper. At Balad they ate frozen yogurt and took salsa classes. We called them Fobbits—people who never left the Forward Operating Base (FOB). We grunts despised them.

We had been in Iraq almost a year, but no days dragged by more slowly than these. It was freezing, and all our cold-weather gear was packed. We scavenged to find wool blankets and anything else to break the cold. It was the perfect insult that on the way out we froze our asses off nearly to the point of hypothermia. The men lounged in our tented shantytown, which looked like a concentration camp, discussing what they would eat, drink, or sleep with first when we finally got home.

New soldiers from arriving units or fresh out of Basic Training stood out like *Playboy* Playmates in Rikers Island. As my guys loitered outside the tents smoking and playing cards, the newbies wandered by with their stuffed A-bags, wide eyes, and starched uniforms. My grizzled soldiers rode them relentlessly with calls of "Fresh fish! Fresh fish!" In ridiculing the incoming new soldiers, they were completing a rite of passage that must have dated back centuries.

The flights in and out of Balad were run entirely by civilian contractors. This was no surprise. They were the second-largest force involved in the Iraq war effort. More than the British. More than the Italians. They were civilians, working for one no-bid contractor or another. Using thousands of contractors allowed Rumsfeld to flex considerably more combat muscle without increasing troop numbers. It was a combat enhancement without the political fallout. Civilian contractors fed us at the bases, which was no bargain.

The powdered eggs were gray and the plastic forks broke in our hands. One day in Baghdad my guys had seen mysterious blue helicopters flying in attack formation overhead. Nobody knew who flew blue helicopters. We thought maybe they were UN. They turned out to be Bremer's privately contracted security force.

The guys at Balad were mostly retired military, running around in DCU bottoms and black T-shirts. I struck up a conversation with one who'd retired from the Air Force just a year before. He told me this was a pretty good job. He earned nearly six figures (tax-free) to do almost the same job he'd done in the Air Force. He lived there at the air base, which he said was relatively safe. His contract guaranteed him air-conditioning, decent chow, and four weeks' paid vacation. He was a nice guy, but on my way out, the whole thing didn't sit very well with me. Why was America paying a contractor six figures to do a job a Sergeant could do for $40K? Soldiers definitely didn't like the contractors. The deal sounded good for him, but I wasn't sure it was good for the war, or for America.

Our plane was finally ready, a massive C-17 Globemaster, sitting alone in the middle of the airfield like a mirage. Its wingspan must have been 170 feet, and the nose seemed to be smiling at us as we approached. Our long walk out to the plane was marked with cheering and hooting.

"Good riddance!" a soldier shouted from off to one side.

It felt like a movie scene again. I could hear the music swell. Apaches scanned the landscape to our flank, checking for SAMs in the tree line. The air was still and dusty.

With one last look behind me, I climbed into the plane. I might have been the only guy in the group who felt nostalgic. I looked forward to seeing Iraq again. I hoped one day I could walk the streets of a peaceful, thriving, and democratic Iraq, alive with happy children. I hoped to see Esam and Mohamed again, and visit the memorial to the American soldiers. I thought of the scene from *Saving Private Ryan* when old Private Ryan cries at the grave of Captain Miller.

> *Old James Ryan:* Tell me I have led a good life.
> *Ryan's Wife:* What?
> *Old James Ryan:* Tell me I'm a good man.
> *Ryan's Wife:* You are.

I wanted to be able to take my future family back to Baghdad one day to show them that we had done a good thing there. I wanted to take pride years later in knowing that my men and I were a part of creating something much greater than ourselves. I wanted Iraq to succeed.

And Iraq could still succeed. It wasn't a probability, but it certainly was a possibility. I wasn't ready to put money on it, but there was always a chance. I had hope.

But hope isn't a course of action.

We walked through the cold, cavernous cargo bay and climbed a twisting metal ladder to the passenger section above. We shoved our giddy asses into the tight seats. No smiling stewardesses on this ride. No in-flight movie. No glossy magazines with pictures of exotic destinations. Just steel, iron, and the roar of the engines. A lone Air Force crewman gave us a quick safety talk, and then congratulated us on surviving. The plane corkscrewed hard and fast up into the clouds, to avoid any hits from people below who allegedly hated liberty.

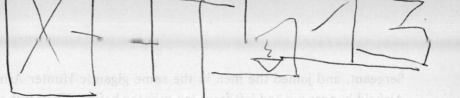

CHAPTER TWENTY-ONE
HOMECOMING

> Older men declare war. But it is youth that must fight and die. And it is youth who must inherit the tribulation, the sorrow, and the triumphs that are the aftermath of war.
> —Herbert Hoover

It was a sunny January morning in Georgia when our plane landed. We all were bouncing and frantic like kids at the end of a long family car trip. A line of smiling pogue Generals and officers shook our hands. A few of my guys kissed the pavement. I did a final head count and watched my men walk into the sunshine as I deplaned last. My boot hit the tarmac, and I exhaled deeply for the first time in ten months. My tax-free days were over. It still didn't seem real. So much had changed. I was different now. We all were. Not everyone returns damaged, but no one comes home unchanged.

Turning in my weapon for the last time made me sad. The same M16 had been with me for fourteen months. I knew where every chip and dent was. I knew how to use my Leatherman to open the bent latch of the buttstock. I thought I'd be liberated by handing away my rifle, but instead I felt empty, weak and vulnerable—like a piece of my body had been amputated. I signed my name on a clipboard, gave away the Platoon's weapons to a

Sergeant, and joined the men in the same gigantic Hunter Army Airfield hangar we had left from ten months before. The great adventure was over. A rear detachment officer welcomed us home and gave us a quick briefing. Our families were anxiously awaiting our arrival an hour away at Fort Stewart. After a quick ceremony, we'd be released on a forty-eight-hour pass. The boys were hoping for more than forty-eight hours. We all were. But I'd take it. I tried to calculate how many beers and burgers I could consume in forty-eight hours. How many restaurants I could visit. Honestly, sex wasn't much on my mind. But I wondered if my girlfriend would even recognize me. Would she look the same? Would she still love me?

We rolled into Fort Stewart in buses, with a Military Police escort. The town of Hinesville was the same dilapidated world of strip malls, Korean dry cleaners, military surplus stores, car dealerships, pawnshops, Wal-Marts, and fast-food joints that rings every military base in the South from Fort Benning, Georgia, to Fort Bragg, North Carolina. As we entered Fort Stewart, there were private security guards at the gates instead of MPs. Most all of the MPs were deployed somewhere in the world. Good to know we don't have enough troops available to guard our own bases. The place looked exactly the same as when we had left. Seasons don't change in Georgia. And neither do the Army bases. The same shitty row houses. The same new cars young soldiers can't afford. The same bowling alleys. The same parade fields. The same Burger Kings. Military bases seem to transcend time.

When our bus passed the parade field, we saw a frenzied mob of women and children standing on the bleachers, desperate for that first view of their long-lost family members. An Army band played. We lunged to the windows, looking for our people. I scanned for Bama in vain. The buses blasted their horns as we passed the assembly. A few kids ran alongside.

We unloaded and mustered in a parking lot two hundred meters from the bleachers, where the families cheered and waved.

It felt like getting off the bus to enter the stadium tunnel right before the homecoming football game. The parade field was lined with newly planted trees, one for each of the Third ID soldiers killed in Iraq while deployed. By 2005, there would be a whole new crop of trees as the Third deployed to Iraq for a second helping.

The gravel crunched under my guys' nervous feet, and I checked the formation. Everyone was online. I yelled over the roar, "Enjoy this moment, fellas. You deserve every bit of it! I am so fucking proud of you. It has been my honor. Welcome home."

Everyone smiled. I was as happy as I have ever been in my life.

I took my position in front and marched my men home across the parade field in formation. Their swelling pride was electric. It was beautiful. I felt like we could march through hell together. The crowd grew louder as we got closer. I called cadence and brought the guys in.

"Mark time, march!"

A fat General I had never seen stood behind a microphone smiling.

"Pla-toon, halt!" I smiled and saluted. "Sir, Third Platoon, Bravo Company, First of the One-twenty-fourth! Reporting! Back from Baghdad!"

The guys let out a resounding *"Hooah!"* And the crowd roared and rushed as we broke formation and gathered our families around us.

Seeing my girl for the first time in almost a year was awkward. It's not like the movies. At least it wasn't for me. I didn't skip across a poppy field and meet her in a passionate, loving embrace. My girl did jump on me and wrap her arms around me, but it didn't feel good. She was the most wonderful woman I had ever met, but it felt wrong. I still had my battle gear on. My warrior's armor on my chest. And my girl in my arms. Something about touching my wonderful girlfriend with the blood and Baghdad sand still on my boots felt unnatural. I wanted to keep the two worlds separate. I didn't want to contaminate my woman with my war.

Too many emotions. I was so used to compartmentalizing them, deep in the back of my mind. Now they were bubbling up. Exposing weakness and leaving me vulnerable. I felt like she was trapping me. Boxing me in. Time to move. I had shit to do, equipment to turn in. I still had to think of my men. Even now that we were home, I had an entire chalk of men who were my responsibility until otherwise notified. I wriggled free as my girlfriend squeezed tighter.

And then, from behind me: "Hey, sir. Sir! Excuse me. I need to talk to you for a sec. We got a problem."

The wife of one of the guys in my chalk was in the hospital. She'd gotten into a car accident on the way down from Chicago. Word was that she was in critical condition. It never seemed to end. Welcome home.

We now had forty-eight hours to reintroduce ourselves to the world. I was overwhelmed. I felt like a newborn. Bama and I went to Buffalo's Restaurant, where I was waited on for the first time in over a year. I always told Esam I missed service. I ate a meal, and was alone with a woman for the first time in a year. I had a Diet Coke. In a glass. *With ice.* I ordered the carne asada and savored every smoky bite. I ate with real silverware and wiped my mouth with a cloth napkin. I drank a cold beer. And three more.

Bama had a room at the Comfort Inn that felt like a suite at the Ritz. I walked barefoot on a carpeted floor pockmarked with cigarette burns. We watched the Super Bowl on TV—live. I almost burned the batteries out of the remote control as I channel-surfed with total selfishness. I slept in a big bed, with a real mattress and sheets. Listened to the hum of the ice machine and the sounds of drunken soldiers and giggling women late into the night.

The hotels around Hinesville were all booked up for miles, with the families of soldiers, some coming, some going. I never thought when we left for Iraq in 2003 that soldiers might have to go after us. Some of my friends in the Guard were jealous that I got to go. We never realized that they'd all get their chance. Careful what you wish for. . . .

The week of outprocessing at Fort Stewart was a purgatory of lines, paperwork, and mind-numbing briefings. The men sat in a closed, on-post sports bar, marginally drunk, hungover, or just anxious, forced to listen to a chaplain deliver hours of "don't beat your wife" briefings.

Most of the guys just wanted to get the hell out of there. This was the cherry on top of a year of bureaucratic jerk-jobs. We didn't want to see anything camouflage. We didn't want to take any more orders. We didn't need any more briefings. We could have used this many briefings on the way in.

There were no mental health screenings, unless you self-diagnosed by checking certain boxes on form DD 2796. Filling out this "Post-Deployment Health Assessment" form was voluntary. Check the box honestly, and you could stand on another line or ten, talk to another round of pogue paper pushers, and be held over at Fort Stewart for a few weeks while your buddies went home to have sex with their wives, play with their kids, and drink beer on a beach.

Form DD 2796 asked such probing and insightful questions as:

No 7. Did you see anyone wounded, killed, or dead during this deployment?

We are a friggin' Infantry unit. Are you really asking me this? Yes, every single one of us did.

No 9. During this deployment, did you ever feel like you were in great danger of being killed?

Who writes this shit? Yes. Only every waking minute. And even when I was sleeping restlessly. Outside of that, not really.

No. 14. While you were deployed, were you exposed to loud noises? Sand and dust?

No. Never. I was a pogue bitch who sat in a silent, sanitary cocoon for the entire ten months in the theater of war. Can I go drink now?

We pencil-whipped through these forms. Some guys told the truth; others lied to keep from being held over, or to protect their civilian jobs as cops or correctional officers. Documentation certifying you as emotionally unstable doesn't do a lot for your employment prospects. In the end, it didn't matter. I doubt if anyone even read the forms. They were dropped into the bureaucratic vortex along with our back pay, months of mail, and credible intelligence on WMDs.

To my utter shock, even physical examinations for returning soldiers were not mandatory. We had been exposed to a year of death and disease, and the Army didn't require us to see a doctor? Nice to know that the military cared about our condition when we deployed, but not after we came home. Now I understood why old vets talked about feeling expendable.

I ordered the men of my Platoon to get physicals. The Army was failing to take care of soldiers properly, so we'd take care of our own. Sergeant Jensen and I agreed that any and all injuries or ailments sustained while on active duty should be fully documented. It might take an extra day, but it would be worth it in a year or two when our guys were going to the VA with claims. The only way they'd be able to get service-related injuries treated then would be if they had those injuries on paper from outprocessing. I knew about the way Agent Orange had decimated Vietnam vets decades after they returned home. Gulf War Syndrome was affecting veterans from the '91 war. The Army had a long history of exposing soldiers to dangerous toxins, denying culpability, and failing to treat and compensate appropriately. We had been exposed to the anthrax vaccine, the woman with TB in the Medical City ER, and ten months of shaking dirty hands, treating the wounded, and handling detainees. Ten years down the line, we'd be lucky if we weren't all dead, leaving behind a generation of three-headed babies.

We counted the final minutes until real freedom like inmates waiting to be paroled after serving twenty years in jail. At the end of each day's formation, I watched my men with their families.

One night Andy, Luis, Bama, and I met some of the guys at a terrible nightclub called Revolutions. Revolutions was hardly revolutionary. It was a meat market full of cheap liquor, plastic cups, and bottle blonds. I got drunk quickly and didn't recognize most of the Top 40 songs the DJ played. Later that night, we sat in a booth at Waffle House and joked about the CO and how great it was to be home. Living together as soldiers for so long, we had forgotten all normal civility. Bama said we acted like a pack of dogs. We shoved food in our mouths with our hands, chewed with our mouths open, burped, farted, and pissed anywhere with total disregard for those around us—even when we weren't drunk.

In the hotel room late at night I watched the nightly news, and a show starring Donald Trump I heard had become pretty popular since we left. As I soaked in all that I had missed, I realized I was glad I had missed most of it. It was crap. Especially the news. There was barely a mention of the war at all. Groundbreaking issues like Janet Jackson's exposed breast at the Super Bowl dominated the news. The names of soldiers dying each day in Iraq weren't even mentioned. It didn't feel like the country even knew we were at war. I felt guilty being home.

I waited for my new cell phone to light up with the number of the Hinesville Police Department. Many of the guys in the Company had already been pulled over for speeding or blowing through stoplights. MPs and local cops were becoming rather used to it. It's tough to obey traffic rules after you haven't considered them in a year. Traffic tickets were the least of my worries. I was just happy none of my guys had wrecked their cars or shot anybody. Six days after we landed in Georgia, the rest of the guys were scheduled to leave Fort Stewart at o-dark thirty (sunrise) for Florida. I woke up before my alarm and stared at the cracked ceiling. I was empty. They were all headed south and I was going north. I felt like a parent when his kid leaves for college. The air conditioner whizzed. It wasn't even hot. I just wanted to enjoy the coolness. I gazed in awe at my girlfriend still asleep beside me. I had a long, hot shower, then took my time shaving before the enormous mirror.

Trying something totally new, I slid on a pair of underwear—the first time I'd done that in over a year. Many Infantrymen don't wear underwear because they chafe, and they never stay dry. I'd had one of my two salvageable DCUs pressed by the cleaners the day after we got back. I pulled the stiff, newly starched uniform from the wire hanger and slid it on. The Korean dry-cleaning places around a military base have the system down to a science, and freshly starched DCUs can almost stand up by themselves. The pants legs cracked apart as I slid them on and laced up my tattered boots. Despite the cleaning, my DCU blouse still smelled like Iraq. It was like the smell of Ground Zero; it didn't seem to wash out. I formed my beret and checked to make sure all my pockets were buttoned: cargo on both sides, both in back, jacket bottom left and right, jacket top left and right, cuffs left and right. Bootlaces were tucked. I pulled out my lighter and burned off a few loose strings. Even though I hadn't done the garrison soldier thing in a long time, it always comes right back. But it never felt so strange.

In the mirror, I stared at the CIB (Combat Infantryman's Badge) and combat patch on my right sleeve. It was all starting to sink in now. CIBs always inspire awe in Infantry soldiers. Sergeant Peavey was the only man in the Company who had one when we left for Iraq. Before Iraq, they were pretty damn tough to find. Not anymore.

I grabbed a cup of tepid coffee in the fluorescent hotel lobby. Nice to have a ceramic coffee cup instead of foam. I added sugar that didn't come from a packet. Outside, the cars in the parking lot wore yellow ribbons and welcome home messages. I could see my breath in the cold morning air as I climbed in my cold Jeep Wrangler, turned the radio up, and drove on-post to bid my men farewell.

It was strange having doors on my vehicle. It was strange driving alone. It was strange driving at all. I didn't feel comfortable wearing a seat belt—I didn't want to be locked in if something happened.

My Platoon loaded up a Bluebird bus, one of three bound for Pensacola, five hundred miles away. Nervous wives and unruly kids packed into pickup trucks, SUVs, and new Mustangs for blocks around. This caravan of private vehicles would trail the buses like a high school football team headed to the state championship game.

I climbed the stairs of Third Platoon's bus with a lump in my throat. My guys grab-assed and cracked jokes between the plastic seats like a class of sixth-graders. I told them I was proud of them. We had faced tremendous obstacles and done amazing things. They had kept each other alive, and kept me alive. They had represented our country well and had done a uniquely honorable thing. No matter what happened to Iraq ultimately, we had done the best we could to give it a shot. We had helped people, and made a difference. Third Platoon had helped change the world. And no one will ever be able to take that away from us. Ever.

I was finally relieved of the burden of command. Honestly, it was like removing a ball and chain. The only plan Bama and I had was to stay away from soldiers and avoid the pressure cooker of New York City for a few weeks. I knew that dealing with the crush of crowds, subways, and my family would drive me insane. I needed to decompress. We jumped in my Jeep, left Fort Stewart behind, and started driving.

It was nice to have no schedule. I could do whatever I wanted without asking someone for permission or considering the impact of my actions on thirty-eight others. It was just me, my girl, and my Jeep. I felt like Peter Fonda in *Easy Rider*. I could drive wherever I wanted, wear whatever clothes I wanted, sleep as late as I needed, and drink whatever I fancied. I didn't have to bite my tongue or censor how I felt. For the first time in a while, I was free to be entirely selfish.

We drove east to Savannah, where we spent a few days, then south down Route 95. We kept the top on my Jeep peeled back and the music loud. Our intent was to keep going south into Florida, until we found the ideal spot for decompression. We didn't know where it was, but we'd know when we found it. Jacksonville was too urban, and we continued south. We barreled through the night, catching up on our lives and making up for lost time. Because of the races at Daytona Beach, every hotel and motel for miles in every direction was full. Seeing the Daytona 500 would have been fun, especially for a Yankee like me, but being in a crowd of 100,000 drunks would have been a nightmare. We kept going.

Late one night, after long hours of open roads, Confederate flags, and truck stops, we pulled off I-95 east and onto Route 1. The road skirted the ocean and there was far less traffic. Exhausted, we pulled into an isolated beach town called Fort Pierce. Nicknamed "the Sunrise City," Fort Pierce is roughly midway between Daytona Beach and Miami. A city of thirty-nine thousand people, with a Manatee Museum and jai alai, Fort Pierce is also the home of the Navy UDT-SEAL Museum. We drove down an isolated inlet and found a hidden place called the German-American Motel. Situated just across a dirt road from the beach, it wasn't really a motel so much as a row of run-down shacks perfect for people surfing or running from the law. Perfect for us, too. An old man answered the doorbell in his boxers, took my $200 for the week (cash only, no questions asked), and handed me a key with a grunt. No military discount.

I spent my days lying on the beach, reading books, and staring at the ocean. I let my mind unwind as I basked in the air-conditioned hut, watching a fuzzy TV without cable and taking long naps. In the evenings, we ate key lime pie and swordfish at outdoor cafés. At night, I drank $80 bottles of Scotch out of a coffee cup on the sand until dawn, listening to Stevie Ray Vaughan, Jack Johnson, Linkin Park, and Johnny Cash on my iPod. I played Cash's devastating cover of Nine Inch Nails' "Hurt" over and over again. The song reduced me to tears.

CHAPTER TWENTY-TWO
THE WAR WITHIN

> War is, at first, the hope that one will be better off; next,
> the expectation that the other fellow will be worse off;
> then, the satisfaction that he isn't any better off; and fi-
> nally, the surprise at everyone's being worse off.
> —Karl Kraus

We drove back home to New York in February, just in time for my brother's birthday. My family was waiting to see me upstate for the first time since I'd left over a year ago.

I drove fast, with the radio tuned to KROQ, blaring the new Incubus song "Megalomaniac." It felt great that I didn't have to wear headphones. I could play my music as loud as I wanted. I didn't have to worry about anyone bitching about the genre, or complaining that I was waking him up after a long night on guard duty. There was only my girlfriend, and she shared most of my tastes. And she was very patient. I loved Incubus, and I couldn't get enough of the new song. Then again, after being gone for a year, almost every song was new to me.

By the time we got to the Sprain Brook Parkway in Westchester County, I had zoned out completely. With the music blasting, I focused on the garbage dotting the sides of the road, and checked my mirrors frantically. Then I glanced over to my right and saw white knuckles gripping the dashboard. My girlfriend had been screaming at me for thirty seconds, and I hadn't even heard her. I was in a trance. My hands were moving in front of me, but I felt like I was watching the road pass on TV. I cranked down the music and pulled my foot off the gas pedal, embarrassed. I didn't even realize I was driving ninety miles per hour and straddling both lanes of the highway, as if I were still in Baghdad. Checking for IEDs and scanning overpasses for ambushes.

"Hey! Can we make it to see your parents alive, please?" Bama snapped with a smile.

She was absolutely right. I hadn't lived through almost a year in a war zone to come home and die in a head-on collision with an ice cream truck in Westchester. I promised Bama that from now on, until I got settled down a bit, we'd take the train to see my family.

I met my family at a place called Bugaboo Creek Steak House, which was nestled in a strip mall next to a video game store. A cross between a Chuck E. Cheese and an Outback Steakhouse, it had a talking moose on the wall and a talking Christmas tree. It was my five-year-old nephew's favorite place in the world.

My family was happy to see me—or maybe they were mostly relieved. They asked polite questions and joked about old times. I could sense when I ate or walked to the bathroom that they were staring at me, both to let it sink it that I was home and to look for changes. Unlike most Americans, they had been watching the news from Iraq very closely. And they were worried.

I drove back to Brooklyn with my belly full, but my mind in a haze. After 9/11, things had changed in New York City. But only slightly. The city felt heavier. The economy wasn't as strong. People didn't spend money like they used to. There were National Guardsmen in Grand Central Terminal and the Port Authority bus terminal. Commuters were more cautious. The music in the bars was darker. There was more serious rock, less house.

In Brooklyn I shared a bed with my girlfriend in a tiny second-story walk-up on Lorimer Street. Most people in New York who are single and not rich have roommates. She shared the two-bedroom with a decent guy who was a struggling comedian and thriving slob. Her bedroom windows overlooked the street and a brightly lit gas station that made it seem like high noon twenty-four hours a day.

I had been in Baghdad one month and Brooklyn the next, and the adjustment was tough. As I walked in New York City, stimuli overwhelmed me. People shouting, horns blowing, sirens wailing. It all seemed to reverberate inside my head like a Ping-Pong ball. I was a 240-pound exposed nerve. I was irritable and hypervigilant. I fought frequently with Bama. A few nights she slept in the bath-tub or up on the roof just to get away from me. I snapped at strangers. They all seemed weak to me.

Especially in Manhattan. The island that was hit so hard on September 11, 2001, couldn't be more detached from the Global War on Terror two and a half years later. My values had changed. I didn't have time for bullshit, velvet ropes, and polite small talk anymore. I only cared about things with real meaning. Solipsistic fashionistas and silk-suited businessmen strutting down the street made me cringe. They were self-appointed Masters of the Universe who cared more about the labels on their clothes than the policies of their country. I laughed at the urban hipsters and hip-hop rough-necks wearing army field jackets and camouflage to be cool.

I walked into a Starbucks, where a woman screamed at the kid behind the counter because he hadn't correctly put the lid on her latte mocha whatever. I thought, "You know, lady, you're lucky you've *got* a latte." My jaw literally hurt from gritting my teeth and holding things in.

Sleeping was difficult. Especially sleeping with a woman. I loved my girl more than anything, but it made me severely un-comfortable to have someone touching me. I hadn't had human contact in a year, and wasn't used to it. And my girlfriend was all over me like a spider monkey.

On my first night back in the apartment, a few hours into a restless sleep, I realized that Lorimer Street was on the main travel route for the Department of Sanitation. The building was about three doors up from an intersection with a stoplight. In the early morning hours, empty garbage trucks would barrel down the hill toward the intersection on their way to Manhattan. One truck hit a large pothole. A hollow, metallic *boooooooooom* echoed through the bedroom. I bolted in the bed, instinctively reaching for my rifle. As I shot up, my unsuspecting girlfriend's 105 pounds were launched from the bed as if she'd been flung from a catapult.

From then on I found it hard to sleep in the bed at night. I became an all-night TV fanatic, addicted to the cable OnDemand channels, where I caught up on all the stuff I'd missed, from *The Sopranos* to *The L Word*.

Out on the streets of New York, I had a hard time letting my guard down. Even after a few drinks, I still found my eyes scanning back and forth across streets, peering into the eyes of people passing by. I especially found myself watching people's hands. I usually hawked strangers' hands and eyes for a few minutes unconsciously before I stopped myself.

One evening, Bama and I went for dinner at an East Village restaurant. It was a beautiful summer night and we sat at a sidewalk table, just across from Tompkins Square Park. We people-watched and chatted about the day as we ate.

As Bama and I sat there that evening, people streaming by, someone caught my attention. I noticed him right away. He was a middle-aged, dark-skinned man, walking toward us more slowly than the rest of the crowd. He wore a coat way too heavy for the warm night.

My eyes locked on him and the hair stood on the back of my neck. I leaned forward. He didn't see me watching him. His head swiveled nervously from side to side, and several times he turned to check behind him. Then he slowed even more, probing. I checked his hands. They were empty. He looked in the door of the restaurant. I tried to get a look at his waistband to see if he had a gun; I thought he was about to shoot the place up. Bama was talking to me, but I was completely zoned out. "Go ahead, fucker. Try it," I thought.

And he did. He lunged into the doorway of the restaurant toward a woman and I heard a scream. In one motion I was on my feet, standing on my chair. As he ran out, our eyes connected. His widened. As he darted past us down the sidewalk, I leaned out to grab him. I would have had him if I hadn't gone for his throat.

Before Bama realized what was happening, I leapt over the three-foot barrier and was running after him down East 7th Street. He looked back once as I closed in on him, dodging pedestrians. When I swerved to dodge an old woman, my foot clipped a parked bicycle and I tumbled hard on the pavement. I did a textbook combat roll and was back on my feet in seconds, huffing after the perpetrator. He rounded the corner and headed south down First Avenue, where the evening crowd was thicker. Then he turned another corner and was gone.

I wished I had my gun. I wished I could have just shot him.

After a few weeks of being surrounded by suits bitching about the foam in their lattes, I had so wanted to grab this guy and pummel him into a bloody pulp. This was my chance to let go of all my pent-up anger and rage, and I blew it.

My elbow bloodied, I walked back to the restaurant. Bama was waiting, stunned, with the waiter, who thanked me for trying to grab the guy, who was probably a local drug addict. The neighborhood had improved, he said, but there were still some rough characters around.

Most New Yorkers don't do anything when they see a minor crime. Some are afraid to, but most just tend to mind their own business. The couples at the surrounding tables whispered and looked at me like I was mad. The waiter thanked me again and generously offered to buy my dinner.

"What are you, a cop?" he asked.

"Nah," I replied sheepishly.

"He's not a cop," Bama explained. "He just got back from Iraq."

All the nearby tables went silent. Half a dozen heads turned, and I felt my face getting hot. On a busy New York street, you could hear a pin drop.

It was as if she'd told them I had leprosy.

A few weeks after I got back to New York City, three good friends invited me to join them on a long weekend of partying in Los Angeles. It would be my first time in L.A. and I figured it would be a blast. I had more than enough steam to blow off, and ten months of tax-free combat pay burning a hole in my pocket.

Todd and I were roommates at Amherst. Todd was a banker in Tokyo for Merrill Lynch and had spent the last year traveling in Asia on business and pleasure. He didn't do things halfway, and he wanted to give me a proper welcome home. When he brought the boys together in any city, he did it right. Todd made good money, had great contacts in every city, and always seemed to get incredible discounts.

I stepped out of the plane at LAX to bask in the trademarked Southern California sun. Gawked at the Capitol Records building and the Hollywood sign as the cab made its way to the Mondrian Hotel on Sunset Boulevard. The Mondrian is the type of exclusive, sophisticated, and ridiculously pricey hotel frequented by movie stars and celebrities. White-jacketed Hispanic valets clustered at the front door, parking Ferraris and Hummers (not the kind I was used to in Baghdad). I pulled my desert camouflage backpack out of the cab, paid the driver, and strolled into the lobby.

The Mondrian's Web site describes the lobby as "an inspired and surreal stage set with diaphanous curtains, glowing glass walls, eclectic furnishings, and a stunning Indoor/Outdoor Lobby that seems to magically transport the indoors out and the outdoors in." It looked like heaven's waiting room. In the luminous glow, gorgeous rich people sized each other up while chatting loudly on the newest-model cell phones. I felt more out of place there than I ever had on Haifa Street.

The whole weekend was like living in a music video. We spent our days lounging by the pool overlooking the world of the common people from high atop Sunset. Celebrities strolled in and out sipping on drinks—Terrence Howard, Jamie Foxx—but the L.A. glamoratti hardly seemed to notice. Gorgeous tanned waitresses in white sarongs brought us food and drinks, flirting for tips and compliments. I was distant with my good friends, who I couldn't seem to relate to. But I still had fun. We sipped good liquor, they told stories, and we stared endlessly at the models basking in the sun. I couldn't stop watching them from behind my dark sunglasses. After a year away, I had forgotten how beautiful American women were. I could smell them from fifty meters away. I felt like a pervert, or a felon just released from prison.

To get us around at night, Todd rented a stretch limo filled with liquor. We ate at fantastic restaurants. He got us twelfth-row tickets to two Lakers games. We sat five rows in front of tennis star Lindsay Davenport. I felt like I was on a weekend furlough. On the final night, we went to a velvet-rope party hosted by Prince at the hotel nightclub Skybar. The bouncer wouldn't let us in at first.

"Dude, give us a break, this guy just got back from Baghdad," Todd said.

"And?" The bouncer shrugged. "Dennis Rodman's here."

It wasn't like I was expecting the red carpet. But it was one of those moments when I wondered if anyone back home appreciated the sacrifices I had just made.

The Skybar bouncer eventually relented and we got in. I found myself surrounded by beautiful people whose shoes alone cost as much as I made in a week in Iraq. I slurped a beer just a few feet away from Prince. Rodman was at the other end of the bar smoking cigars. It was too much to digest. Two months ago, I was with an Infantry Platoon getting mortared in Baghdad and eating MREs. Now I was sipping twelve-dollar cocktails at a bar with

Prince and Dennis Rodman. These people couldn't have been more removed from the geopolitical crisis going on half a world away. Part of me wanted to toss a grenade into the well-dressed crowd and kill them all.

Throughout the weekend, I felt like I wore a scarlet V on my forehead indicating my status as a newly returned Iraq vet. I was an outsider. My driver's license had expired while I was gone, so I used my military ID to get into bars and clubs. Some bouncers looked twice, but unlike in New York and Georgia, not a single one in L.A. comped me for it. Then again, my buddies used what they called "the Iraq factor" as an extremely effective tool to meet women. Some women were fascinated to meet me; others were outright terrified. By the end of the weekend, I was sick of it all.

My trip to L.A. was full of fabulous and terrible contrasts. It was fun, but in the back of my mind it didn't feel right at all. I felt terribly out of place. I was in my homeland, but I felt like a stranger in a foreign land. The opulence, the glamour, the detachment from reality disturbed and angered me. Everyone was too busy primping, chatting about *Desperate Housewives*, and looking to see who would walk in next. There were American kids dying a world away, while the glamoratti sipped Vitamin Water and tanned. I felt guilty knowing that as I listened to the latest Usher remix by the pool, there were guys on patrol in Ramadi.

America was a country at war. But it sure didn't look like it. Everywhere I went I saw Americans living their lives entirely uninterrupted. No threat of the draft, no increase in taxes, no sacrifice whatsoever. All the benefits with none of the risks. Patriotism Lite. It was hard not to hate them all.

Didn't these people understand there was a war going on? Weren't they concerned about the future of their country? Didn't they care? No. And no one was making them care. Certainly not the president.

After my trip to L.A., I focused more than ever on the news and general discourse in America regarding the war. Stories like

Martha Stewart's jail time continued to dominate the headlines, while the insurgency grew in Iraq. The American public had no idea that thousands of soldiers were on their second tours in Iraq, without body armor, in thin-skinned Humvees.

Richard Clarke, who'd served as a terrorism advisor to every president from Reagan to George W. Bush, finally stirred some debate that March with his book *Against All Enemies*, an insider's account of foreign-policy decisions in the White House. His March 24 testimony before the 9/11 Commission was sincere and vital. He was the first public official I had ever seen apologize to the family members of 9/11 victims for the failure of the government to protect them. That was inspiring.

Not surprisingly, the White House launched a ferocious campaign to smear and destroy him. It was strikingly similar to the way they attacked former ambassador Joe Wilson, a harsh critic of Bush's WMD rationale for invading Iraq. (In Wilson's case, the White House fought back by outing his wife, Valerie Plame, as a CIA agent, possibly breaking the law and flagrantly endangering her life.) The message was clear: those who challenge the White House on the war in any way will be crushed.

The old saying had never been more true: truth is the first casualty of war.

Martha Stewart's jail time continued to dominate the headlines while the insurgency grew in Iraq. The American public had no idea that thousands of soldiers were on their second tour in Iraq, without body armor in thin-skinned Humvees.

Richard Clarke, who'd served as a terrorism advisor to every president from Reagan to George W. Bush, finally stirred some debate that March with his book Against All Enemies, an insider's account of foreign-policy decisions in the White House. His March 24 testimony before the 9/11 Commission was sincere and vital. He was the first public official I had ever seen apologize to the family members of 9/11 victims for the failure of the government to protect them. That was inspiring.

Not surprisingly, the White House launched a ferocious campaign to smear and destroy him. It was strikingly similar to the way they attacked former ambassador Joe Wilson, a harsh critic of Bush's WMD rationale for invading Iraq. (In Wilson's case, the White House fought back by outing his wife, Valerie Plame, as a CIA agent, possibly breaking the law and flagrantly endangering her life.) The message was clear: those who challenge the White House on the war in any way will be crushed.

The old saying had never been more true: truth is the first casualty of war.

CHAPTER TWENTY-THREE
FINDING A VOICE

> Loyalty to the country always, loyalty to the government
> when it deserves it.
> —Mark Twain

Testifying in Congress about the failure

to find weapons of mass destruction in Iraq, arms inspector David Kay said that the prewar intelligence selected by the White House to justify the invasion was "almost all wrong."

Based on my own experiences, I knew that the planning and direction of the postinvasion occupation were "almost all wrong" as well. There were never enough troops on the ground. Officers and soldiers in the field were being deployed with no training in Iraqi culture and customs. They received little direction from above, and were vulnerable to attacks. Far more troops were dying in the peacekeeping phase than had been killed during the invasion and defeat of Saddam's military. I was certain about my assessment of the war. I knew that it was the wrong battle, fought at the wrong time, for the wrong reasons.

By April, I was fed up. I had to speak out.

I spent a few days sending letters to every major news and talk radio station in New York. In FedEx packages with a nice cover letter, I sent a copy of my résumé to WABC Radio (home of Rush

Limbaugh and Sean Hannity), National Public Radio, and a few others. I dug around on the Internet and found some other stations that were more obscure, like an Internet site called Outrage Radio, and a new network called Air America.

I complained that nobody on their stations talking about Iraq had actually *been* in Iraq. The White House and Pentagon had a stranglehold on the flow of information about the war, and there were very important issues that the American public needed to know about. I was sick of policy wonks, retired Generals, and guys like Sean Hannity talking about something they knew nothing about. The wonks sat behind desks in Washington while we got shot. The retired Generals didn't serve in this war, and were on the network payroll. And the talk show hosts were just full of shit, overtly partisan or dangerously uninformed. Soldiers had been on the ground and could cut through the propaganda spin, talking points, and press conferences.

The media needed to start putting soldiers on the air. I offered to be the first. I told them I'd be a regular, do research, get them coffee—anything. I just wanted a chance. The war was a mess, and people needed to know the truth. I told them that I had just gotten back from Iraq, was passionate about politics, and had even had a radio show in college. It was a long shot, but I had nothing to lose.

I also called the Bush and Kerry presidential campaigns. For both campaigns, Iraq was just a political football. Both men made it clear to me that they did not have a handle on what was really going on over there. I doubted that either wanted to hear a combat officer's perspective on the truth, much less convey that to the American people. Politicians tend to be uncomfortable with the truth. My grandfather used to say, "The only promise a politician ever kept was when he told his mother he would never have to work for a living."

Still, I had to try to get my voice heard. Maybe there were other returning soldiers who felt the same way.

I started with the Bush campaign. My expectations weren't

high. Bush was telling everyone that everything was fine and jolly in Iraq. The insurgents were dead-enders. There were only a few thousand of them, and they were mostly foreign fighters. We were making progress. Freedom was on the march.

I didn't agree with the president's assessment of Iraq, but I wanted to give him a chance. He could always come clean and admit his mistakes. Maybe some staffers in his campaign would have me and a few of my guys down to D.C. to talk to them. Maybe they'd ask me to write a brief for them, or give a talk to some policy guys.

So I called the Bush campaign headquarters. I told the kid who answered the phone that I had just returned from Iraq. That I had some serious issues about how policies had affected my men during our time at war. I also left messages with the Veterans for Bush campaign.

No one called me back. Big surprise.

Kerry didn't really seem to want to address Iraq either. The only thing more disturbing to me than the Republican mismanagement of the war in Iraq was the Democrats' inability to capitalize on it politically. Kerry seemed afraid to attack Bush on the war, maybe because he was one of the seventy-seven senators who had voted for Joint Resolution 114 on October 11, 2002, giving the president the power to wage war on Iraq.

Kerry focused on the Vietnam War instead. This was clearly a strategic move much more than a moral one. Since Kerry had served in combat in Vietnam and Bush had not, some overpriced political operative must have convinced the candidate that his military service was a winning issue. The Swift Boat Veterans for Truth proved that guy wrong. I'm sure he'll be the lead political advisor to whomever the Democrats pick as their presidential candidate in 2008.

Still, as a young vet, Kerry had courageously protested the war he had fought in. I figured that he'd appreciate a chance to hear the truth from the front, and that he'd understand its political power.

I called Kerry campaign headquarters both in New York and in Washington. Repeatedly. I was ready to give up hope on them, too, when I got a call from a Vietnam vet from New York who worked for the campaign. He asked if I'd like to meet the senator at La-Guardia Airport two days later. We'd had a few talks about my time in Iraq and he felt that Kerry should meet guys like me who had actually served in the war.

I was skeptical. It wasn't like I'd really get a chance to "meet" John Kerry. The campaign wanted to have a group of veterans for the senator to shake hands with as he got off the plane. A staged photo op. But I figured that I'd give it a shot. Maybe I'd actually get five minutes to talk to Kerry about how screwed up things were in Iraq.

I agreed to go. The campaign staff asked for my Social Security number to give to the Secret Service. Apparently they needed to have it on record or run some background checks or something. I thought that was a little fishy, but I complied.

Displaying what would become typical for the unorganized Kerry campaign machine, two different campaign people called to ask me if I'd like to go to LaGuardia Airport to meet John Kerry. I hoped that if Kerry got elected his staff wouldn't be that uncoordinated with smart bombs.

It was freezing when I got to the airport on Wednesday, April 14. After months in the Middle East, my body hadn't really adjusted yet to the New York winter. I paid some ridiculous rate to park my Jeep for a few hours and walked in the cold toward a distant terminal, wearing the only suit I owned, with a rip in one pants leg. It was tough to keep my wardrobe in good shape after it had sat in boxes in my dad's garage for a year and a half. Hopefully the Secret Service wouldn't have a minimum fashion standard.

I finally found the terminal. A dude who looked like a vet stood outside. Mid-fifties, tough stare, scanning. He had a beard and a long braided ponytail that hung like a rope to the middle of his back. Oh yeah, he was a vet. Or a biker. Maybe both.

He was Bruce Smith, a Navy vet from the Vietnam era, and a good guy. He'd gotten the string of calls from campaign intern flunkies too. We chatted about Kerry and the war. He asked about my time in Iraq, and the brotherhood of vets was in full bloom.

Three black SUVs with tinted windows pulled into the parking lot. It was like a scene from a Tom Clancy movie. Hard-looking Secret Service guys in sunglasses and suits with bulging jackets popped out of every door like they were clown cars. A few uniformed guys with bomb-sniffing dogs went to work checking out some shuttle vans parked nearby.

Bruce and I mustered next to the SUVs with a group of maybe nine vets freezing their asses off in various VFW and campaign hats. It was an impressive assembling of heroes. Most were from Vietnam, a few from Korea, and one younger guy had been with the Third ID in Baghdad working as a medic.

He and I were the youngest in the group by thirty years. It sank in for me that almost thirty years had passed since America had fought in a protracted war. That was a good thing. These men had given their blood decades earlier and were responsible for protecting the freedoms I enjoyed today. The oldest gentleman had fought in the Battle of the Bulge with the 101st. He walked with a cane. We all circled him to help him move around and offer him our support. It is instinctive to soldiers to put themselves last. I felt proud to be in their company, like I was in a club and knew the secret handshake. And I felt dwarfed in the company of heroes. We swapped a few stories, snapped off cynical cracks, and waited for instructions. The training and discipline of military service stays with a veteran forever.

A few suits from the campaign joined us, but none seemed to know much about the plan for the day. They didn't know where we were going or when Kerry was coming in. They talked on their cell phones and ignored the vets, which pissed me off. These old guys had driven to the airport at ten a.m. on a weekday in the freezing cold to be here. The least the campaign people could do was give them some attention, a thank-you—or at least have a plan together. One of the old-timers cracked, "This is just like the Army! Everyone is excited, and miserable, and nobody in charge knows what the hell is going on!" We all roared.

The organizer finally appeared. She looked about nineteen years old and was definitely not a vet. She meant well but had no idea what the hell she was doing. No buttons for the vets. No handshakes. Not even a thank-you. She just stood there with a list of names and checked them off one by one. She rushed us onto the buses, where we waited for almost an hour. She told me she'd worked on the Dean campaign the week before. She clearly didn't know the difference between General Patton and General Motors. This gave me a quick indication about where vets stood on the campaign's priority list.

We finally cruised out to the tarmac to wait for Kerry's plane. It was an impressive chartered jet of some kind. "Damn. I bet Mike Dukakis didn't have one of those!" one of the vets called from the back of the van. Politics had gone to a new level since the 1980s.

One door opened in front of the plane's wing and another behind it as trucks pulled up with steps. The rear door was for press, the front for the campaign. Staffers shuffled the gaggle of vets out of the vans and into a receiving line, just like at a wedding. We lined up shoulder to shoulder, staring across the tarmac at the press corps lined up with their cameras like a firing line. The vets were anxious and excited. I was fascinated. I had never met a U.S. senator before, much less one who was a presidential candidate. I'd be shaking the hand of the man who could be president in a few months.

A few of the vets were really inspired by the possibility of Kerry, a veteran, becoming president. It was like electing a guy from our fraternity. He'd take care of his brothers. Kerry would be the first veteran president since George H. W. Bush, who had been a fighter pilot in World War Two. Some vets said that Kerry had their vote simply because he had been in the shit. That was important.

From George Washington to Ulysses S. Grant to John F. Kennedy to John McCain and the senior Bush, combat leaders have returned as veterans to continue to serve their country in elected office. A nonveteran had gotten us into this war; maybe a veteran could get us out. Only after my time in Iraq did I realize how much combat experience honed leadership and tested mettle. Veterans have been trained and hardened in the most extreme conditions, and possess a unique set of skills that make them exceptional political candidates. Veterans will not shy away from difficult decisions. They have seen firsthand the need for strong leadership in difficult times. They have demonstrated the courage to take the difficult path. General Colin Powell demonstrated such courage in his role as secretary of state. Senator McCain has done the same in leading the fight on issues ranging from campaign finance reform to the anti-torture amendment. Both proved that the courage and fortitude they demonstrated in combat was not left on the battlefield. Veterans of World War Two, Korea, and Vietnam currently filled the ranks of government. One day, so too would the veterans of the current conflicts in Iraq and Afghanistan.

Honestly, I feel that military service should be mandatory for a presidential candidate. Especially in a time of war. President Eisenhower once warned, "God help this country when somebody sits at this desk who doesn't know as much about the military as I do."

But although I knew about Kerry's service, I was never really inspired by him as a leader. He seemed like a nice enough man, but he didn't exactly have the mojo I looked for in a national leader. I liked General Wes Clark. He was not a professional politician. He appreciated and emphasized diplomacy, but he also knew military and defense issues. A Rhodes scholar and a combat vet. He was an ass-kicker. John Kerry just seemed to play one on TV.

Then again, John Kerry was not George Bush. He hadn't sent me and thousands of other troops around the world to die for weapons of mass destruction that we couldn't find. And that was enough for me. I would give him a shot. The 2004 presidential campaign was like the war in Iraq: there were no good choices, just some that were less bad.

Kerry came off the plane with a bounce. He was taller than I expected. The line of vets curled inward as he made his way to each of the men, who were asking questions, cracking jokes, taking pictures. Every guy seemed to want a picture. The candidate wore a checkered shirt with no tie, and an American flag pin on his left lapel. He looked each of us in the eye and talked a bit before moving to the next man, like an officer proudly conducting an inspection. When one vet fumbled with his camera, Kerry was patient. He seemed regal. He was good at working the line. Clearly he had been doing this type of thing for almost two decades.

I was the last guy on the line. As he approached me, I stood ready, took a breath, and felt the cold wind on my ears. I had no idea what I wanted to say to him. I had not practiced anything in my head. Some of the other men were there to get their pictures taken. But this was my shot. I wanted this man to know that my guys and thousands like them had gotten screwed. I wanted him to know that America was not better off as a result of the Iraq war. I wanted him to know the truth about Iraq from a man who had served. I wanted him to understand why the war was keeping me up at night. I wanted him to feel the urgency. And I wanted him to tell the world.

He extended his hand and I introduced myself. I told him not to worry. I didn't have a camera. He chuckled. The lines in his face were deep and his eyebrows turned up in the middle in a way that said, "Yes, I see." He said I looked too young to have been in Vietnam or the Gulf. I told him he was right. I had been in Iraq. His eyes focused tighter and the smile dropped. He seemed wise to me, like a thoughtful old professor. He asked me when I had gotten home. I told him about two months ago.

"How is it?"

"It's messed up, Senator. It's much worse than the president is telling people."

He was listening. I had a window. There were dozens of people in the area, but for this moment it was just him and me. I had a minute or two with one of the most powerful men in the world. I didn't want to blow it. I went into rapid-fire mode, talking quickly and ticking off issues. He focused on what I was saying. He listened and nodded.

I told him about the inadequate number of troops. I told him about the insurgency. I told him about the body armor and equipment issues. I told him about stop-loss and repeated extensions crushing the morale of soldiers.

"Senator, it's not getting better. It's bad. And it's getting worse." He didn't talk at me. He just listened. At some point a staffer interrupted us to pull him away, and Kerry brushed him off, telling me to continue. We had made a connection. Even if for only a few minutes, John Kerry listened. I will never forget that.

He asked me, "Are you involved in the campaign?"

I said, "Senator, I want to be, but your campaign is screwing it up. I want to fix this problem. And there are lots of other guys like me." I offered to be on the plane with him daily. Whatever it took to help him understand Iraq.

He told me he wanted me involved. He called a staffer over and told her to make sure she followed up with me soon. I took her card. And a deep breath.

to me, like a thankful old professor. He asked me when I had gotten home. I told him about two months ago.

"How is it?"

"It's messed up, Senator, it's much worse than the president is telling people."

He was listening. I had a window. There were dozens of people in the area, but for this moment it was just him and me. I had a minute or two with one of the most powerful men in the world. I didn't want to blow it. I went into rapid-fire mode, talking quickly and ticking off issues. He focused on what I was saying. He listened and nodded.

I told him about the inadequate number of troops. I told him about the insurgency. I told him about the body armor and equipment issues. I told him about stop-loss and repeated extensions crushing the morale of soldiers.

"Senator, it's not getting better. It's bad. And it's getting worse."

He didn't talk at me. He just listened. At some point a staffer interrupted us to pull him away and Kerry brushed him off, telling me to continue. We had made a connection. Even if for only a few minutes. John Kerry listened. I will never forget that.

He asked me, "Are you involved in the campaign?"

I said, "Senator, I want to be, but your campaign is screwing it up. I want to fix this problem. And there are lots of other guys like me." I offered to be on the plane with him daily. Whatever it took to help him understand Iraq.

He told me he wanted me involved. He called a staffer over and told her to make sure she followed up with me soon. I took her card. And a deep breath.

CHAPTER TWENTY-FOUR
SPEAKING OUT

For a war to be just three conditions are necessary—
public authority, just cause, right motive.
—Ernest Hemingway

A week after meeting Senator Kerry, I voiced
my concerns about the war in Iraq publicly for the first time. I'd
been contacted by a fellow Amherst College alumnus who wanted
to do a story on my time in Iraq for the college magazine. I was a
bit reluctant, but he was a former military guy himself, and interested in showing the Amherst community the unique value of military service. It's extremely rare for Amherst grads to join the
military, so I felt compelled to share my experience with others to
help them understand a world that was foreign. Amherst was all
about sharing experiences for the sake of education. I hoped I
could reveal to the Amherst community that the military was not
the boogeyman it was portrayed to be.

The article covered everything from why I joined the Army to
the realities of the Iraq battlefield. As a result of that interview, the
president of the college invited me to come speak to students.

The day I drove back to Amherst, in the Pioneer Valley of Western Massachusetts, was sunny and cold. Founded in 1821,
Amherst reeks of tradition. It is situated on an idyllic campus,

perched on a hill just above the town, which contributes to the loftiness of the place. When I was a student there, people jokingly and accurately called Amherst "the bubble." It's a place wonderfully isolated from the rest of the world. Just like when I was there, smiling students bustled among gray stone buildings along manicured paths. They looked so young. And innocent. A group barbecued and played Frisbee on the lawn in front of a dorm, making me feel nostalgic and a bit envious.

I walked around the quad in my Class-A dress uniform, heading for my favorite place on campus—the War Memorial, dedicated in 1946 to the memory of the Amherst men who died in World Wars One and Two. A granite circle lists their names. The site offers a breathtaking view of the Mount Holyoke Range. That memorial had always given me a somber and peaceful feeling. Never more so than on that day.

Still, I felt out of place once again. On the campus of a small liberal arts school in Massachusetts, the only sight more unusual than a soldier in uniform would be a blue elephant riding a unicycle. Amherst is an open-minded and respectful place, but like many of the more exclusive New England colleges, it's detached from the military. The political clouds of the Vietnam War still hang heavy over Amherst. Although not a single graduate was killed in Vietnam, the college was the site of a famous graduation day antiwar protest in 1966, when an architect of that war, Secretary of Defense Robert McNamara, was awarded an honorary degree. Graduating seniors wore black armbands and turned their backs to McNamara as he spoke.

McNamara later wrote in *In Retrospect*, "What disturbed me most during my campus visits was the realization that opposition to the administration's Vietnam policy increased with the institution's prestige and the educational attainment of its students. At Amherst, those protesting my presence wore armbands. I counted the number and calculated the percentage of protesters in each of four groups: graduates, cum laude graduates, magna cum laude graduates, and summa cum laude graduates. To my consternation, the percentages rose with the level of academic distinction."

As at many of the Ivy and Little Ivy League colleges, Amherst doesn't have an ROTC program. Schools had forced the military off campuses in response to Vietnam and kept it off decades later to protest the policy on homosexuality.

In removing the military influence from the campus, Amherst also removed the influence of the college on the military. Amherst graduates were in positions of power in every critical area of American culture *except* the military. No one in a military uniform had spoken on the campus since the 1970s. I didn't know if the students would applaud or throw eggs at me.

I wrote a speech hastily, in the car on the way up from New York, while Bama drove. As we got closer, I grew more nervous than I had been in a long time. I was scheduled to speak in the historic Babbott Room of the Octagon Building, originally built as an observatory in 1848. With its spiral staircase and domed ceiling, the Babbott Room looked like it was straight out of *Dead Poets Society*. Oil paintings of rich, old white men stared down from the walls. A marble tablet commemorating Mr. Babbott had been cut from the same block of stone that was quarried for the Tomb of the Unknown Soldier in Arlington, Virginia.

The event had been well advertised, and I was relieved to see no pickets or protesters outside. We got there early, which gave me a chance to catch up with some old friends, coaches, and faculty. From across the room, a couple of older men, one white and one black, stared at me. They looked serious, even angry. When they approached me, I thought I might be in for a fight before I even stepped up to the podium. They thrust out their hands.

"Welcome home, brother," one of them said. "We both served in Vietnam. We just want you to know that we support you and wanted to be the first to welcome you home."

I was speechless. I had always heard about the brotherhood

combat vets shared, but this was the time I really needed it. I felt proud and humbled.

Game time. My friend Ben Lieber, the Dean of Students, gave me a warm, funny introduction. I checked my uniform one last time and stepped up to the lectern. The room fell silent. I shuffled my papers, raised my head, and faced a couple hundred people. My stomach and groin tightened the way they do when you lean over the railing of a high balcony—probably a fitting reaction. The octagonal shape of the room made for a very intimate setting. It felt like an intellectual version of Thunderdome. I was as nervous as I had ever been in Iraq. I cracked a joke or two about Amherst life to warm things up. Then I went to the heart of my speech.

"I love Amherst deeply, and I hope that tonight I can offer you all some insight, but most importantly some perspective: about the war in Iraq, about how it affected me, and ultimately how it affects all of you."

My palms were sweaty. I tried to enunciate as I struggled to read my own handwriting. I only mentioned the president's name once in the whole speech, but that was enough.

"I was against the war in Iraq. George Bush did not convince me that we, as a nation, needed to invade Iraq. There was a constant changing of the rationale, a multitude of reasons the administration used to justify the war. First it was the connection to 9/11. Then it was to free the oppressed Iraqi people from a ruthless dictator. Then it was the weapons of mass destruction. In the end, I didn't understand the urgency and I was not convinced we needed to go."

I knew how risky mentioning the president was. I had just returned from Iraq and I had called the president out. As cathartic as it was, I didn't know if I could end up in jail for saying what I had. Service members have free speech rights, but these rights are limited. There are some obvious things they can't do, like violate operational security, communicate with the enemy, encourage violence (other than official military operations), or urge people to violate military regulations. But they also can't take part in partisan political letter-writing campaigns, or distribute materials that present "a clear and present danger to the loyalty, discipline, or morale of military personnel." They can't use words that undermine "the good order and discipline of the armed forces" or bring "discredit upon the armed forces." And if they're commissioned officers, they can't utter "contemptuous words" about anyone in their chain of command, including the president and vice president.

If the MPs showed up at my house the following night, I'd know why.

But I was willing to go to jail for the truth. Things were not going well in Iraq. U.S. forces were planning to transfer power to a new civilian government on June 30, and the insurgents had ramped up the violence in protest. The war was entering a bloody new phase.

"Iraq needs lots of time, and it needs support, understanding, and patience. And I fear that we have none of those right now. Our republic is two hundred years old, and we still haven't gotten it right here, so assuming we'll have democracy, a healthy democracy, in Iraq after a year is ridiculous. And even worse, it's dangerous."

When I finished, I felt like I was going to pass out. I looked to the Vietnam vets. Their eyes met mine; then they gave me a thumbs-up and applauded loudly. I was relieved.

I got a standing ovation, even from the kids. I felt a storm of emotions. The response was exhilarating, yet I felt exposed and uncomfortable, like I was telling family secrets. But I was angry and driven, and in my heart I knew I had done the right thing. For weeks I had felt an obligation to share what I knew. It was the same sort of calling I felt when I joined the Army. I wanted to wake people up a bit, prepare them for a long fight, and issue a public warning. I wanted them all to think about this speech when they voted later that year.

The next day, a local newspaper ran a story with the headline "Army lieutenant, an Amherst grad, questions war he fought," with the subhead "Rieckhoff disagrees with Iraq War."

Momentum was building. The Bush White House was not leveling with the American people about the state of affairs in Iraq. Things were not going well. I saw it. I was there. And I was ready to tell it to the world.

CHAPTER TWENTY-FIVE
TAKING ON THE PRESIDENT OF THE UNITED STATES

> TRENT: They're gonna give daddy the Rainman suite—you dig that?
> MIKE: Do you think we'll get there by midnight?
> TRENT: Baby, we're going to be up five hundy by midnight!
> MIKE: Yeeeeaaaaahhhhhhh!
> TRENT: Vegas baby! Vegas!
> MIKE: Vegas!
> —*Swingers*

But before I could tell the world and all that, I was going to Vegas. My dad, my brother, and I flew to Las Vegas for a few days of partying and catching up. Four days of male bonding, drinking, gambling, and ogling bikinis by the pool at the Palms Hotel and Casino. It was a perfect spot, with a tattoo parlor in the lobby and a dance club on the roof. Sports greats like Eric Dickerson and John Salley roamed the lobby as *The Best Damn Sports Show Period* filmed live all week by the pool. The Palms was a fantastic place to make up for all the vices I had missed for the last year.

We passed the first night with six hours of Jack Daniel's and blackjack. At five in the morning, the sun just barely showing, I crept out of the casino. I bounced, sweaty and nauseated, in the back of a dank cab, piles of shiny hooker postcards stacked on the dashboard. The driver was railing on in a thick accent about something or other. Still drunk and woozy, I dreamed of a hot shower and a long sleep on my way back to the Palms. Then I noticed a message on my voice mail.

It was the Kerry campaign. I had e-mailed them the text of my Amherst speech. They must have liked it.

"We are kicking around the idea of having you do a national radio address a week from today. May first, the day that Bush declared 'Mission Accomplished' last year. Are you free that day?"

Not really. I was in Vegas. My dad and brother had been planning this trip for months.

But I couldn't turn it down. I had seen our country turned inside out. The entire world was behind the United States and its people after 9/11, and now Americans were hated around the world. The last three years of my life had led me to this precise moment. It was time for me to tell the truth about Iraq to the American people.

I had very little time. Nursing a mean hangover, I spent the next two days writing my speech in self-imposed solitary confinement in the City of Sin. My bro and dad pleaded with me to come hang with them, but I was laser-focused on anything but women, cards, and liquor. I was ready for a whole new kind of fight.

In my swank hotel room, I worked like a dog. It felt like I was writing the term paper from hell. Every word had to be carefully chosen. Kerry's people and I went back and forth through numerous revisions of the text. Everyone at the highest levels of the Democratic National Committee (DNC) had to sign off on it. I also had to ensure I didn't get myself sent to jail. I was still in the National Guard. There really was no legal precedent that anyone could find for this sort of thing. I was taking a huge risk. Kerry bankrolled some of the best lawyers in the country, but not one of them was sure I wouldn't be court-martialed over the speech.

Everyone told me not to cross the line, but nobody really knew where the line was. It wasn't exactly reassuring. The best I got was a "good luck, kid." I figured that if my government came after me legally, or sent me to jail, it would at least get some decent press coverage. At least I would go out guns blazing.

So I did my own research and found that Article 2 of the Uniform Code of Military Justice expressly states that the scope of the legislation covered in the UCMJ only applies to service members active in the armed forces and federalized Reservesmen or National Guardsmen. If you are not on active duty and you do not have federalized status, your actions are not restricted by the Uniform Code of Military Justice: you have all the rights that civilians enjoy. Good enough for me.

I dove headfirst into a shark tank with a steak tied around my throat. I figured people would attack my family, my girlfriend, my goldfish. I knew this was politics, and that the Kerry campaign was using me, but I intended to use them too. I didn't even plan to mention John Kerry's name. It wasn't about him. It was about the commander in chief.

I was not working for the Kerry campaign or for the Democratic Party. I wasn't even a Democrat. I read once that political affiliation is the shortest distance between two points. My grandfather used to volunteer at the voting booth when I was growing up. He told me, "Vote for the man, not the party." I was independent and proud of it.

The radio address was a chance for an ordinary guy to speak on a national stage. The issues that my soldiers faced needed to be aired. And this would be one hell of a way to do it. I made it clear, through my carefully crafted words, that I was not representing the Army or any unit. I spoke as a private citizen exercising my constitutional right to free speech.

I found that Senator Lindsey Graham, a Republican from South Carolina, was also an officer in the Air Force Reserves. There were five other members of Congress who served as active members of the National Guard or Reserves. If it was legal for them to speak out every day on the floor of the Congress about their ideas and political beliefs, then so could I.

It is important for veterans to know that there is nothing unpatriotic about speaking up about their experiences in the military. They had served their country as soldiers. To continue to serve their country as civilians, it is imperative that veterans demand attention and inform the government of their opinions so that problems can be addressed and solved. So I believed I had not only a right, but an obligation to talk about my experiences in Iraq. As Vietnam veteran and Republican Senator Chuck Hagel said: "To question your government is not unpatriotic—to not question your government is unpatriotic." The Pentagon maintained a stranglehold on the information about the war, and the press was dropping the ball. America desperately needed to hear the "ground truth." I was not speaking out against the war. It was much more complex than that. The country had to initiate a real dialogue about the Iraq war. I was speaking out *about* the Iraq war.

After two days of feverish writing, I caught a plane out of Vegas that landed in New York at two a.m. The speech had to be recorded by seven a.m.

Jumping in a cab, I went immediately to a recording studio at the top of the ABC Radio building. Bama met me outside and we took the elevator up. To say I was nervous would be a hell of an understatement. ABC put me in a big-time Howard Stern radio studio with an in-house producer. I had no idea what the hell I was doing. My voice was gravelly from lack of sleep. I had been living on Diet Cokes and Snickers bars for days and felt like crap. Three cups of coffee later, I read the speech into the microphone, my musician girlfriend coaching my voice inflections from behind the glass. When we finished, at about five a.m., the producer gave me thumbs-up. I was spent. Bama and I headed home. I collapsed on my bed with a thump. I passed out thinking that the next day I'd do a radio interview or two, and then get my paperwork ready for Special Forces on Monday. I had no idea what was about to happen.

A few hours later, President Bush gave his weekly radio address to the nation. "A year ago, I declared an end to major combat operations in Iraq, after coalition forces conducted one of the swiftest, most successful and humane campaigns in military history," he said. "On that day, I also cautioned Americans that, while a tyrant had fallen, the war against terror would go on." He went on to say that the coalition was "implementing a clear strategy in Iraq," and that a new government would take power on June 30.

And at about eleven a.m. on May 1, 2004, my recorded voice delivered a response.

REMARKS OF PAUL RIECKHOFF
DEMOCRATIC RADIO ADDRESS TO THE NATION
SATURDAY, MAY 1, 2004

"Good morning. My name is Paul Rieckhoff. I am addressing you this morning as a U.S. citizen and veteran of Operation Iraqi Freedom. I served with the U.S. Army in Iraq for ten months, concluding in February 2004.

"I'm giving this address because I have an agenda, and my agenda is this: I want my fellow soldiers to come home safely, and I want a better future for the people of Iraq. I also want people to know the truth.

"War is never easy. But I went to Iraq because I made a commitment to my country. When I volunteered for duty, I knew I would end up in Baghdad. I knew that's where the action would be, and I was ready for it.

"But when we got to Baghdad, we soon found out that the people who planned this war were not ready for us. There were not enough vehicles, not enough ammunition, not enough medical supplies, not enough water. Many days, we patrolled the streets of Baghdad in 120-degree heat with only one bottle of water per soldier. There was not enough body armor, leaving my men to dodge bullets with Vietnam-era flak vests. We had to write home and ask for batteries to be included in our care packages. Our soldiers deserved better.

"When Baghdad fell, we soon found out that the people who planned this war were not ready for that day either. Al-Adamiyah, the area in Baghdad we had been assigned to, was certainly not stable. The Iraqi people continued to suffer. And we dealt with shootings, killings, kidnappings, and robberies for most of the spring.

"We waited for troops to fill the city and Military Police to line the streets. We waited for foreign aid to start streaming in by the truckload. We waited for interpreters to show up and supply lines to get fixed. We waited for more water. We waited and we waited and the attacks on my men continued . . . and increased.

"With too little support and too little planning, Iraq had become our problem to fix. We had nineteen-year-old kids from the heartland interpreting foreign policy, in Arabic. This is not what we were designed to do. Infantrymen are designed to close with and kill the enemy.

"But as Infantrymen, and also as Americans, we made do, and we did the job we were sent there for—and much more.

"One year ago today, our president had declared that major combat operations in Iraq were over. We heard of a 'Mission Accomplished' banner, and we heard him say that 'Americans, following a battle, want nothing more than to return home.'

"Well, we were told that we would return home by July Fourth. Parades were waiting for us. Summer was waiting for us. I wrote my brother in New York and told him to get tickets for the Yankees–Red Sox series in the Bronx. Baseball was waiting for us. Our families were waiting for us.

"But three days before we were supposed to leave, we were told that our stay in Iraq would be extended, indefinitely. The violence intensified, the danger persisted, and the instability grew. And despite what George Bush said, our mission was not accomplished.

"Our Platoon had been away from their families for seven months. Two babies had been born. Three wives had filed for divorce and a fiancée sent a ring back to a kid in Baghdad. Thirty-nine men missed their homes. And they wouldn't see their homes for another eight months.

"But we pulled together—we took care of each other and we continued our mission. The mission kept us going. The mission was to secure Iraq and help the Iraqi people. We saw firsthand the terrible suffering that they had endured. We protected a hospital and kept a school safe from sniper fire. We saw hope in the faces of Iraqi children who may have the chance to grow up as free as our own.

"And still, we waited for help. And still, the people who planned this war watched Iraq fall into chaos and refused to change course.

"Some men with me were wounded. One of my Squad Leaders lost both legs in combat. But our Platoon was lucky—all thirty-nine of us came home alive.

"Too many of our friends and fellow soldiers did not share that same fate. Since President Bush declared major combat operations over, more than five hundred and ninety American soldiers have been killed. Over five hundred and ninety men and women who were waiting for parades. Who were waiting for summer. Who were waiting for help.

"Since I've returned, there are two images that continue to replay themselves in my mind. One is the scrolling list of American casualties shown daily on the news—a list reminding me that this April has become the bloodiest month of combat so far, with more than one hundred and thirty soldiers killed.

"The other image is of President Bush at his press conference two weeks ago. After all the waiting, after all the mistakes we had experienced firsthand over in Iraq, after another year of a policy that was not making the situation any better for our friends who are still there, he told us we were staying the course. He told us we were making progress. And he told us that, 'We're carrying out a decision that has already been made and will not change.'

"Our troops are still waiting for more body armor. They are still waiting for better equipment. They are still waiting for a policy that brings in the rest of the world and relieves their burden. Our troops are still waiting for help.

"I am not angry with our president, but I am disappointed.

"I don't expect an easy solution to the situation in Iraq. I do expect an admission that there are serious problems that need serious solutions.

"I don't expect our leaders to be free of mistakes. I expect our leaders to own up to them.

"In Iraq, I was responsible for the lives of thirty-eight other Americans. We laughed together, we cried together, we won together, and we fought together. And when we failed, it was my job as their leader to take responsibility for the decisions I made—no matter what the outcome.

"My question for President Bush—who led the planning of this war so long ago—is this: when will you take responsibility for the decisions you've made in Iraq and realize that something is wrong with the way things are going?

"Mr. President, our mission is not accomplished.

"Our troops can accomplish it. We can build a stable Iraq, but we need some help. The soldiers I served with are men and women of extraordinary courage and incredible capability. But it's time we had leadership in Washington to match that courage and match that capability.

"I worry for the future of Iraq and for my Iraqi friends. I worry for my fellow soldiers still fighting this battle. I worry for their families, and I worry for those families who will not be able to share another summer or another baseball game with the loved ones they've lost. And I pledge that I will do everything I can to make sure they have not died in vain and that the truth is heard.

"Thank you for listening."

When I woke up at about noon, my voice mail was full of messages from producers and reporters from places like CNN and ABC News, who wanted to know about me, my mission, my speech, and my understanding of the war's deepest flaws.

I spent the day dashing in cabs from one studio to the next on a whirlwind marathon of national television and radio appearances. People said I was the voice of dissent on the Iraq war. They said I might be "the next John Kerry." The next John Kerry? A week ago I had been an ordinary guy just back from Iraq, sitting across from a hairy fat blackjack dealer named Chi Chi, debating whether to split a pair of fours. Now people were calling me a hero or a traitor on the Internet? My head hurt.

One phone call shook me.

"Is this Lieutenant Paul J. Rieckhoff?"

"Yes, it is."

It was a Colonel from the Pentagon. Uh-oh. How did he get my cell phone number? I asked him if I could call him back to verify. He answered.

He asked, "Are you off active duty, son?"

"Yes, sir."

"When did you come off active duty?"

"March fifteenth, sir."

"You better hold on to your DD 214. Make sure you have proof."

"Yes, sir."

"Good luck, son."

Click.

I hadn't eaten all day and was running on pure adrenaline. Bama was a saint. She calmed me down and coached me after each interview. A CNN crew couldn't fit in my apartment with all its equipment, so it followed me around Tompkins Square Park as I chatted with Alina Cho about the war's shortcomings. All my nice clothes were still packed in boxes in my dad's garage. I didn't even have a suit that fit. I had worn a uniform every day for the last year and a half. The only clean clothes I could get my hands on were a pair of jeans and a CBGB T-shirt.

Wednesday night I sat across from CNN's Paula Zahn in a studio that looked like something from *Star Trek*. She was kind and charming, and genuinely concerned for the troops' welfare, and before I realized it, the camera rolled, and I was talking to millions of people.

I also ran into the cross fire of FOX's *Hannity & Colmes*. I knew this one would be fiery. Sean Hannity (a guy I had grown up listening to in New York) came into the greenroom just as I left the makeup chair. I introduced myself, and once he realized who I was, he blurted, "What are you doing to my president?"

"What is your president doing to my country?" I snapped back. We saved the rest for the cameras.

Of course, he came after me. He shamelessly defended the president, and tried to talk over me in his typical fashion. I told him that if he wanted to engage in a conversation, he'd have to let me finish a sentence. It was rapid-fire with a master of the craft, but as the cameras went off, I felt like I had held my own. As an assistant leaned in to remove my microphone, Hannity nastily warned me to watch what I said. I wanted to body slam him. Hannity's comments were a shot across the bow. From now on, everything I said was going to be examined by people who were out to impugn me.

Karl Rove probably knew my name. My brother called and said, "Dude, Bush himself knows your fucking name by now! You are in more danger from GOP snipers now than you ever were in Baghdad."

ABC, CNN, CBS, FOX News, NPR, AP, *Los Angeles Times*, *New York Times*, *Washington Post*. It turned out that a soldier calling for accountability from the Bush administration was a much bigger story than I ever imagined. People I hadn't talked to in years were calling my dad's house. My friend Todd e-mailed me to tell me he saw me on TV while he was on vacation in Phuket, Thailand. He also told me I looked like shit and should get some sleep. My girlfriend and I had just moved from Brooklyn into a tiny four-hundred-square-foot studio apartment in the East Village, and I didn't even have a landline telephone. I did most of the radio interviews on a cell phone in a minuscule bathroom that Bama called the phone booth. It was the only spot in the apartment where I could talk on my phone without the reception conking out. I did most of the interviews sitting on the toilet seat with my leg perched on the bathtub so I wouldn't lose the signal.

Reporters called my eighty-six-year-old grandmother's house, and dug up old articles about a protest for students' rights I had led my junior year of college. Conservative pundits questioned my patriotism, and some fellow soldiers wrote disparaging articles. A classmate from Infantry Officers Basic Course (IOBC) e-mailed, "I feel that you have shamed those you served with. I am embarrassed that you would make such statements."

George Stephanopoulos called me on my cell phone and asked if I would be on his Sunday morning show, ABC's *This Week*. Hold on, George. Let me see if I'm free. I thought it was Rydberg or Phil playing a trick on me.

The next morning I sat in an office full of important-looking books with an earpiece in my head. Just before he introduced me to the Sunday morning news junkies, Stephanopoulos was finishing up an interview with General Myers, who was not exactly thrilled with my statement. It wasn't too often a General had to respond to a lowly Lieutenant.

Senator John McCain, one of my personal heroes, criticized me, saying, "I think it's important for us not to try to involve our men and women who are serving in the military, no matter how strong their views are. There's a clear line between civilian and military in America, as far as politics is concerned. I respect and cherish the opinion of all young men and women, but I don't think it has a place in this presidential campaign." I had great respect for Senator McCain, but I think he was misinformed. I was off active duty. And that meant the line was gone.

The critical responses didn't surprise me. What did was the flood of support I received from other returning vets. I got e-mails from soldiers all over the country I had never met. Within days it became clear that there were other troops who wanted to tell America the truth about Iraq from the perspective of those who served. I wasn't the only one pissed off. I was just the tip of the iceberg.

CHAPTER TWENTY-SIX
OPERATION TRUTH

The willingness with which our young people are likely to serve in any war, no matter how justified, shall be directly proportional to how they perceive how the veterans of earlier wars were treated and appreciated by their nation.
—General George Washington

Not long after the radio address, I got a late-night call from my good friend Kevin in Florida. We had served in Iraq together and stayed in close touch. He was upset. Jason Bonts, a Specialist from Kevin's Platoon, had been reported missing by his family in Florida. A great kid, Bonts always smiled and never complained. While on mounted patrol one day, he took some shrapnel when an IED hit his vehicle, and was back out on patrol with his Squad the next day. The Army awarded him a Purple Heart for his wounds.

Bonts had been battling with PTSD (post-traumatic stress disorder) since he'd gotten home. Everyone in the Company was worried. Bonts had apparently left home without his antidepressant medication, and no one had seen him for over a week.

On May 28, a county work crew found his blue pickup truck in the woods just off a highway in Hilliard, Florida. The police found his body nearby. Jason Bonts was only twenty-five years old.

Over one million troops have deployed to Iraq and Afghanistan since 9/11. As many as one in four troops is returning home from Iraq with PTSD, and thousands like Jason Bonts face an entirely new battle, alone and inadequately cared for by our government and our nation. Mental health issues could be the Agent Orange of the Iraq war. Incredibly, no government agency keeps track of the number of veterans who kill themselves after their service has ended—another sign of how little value is placed on veterans' long-term well-being.

The VA health care system, drastically underfunded for many years, is hampered in its ability to provide timely care to veterans. In 2003, a backlog of vets sought treatment at a number of VA facilities. Some had to wait months for an appointment. Returning National Guardsmen and Reservists, because they don't live near military bases, are often obliged to stay far from families during rehabilitation, which can last months. After a long deployment, this added period of isolation weighs heavily on military families.

You don't need a crystal ball to predict the outcome in the coming decades. We saw it during and after Vietnam. Physical wounds, untreated PTSD, and weak or nonexistent transitional programs often lead vets down a dangerous path of marital problems, criminal activity, alcohol abuse, drug problems, homelessness, and suicide.

The moment I went public with my critique of the war, I started to hear from hundreds of young men and women eager to speak out on these issues. But in the 2004 political arena, who was listening? It sure wasn't the Bush campaign. For a while, by default, we still pinned our hopes on Kerry.

I met with Kerry in person for the second and last time one hot June night in Minneapolis, in an intense closed-door meeting with him, former Senator Max Cleland of Georgia, some of the Vietnam vets known as the Band of Brothers, and a few Kerry advisors. We were supposedly there to offer advice for the final push of the campaign. We pulled our chairs in a circle and talked over bottles of beer.

At one point Kerry asked us all who we thought he should

choose as his running mate. A few in the room mentioned John McCain. Rumors had circulated in the press for weeks about secret meetings between Kerry and McCain. Getting McCain to abandon Bush to run as Kerry's VP would change history. Together they could beat Bush. But Kerry made it clear the McCain option was not on the table.

One vet suggested Senator Cleland. Max is a hero and role model to every veteran. After losing three limbs in Vietnam from a grenade explosion, he ran for and won a seat in the Georgia state senate, and then became the youngest head of Veterans Affairs (VA) in history. An incredibly effective advocate for veterans, Max introduced America's first Vet Centers, revolutionizing VA care by providing Vets with peer-to-peer counseling led by older combat vets. Max went on to be elected to the U.S. Senate. He was a guy with the most mojo I had ever been around.

But Max wouldn't be Kerry's choice either. Instead, Kerry asked us about Dick Gephardt. Everyone reacted tepidly. Then I proposed Wes Clark, arguing that in times of war, Americans trust a General. Generals project strength, which Democrats seriously needed. And Clark would bring in the most Independents and Republicans.

I came back from Minneapolis sorely disillusioned and angry. John Kerry was not the passionate activist he had been thirty years ago. He seemed like a good man, but over the decades in Washington he had morphed into a calculating and coached politician.

A few weeks later, ignoring our advice, Kerry chose Senator John Edwards. Politics as usual.

Campaigning that summer for election in 2004—an election that would have an atomic-blast impact on the course of history— the Democrats did not have the foresight, or maybe the guts, to carve out a real policy on Iraq. After the initial flurry of media coverage following my radio speech, the Democratic leadership made a strategic decision not to focus on the Iraq war. They didn't view it as a "winning issue." There were no Iraq vets among Kerry's inner circle of advisors, briefing him on the state of the war. We had tried to get through to him. We thought he'd appreciate what we had to say.

In the summer of 2004, a friend of mine, an impassioned Iraq vet, drove four hours to meet with the Veterans Outreach Coordinator for the Kerry campaign two days after he got home from Iraq. This guy had been stationed at Abu Ghraib, without proper body armor. When his mother bought him some real bulletproof armor on eBay and sent it to him in Iraq, the media got wind of the story and published a slew of articles about the underequipping of the military. So this soldier thought that the Kerry campaign would be happy to receive him.

But when he arrived at the Kerry HQ, the staffer said she didn't have time to meet with him. He protested, and somehow a staffer "found" time to meet with him in the lobby. He gave her about a dozen articles from major media outlets talking about the body armor story, including one in which John Kerry himself talked about his family by name on the floor of the Senate. She said, "Don't call me, we'll call you," and thanked him for his time. He said, "Can I see the HQ?" She said no, "for security reasons." He told her he had a security clearance and had guarded members of al-Qaeda, but she said sorry, rules are rules.

Later he went to a press conference to defend Kerry from the Swift Boat Vets. Kerry's cronies actually forbade him from speaking to the media, and they hid his famed body armor in a box under a table, telling him to stay on message!

Clearly, the John Kerry of 1971 never could've gotten in to see the John Kerry of 2004.

I realized then that I had no candidate and no party. Just as in Iraq, veterans back home were given limited resources, left to fend for themselves, and to make their own plans. A tremendous gap between the public and the truth existed in the national dialogue about Iraq, because the firsthand perspective, which only those who served on the ground could provide, was not being told.

It was clear we veterans would have to do it ourselves. Adapt, improvise, and overcome. We needed to abandon convention and take care of our own. We created our own nonpartisan forum for the troops to tell their stories so the American people could make informed decisions about the issues affecting America and hold leaders from both parties accountable.

I invited a few Iraq vets volunteering for the Kerry campaign to defect and join me. One was Dave Chasteen, a former Chemical Officer with the Third Infantry in Iraq who told searing stories about his exposure to the flaws in war planning at the Brigade level. A Bible-toting Midwesterner and registered Republican, Dave did not support George Bush, but was also disillusioned with Kerry. He became one of our most potent spokesmen.

Every effective combat unit depends on logistical support. The same is true for a political movement. I needed to recruit a team of operators to provide that foundation for the vets battling out in front. I met Eric Schmeltzer in a Lower East Side bar at a mutual friend's birthday party. A tall, grinning Jewish kid from Philadelphia, Schmeltzer wore a tiny soul patch. Fearless and fed up with conventional politics, he had tons of connections from working on Capitol Hill and for the Howard Dean campaign. He cared about the war and about veterans. His grandfather had served in World War Two, and Eric wore his dog tag every day. He became my political Radio Telephone Operator (RTO), my trusted press and strategy man.

But I knew next to nothing about how to start up a nonprofit organization, so I called around to my old Wall Street friends for advice. Yannick Marchal stepped up in the clutch like Reggie Jackson. A driven and intense business genius, Yannick knew how to pull numbers and figures apart like a surgeon. He also had a heart of gold, and loved a good challenge. His nickname on Wall Street was "Smackface," because his swagger made us want to smack his face every time he talked. We would need some of that attitude.

Vanessa Williamson had just finished graduate school in New York when she volunteered to join our fight. Directing outreach to all fifty states, Puerto Rico, and Guam, Vanessa maintained our Web site, organized grassroots supporters, and managed veterans with the patience and kindness of a saint.

That summer, our small band of pissed-off patriots lunged into the dangerous world of American politics at the peak of the fight and attacked both parties head-on. Overhead, Web design, lawyers' fees—it all cost money we didn't have. I cashed out the Apple stock I'd bought in Iraq and maxed out my credit cards to fund our fledgling operations. It would be several months before we could pay staff. Our office space was generously donated and everyone worked for free. We mortgaged the farm on the hope that concerned Americans would support some vets trying to tell the truth.

But hope is not a course of action. We needed a plan. We were ahead of the curve, and America was still suffering from a Vietnam hangover. The country viewed everything through Vietnam goggles, and that needed to change.

Iraq was a new kind of war in a new geopolitical climate, and demanded new policy ideas. Right from the start, we made it crystal clear that Operation Truth was not part of the "antiwar movement." We weren't antiwar or prowar—both were outdated ways of looking at the situation.

We weren't tree-hugging peaceniks and we weren't throwing our medals at the White House. Sometimes military action is necessary—all of us understood that. We represented veterans proud to have served their nation at a time of war, but deeply concerned about the ways our leaders had mishandled that war, created more enemies, and jeopardized our national security. We argued that what America needed was a *sensible* war movement. The Pentagon continued to approach the war in Iraq as business as usual, which wasn't working. It wasn't helping the Iraqi people, and only made life more dangerous for our troops in harm's way. As framed by the media and by politicians on both sides, the debate about the war in Iraq presented a false choice: Stay the course, or Bring 'em home now. But there were third, fourth, fifth courses of action somewhere in between. We called on the president to outline a clear mission, with measurable goals and a defined end state. Enlist the wisdom and experience of Generals Zinni, Powell, Schwarzkopf, and Shinseki to create a plan to get America out of Iraq while preserving our national interests, minimizing the loss of life, and honoring our commitment to the Iraqi people.

We also made the strategic decision that we would not be joining any antiwar protesters marching around with signs ranging from "End the Blockade of Cuba!" to "Free Palestine!" Public demonstrations and rallies were outmoded, Vietnam-era tactics that failed to move either the public or the policy makers. Demonstrators had every right to protest the Iraq war, but when they marched outside military bases, for example, their efforts came across, to veterans, as insensitive and counterproductive. Although their intentions may have been otherwise, they appeared to blame the warriors, instead of the decision makers, for the war. Rallying against the war by marching at a military base was like protesting the cows if you don't like McDonald's.

Operation Truth comprised a new generation of activists, criticizing a new kind of war, and that required new tactics. We took the fight for American hearts and minds to where it could be waged most effectively: the media. News stories only pictured smiling wounded veterans and welcome home parades. The names of the dead weren't mentioned and the troops' opinions were ignored.

With less than 1 percent of the American population having served in Iraq, the veteran population was relatively small. We needed to amplify the voices of a few soldiers and vets to reach out to all Americans, reminding them that there was a war going on, and that it affected them personally. We sought to drive home that even though the war was being waged far away, in a place very few Americans knew or even cared about, the troops fighting that war were the kids who lived down the block or right next door. And those troops had something important to say.

Troops like Robert Acosta, an inspiring twenty-one-year-old

former ammunition Specialist from California. He'd joined the Army to get away from a dead-end life in Orange County. In Baghdad in 2003, someone threw a grenade into Robert's Humvee. Robert scooped it up to toss it out when it detonated, blowing off his right hand and shattering both his legs. He spent months rehabilitating at Walter Reed Army Medical Center. In July 2004 he heard me on a public radio talk show and sent me an e-mail with the header "From One Soldier to Another!"

A laid-back, tattoo-covered smart-ass with a goatee, Robert became a powerful voice for the wounded, and a charismatic leader. He was featured in Operation Truth's first national television ad, a brave single vet representing a legion of others. That historic and moving statement ran on CNN worldwide during the final debate between Bush and Kerry. It was featured on the front page of the *New York Times*, raised hundreds of thousands of dollars in online donations, and attracted legions of recruits to our cause.

Herold Noel walked into our New York office in the winter of 2004 wearing the same clothes he'd had on for weeks. A skinny, fierce, effective speaker, he aspired to be a music producer. Born to a Haitian family in a Brooklyn housing project, Herold joined the Army to get out of the ghetto. He served at the tip of the spear during the invasion of Iraq, driving fuel trucks for the tanks in the Third ID's 3/7 Cavalry.

Now, a year later, Herold lived in his beat-up Nissan Pathfinder on the streets of Brooklyn. His wife and young son slept on a couch with family. He couldn't ride the subways because of his overwhelming paranoia. One night in a shelter, someone stole his war medals. Herold had served his country nobly, and now he was homeless and on the verge of suicide.

Through our efforts, the *New York Post* ran a full-page story on Herold, with the stark headline "HERO HOMELESS." TV and radio stations followed up. An anonymous donor provided Herold and his family the funds for a year of rent and therapy—and probably saved his life.

Herold later testified before the New York City Council on Veterans Affairs, an unlikely leader of the veterans' movement bringing a much-needed focus on PTSD and its consequences. And within a year of his association with Operation Truth, Herold found himself in private meetings with Senators Hillary Clinton and Chuck Hagel, pleading with them to pay attention to the needs of our country's great heroes.

And there were many others—male and female soldiers, from every ethnic background and political persuasion, some homeless, some wounded, some just pissed off. True American heroes. Each had a unique and powerful personal story to tell. And every time they told those stories—on television and radio, in person and on the Internet—the movement grew and spread. Like a wildfire. . . .

In 2005, Operation Truth was renamed Iraq and Afghanistan Veterans of America (IAVA). IAVA is America's first and largest nonpartisan, nonprofit organization for veterans of the wars in Iraq and Afghanistan. The mission of IAVA is to educate about the wars in Iraq and Afghanistan and the issues facing returning veterans, and to advocate on behalf of those veterans. Because we believed so strongly that the Bush administration was leading our country down the wrong path, we tried one last time to appeal to John Kerry and the Democrats. We were invited to attend the Democratic National Convention at the Fleet Center in Boston in July, but once there we were repeatedly ignored and blacklisted, even from events that we had been invited to attend. And nobody—absolutely nobody—at the convention wanted to talk about Iraq. Vietnam, sure, but not Iraq. We actually heard from an insider that several of the delegations had uninvited us from our speaking engagements because of a secret pact among DNC higher-ups in those states not to talk about "the war." Since it wasn't a winning issue for the Dems, they wanted it off the table. We wanted to help them *make* it a winning issue, and put it back on the table. No dice.

So we tried the Republicans. The Republican Party denied our requests to attend its shindig, but we got in anyway. An internationally focused upstart news network called LinkTV allowed me to be an on-camera correspondent for a segment on the convention involving veterans critical of the war, "Embedded: Live inside the RNC." That got us inside the legendary Madison Square Garden, where the scene included more cowboy hats and fewer dreadlocks than at the Fleet Center, but otherwise was very similar. Lots of suits running around smiling, shaking hands, applauding, drinking the Kool-Aid. They loved their man, the president. And he gave a damn good show. His speech was masterful. As he spoke, old ladies erupted in tears of joy. I watched the people's faces. They believed. They were inspired.

In his first four years as president, George W. Bush had sent my beautiful and revered country careening over a cliff like a drunken sixteen-year-old behind the wheel of a Ferrari. America had rushed into war based on faulty intelligence. Iraq was a mess, and getting worse every day. Diplomacy had been virtually abandoned, and most of the world hated us. Our military was being run into the ground. Bush exaggerated our progress. He admitted no mistakes. He offered no new initiatives to deal with Iraq. America was not safer.

And it was his fault. And despite all this, he was going to win the presidential election in November. I was sure of it.

Three months later, Kerry lost. We weren't surprised. Blinded to the issues that mattered, focused on a war that happened thirty years ago, he sealed his own fate. The Bush administration may have failed to understand the Iraqi people, but the Kerry campaign failed to understand the *American* people.

Bush sealed his fate less than a year later, by ignoring the same issues that Kerry refused to acknowledge.

Nobody in America had their eyes on the ball in Iraq.

So my new band of brothers and I focused our eyes on the ball. We would fix what the most powerful people in the world had broken.

CHAPTER TWENTY-SEVEN
THE SENSIBLE
WAR MOVEMENT

> Our country is not the only thing to which we owe our
> allegiance. It is also owed to justice and to humanity.
> Patriotism consists not in waving the flag, but in striving
> that our country shall be righteous as well as strong.
>
> —James Bryce

The generation of politicians currently in power failed America's veterans—and the American people—in 2004. They refused to hear us, and treated us as outsiders. They continue to do so.

But we won't be outsiders much longer. Iraq is the most important issue facing this nation. The Iraq war has been riddled with serious problems. The war on terrorism is creating more terrorists every day. The America I fought for is not safer now than before.

I hope I am wrong, but I believe that terrorist attacks on New York or Los Angeles are only a matter of time. By overextending its military (especially our National Guard and Reserve forces), America has left its back door wide open. President Bush has always said that America must fight its enemies in Iraq so we don't have to fight them over here. Well, what if we have to do both? Hurricane

Katrina revealed to America (and the world) that if forced to fight on two fronts, this country would be in deep trouble.

America will start to draw troop numbers down in Iraq in the next three years. It won't be because the political situation stabilizes in Iraq. And it won't be because domestic political pressure increases on President Bush (although it will). It will be because the bottom will start to drop out of America's military. Given the current size of the military and the extent of this country's global military commitments, the present operational tempo is unsustainable. It's simple supply and demand. We must either increase the supply of military personnel, or decrease the demand for them. The president can't have it both ways.

And yet nobody has come up with a viable alternative. The Democrats scream about Bringing Troops Home Now, and the Republicans strike back, calling the Dems unpatriotic and weak. They're both wrong. Staying the course has reached the point of diminishing returns, and bring 'em home now is not only naïve—it's also possibly the cruelest and easiest way to screw up Iraq more than we already have. Although the rationale for war was flawed, and George Bush was not fucking right, America is stuck in Iraq without an easy exit. Americans need to realize that there are no easy solutions. There are no silver bullets. If we stay it will be bad; if we leave it will be bad.

The severity of the situation is becoming increasingly clear to American voters, and they're looking for public servants who can lead us out of this fog of war.

In August 2005, Iraq war veteran and Democrat Paul Hackett came within 3.5 percent of victory in an Ohio congressional district where President Bush had gotten 64 percent of the vote and a Republican win had been considered a sure thing. Newt Gingrich said Hackett's performance "should serve as a wake-up call to Republicans." It should serve as a wake-up call to both parties.

Hackett is the tip of the iceberg. Many more Iraq and Afghanistan war vets will be running for office. America's most courageous and competent leaders have always been veterans. To-day far too few veterans of World War Two, Korea, and Vietnam fill the ranks of government. But veterans of the current conflicts will soon be joining them. In the media, and among politicians, there is a credibility vacuum in America on the war in Iraq, and the war-riors are now ready to fill it.

Iraq veterans will change the course not only of the war in Iraq, but also of America's path for the next generation. The movement will start to emerge in the critical 2006 congressional elections. The Republicans have gotten us into this mess, and the Democrats don't have a plan to get us out. Only veterans have the credibility to reach across party lines and represent all Americans. George Washington once wrote, "When we assumed the soldier, we did not lay aside the citizen." Our combat veterans understand service better than anyone. America's next generation of leaders will be forged on the battlefields of Fallujah and Ramadi. They will lay the groundwork for a populist political movement that challenges the status quo in America and propels veterans into Congress for decades to come. Iraq vets can heal our divided country, strengthen our tattered reputation, and remind us what is important.

They are serving in Iraq and Afghanistan right now. Or they served nobly and have returned.

If you really want to support the troops, listen to them. Vote for them. A future president of the United States is among them somewhere.

George Bush wasn't fucking right. But now we have the means to fix what he broke.

We fought for America in Iraq. It is time for the next fight—the fight for America back home.

Bring it on.

GLOSSARY

AAR After Action Review

A-bag Army-issue green duffel bag, one of two, along with B-bag

AIT Advanced Individual Training; follow-on specialty school, completed after Basic Combat Training

B-bag Army-issue green duffel bag, one of two

BDUs Battle Dress Uniforms; camouflage issue clothes, intended for woodland environments

CasEvac Casualty Evacuation

CCP Casualty Collection Point

CENTCOM Central Command, the Army's highest levels of authority

CID Criminal Investigation Division; Army Internal Affairs

CO Commanding Officer, often a Captain serving as a Company Commander

Cope Copenhagen chewing tobacco

COR Commander of the Relief

CP Command Post

CPA Coalition Provisional Authority, formerly known as ORHA, led by Paul Bremer

DCUs Desert Combat Uniforms; brown camouflage, intended for use in desert environments

DD Sometimes short for Department of Defense, usually referenced on forms; for example, DD 214

DOD Department of Defense

deuce-and-a-half two-and-a-half-ton, large Army truck, usually open-back or covered with canvas, sometimes outfitted with a .50-cal machine gun

ECP Entry Control Point

EPWs Enemy Prisoners of War

FOB Forward Operating Base

GOP Grand Ol' Party, the Republican Party

GPS Global Positioning System

HHC Headquarters and Headquarters Company

HQ Headquarters

IAVA Iraq and Afghanistan Veterans of America

intel intelligence

IOBC Infantry Officers Basic Course

JAG Judge Advocate General

JDAM Joint Direct Attack Munition

KIA Killed in Action

LBE Load-Bearing Equipment; web gear

L.T. Lieutenant

medevac medical evacuation

MOS Military Occupational Specialty; an enlisted soldier's job

MOUT Military Operations on Urbanized Terrain; urban warfare

MP Military Police

MRE Meals Ready to Eat; Army-issue rations in a desert brown, hard plastic envelope

MSG Madison Square Garden; New York site of the 2004 Republican National Convention

NBC Nuclear Biological Chemical; often jokingly said to stand for "No Body Cares"

NCO Non-Commissioned Officer; enlisted soldiers pay grade E-5 and up

NODs Night Vision Optical Devices, aka NVGs, Night Vision Goggles

Op Order Operations Order

OpSec Operational Security; the initiative of denying the enemy usable sensitive information (military operations, capabilities, limitations, intentions, personnel, programs)

ORHA Office of Reconstruction and Humanitarian Assistance, pronounced "or-ha," led by General Jay Garner; renamed CPA at the end of May 2003

PLGR Precision Lightweight GPS Receivers, or "Plugger"

pogues People other than grunts; non-infantry support soldiers

pro mask Army-issue protective mask; gas mask

QRF Quick Reaction Force

ROTC Reserve Officer Training Corps; a college scholarship commissioning program, and the source of roughly 50 percent of the officer corps

RPG Rocket Propelled Grenade, the most commonly used anti-tank weapon

RTO Radio Telephone Operator, the communications guy who carries the radio and is always alongside a Platoon Leader

SAMs Surface-to-Air Missiles

SF Special Forces

SGLI Serviceman's Group Life Insurance, the Army's optional life insurance. The policy is worth $250K—recently raised to $400K.

TOC Tactical Operations Center, also called the "head shed"

TOW Tube-launched, Optically tracked, Wire command-link-guided missile system

twenty-mile-an-hour tape What soldiers call the green Army version of duct tape

240 240-B heavy machine gun, a two-man crew-served weapon

UN United Nations

USO United Service Organizations

WMD(s) Weapons of Mass Destruction

XO Executive Officer, usually a First Lieutenant; second in command

U.S. ARMY SOLDIER RANKS AND TITLES

ENLISTED MEN (E-Ms, JOEs)

Rank	Pay Grade	Title/Nickname
Private	E-1	Private
Private	E-2	Private, mosquito wings
Private First Class	E-3	Private, PFC
Specialist/Corporal	E-4	Speck Four, Corporal
Sergeant	E-5	Sar'nt
Staff Sergeant	E-6	Sar'nt
Sergeant First Class	E-7	Sar'nt
First Sergeant/ Master Sergeant	E-8	First Sar'nt, Top
Sergeant Major/Command Sergeant Major	E-9 +	Sar'nt Major

OFFICERS (ALL RANKS ADDRESSED BY ENLISTED SOLDIERS AND SUBORDINATE OFFICERS AS "SIR")

Rank	Pay Grade	Title/Nickname
"Company Grade"		
Second Lieutenant	0-1	Lieutenant, L.T., Butter Bar, Cherry
First Lieutenant	0-2	Lieutenant, L.T., the XO
Captain	0-3	Captain, the CO
"Field Grade"		
Major	0-4	Major
Lieutenant Colonel	0-5	Colonel
Colonel	0-6	Colonel, Full-Bird
"Flag Grade"		
Brigadier General	0-7	General
Major General	0-8	General
Lieutenant General	0-9	General
General	0-10	General

TIME LINE

SEPTEMBER 15, 1998: Five months after graduating from Amherst College, I enlist in the Army.

SEPTEMBER 11, 2001: Al-Qaeda attacks on America in New York City and Washington, D.C. My National Guard unit is activated to respond and participate in the rescue efforts at Ground Zero in New York City.

JANUARY 3, 2003: After volunteering for the war, I am called to active duty to take part in the invasion of Iraq (later called Operation Iraqi Freedom)

JANUARY 6, 2003: I arrive at Fort Stewart, Georgia, and I am assigned as Platoon Leader for Third Platoon, B Company, 3/124th INF FLNG.

MARCH 19, 2003: The United States commences Operation Iraqi Freedom.

APRIL 3, 2003: Third Platoon is deployed to the Middle East.

APRIL 5, 2003: U.S. troops storm Baghdad. Saddam Hussein speaks publicly for the last time.

MAY 1, 2003: Third Platoon arrives in Baghdad. President Bush delivers his infamous "Mission Accomplished" speech and declares that major combat operations have come to an end.

MAY 12, 2003: L. Paul Bremer, previously head of the State Department's counterterrorism department, becomes the new civil administrator of the Coalition Provisional Authority (CPA) in Iraq. He is widely deemed ineffective at controlling the rapidly mounting violence in Iraq.

MAY 23, 2003: Secretary of Defense Donald Rumsfeld orders L. Paul Bremer to disband the Iraqi army and civil service. This colossal blunder establishes approximately 400,000 disgruntled unemployed Iraqis. Thousands move directly to the ranks of the insurgency—many with military experience and their own weapons. The civil servants take with them valuable knowledge of Iraq's electrical, water, and sewage systems. Third Platoon feels the repercussions immediately.

MAY 30, 2003: A team led by David Kay is established to search for WMD in Iraq. Some say that this move redistributes valuable intelligence assets, weakening America's fight against the insurgency.

JUNE 1, 2003: In al-Adamiyah, our neighborhood in eastern Baghdad, Iraqi soldiers inside the Abu Hanifa mosque throw grenades at U.S. Army soldiers from the First Armored Division. Two American soldiers are injured; two Iraqis are killed by return fire. First sign of a coordinated resistance in our sector.

JUNE 13, 2003: Lieutenant General McKiernan, head of U.S. military land component, is ordered to move his HQ to Florida. Hundreds of intelligence officers leave with him. Removal of these assets proves to be one of the biggest errors in battle versus the insurgency.

JUNE 16, 2003: A soldier from the First Armored Division takes sniper fire and is killed while riding in a Humvee in Baghdad. Another sign the insurgency was forming in our area.

JULY 2, 2003: "Bring 'em on" speech. President Bush says, "There are some who feel like the conditions are such that they can attack us there. My answer is, bring 'em on. We've got the force necessary to deal with the security situation."

JULY 22, 2003: Uday and Qusay Hussein are killed by U.S. forces in Mosul. First Platoon accidentally shoots a little girl amid the chaos that follows in Baghdad. Gunfire erupts in central Baghdad, as journalists take refuge in the Palestine Hotel.

AUGUST 7, 2003: At Jordanian embassy in Baghdad, a car bomb kills nineteen people.

AUGUST 19, 2003: UN headquarters in Baghdad is destroyed by suicide bombing—a key turning point in the occupation. Twenty-two people are killed, and a hundred are wounded. Among the dead is top U.S. envoy Sergio Vieira de Mello. This attack was a sign the insurgency was becoming more sophisticated, and an indication that the security situation in Baghdad was in trouble.

AUGUST 26, 2003: Bush makes his "no retreat" vow, indicating that the occupation of Iraq will not soon end.

SEPTEMBER 6, 2003: Two surface-to-air missiles are fired at a U.S. military plane leaving Baghdad airport, indicating a new level of threat to U.S. forces.

OCTOBER 2, 2003: According to an interim report by David Kay, the lead investigator searching for weapons of mass destruction in Iraq, no WMDs have been found as yet.

OCTOBER 14, 2003: A car bomb explodes outside the Turkish embassy in Iraq, killing the bomber and a bystander. The bombing is interpreted as a reprisal for Turkey's plan to send troops into Iraq. Third Platoon responds.

OCTOBER 26, 2003: Coalition authorities lift Baghdad's nighttime curfew in time to facilitate observations of Ramadan. This marks the beginning of a dramatic rise in American casualties.

OCTOBER 27, 2003: The first major coordinated insurgent strike targets four Iraqi police stations and the head of the International Red Cross, killing at least thirty-five people. The attack is an indication that violence is now focused on Iraqi police and security forces, rather than on coalition troops. Fear of being labeled "collaborators" permeates the Iraqi people. Iraqi police stop showing up for duty. Battalion interpreters start to quit.

OCTOBER 31, 2003: The UN pulls all foreign staff out of Iraq.

NOVEMBER 12, 2003: Veterans Day. Our Battalion suffers its first KIA. Specialist Robert Wise, 21, is killed on a mounted patrol just south of our FOB.

NOVEMBER 22, 2003: A German Airbus freighter makes an emergency landing after taking missile fire. Third Platoon mail delivery is disrupted for weeks.

NOVEMBER 27, 2003: U.S. President George W. Bush flies into Baghdad unexpectedly on Thanksgiving Day, in an effort to boost morale among American troops. Third Platoon patrols in Sector 17 as usual.

DECEMBER 13, 2003: U.S. soldiers capture Saddam Hussein in a spider hole near Tikrit.

DECEMBER 17, 2003: Because he has found no WMD in Iraq, David Kay announces that he will leave the country.

DECEMBER 23, 2003: Sergeant Tuller and Sergeant Crawford are wounded.

DECEMBER 24, 2003: Christmas Eve. Command Sergeant Major Eric Cooke is killed by an IED in front of Third Platoon in an attack during a night mission north of Baghdad

JANUARY 28, 2004: David Kay tells a Senate committee that he did not find WMD in Iraq and that prewar intelligence about Saddam's weaponry was almost entirely wrong.

JANUARY 31, 2004: B Co. redeploys from Iraq.

MARCH 31, 2004: An angry mob of Iraqis in Fallujah kills four American civilian contractors and drags them through the streets.

APRIL 4, 2004: U.S. troops launch an assault on Fallujah as a response to the slaughter of American contractors on March 31.

APRIL 20, 2004: The Abu Ghraib prisoner abuse scandal breaks when the media obtains shocking photographs of sexual harassment and humiliation. The entire world is outraged. Criminal charges are brought against seven U.S. soldiers.

APRIL 22, 2004: The United States announces that certain former Baath Party officials forced to resign after the fall of Saddam will be reinstated. In total, nearly 400,000 Iraqis had been forced out of jobs ranging from education to military leadership.

MAY 1, 2004: On the anniversary of the "Mission Accomplished" speech, I deliver the Democratic response to President Bush's national weekly radio address.

MAY 28, 2004: Specialist Jason Bonts, who served in Iraq with Bravo Company's Second Platoon, is found dead in Nassau County, Florida, in an apparent suicide.

JUNE 28, 2004: Two days ahead of schedule, the United States transfers power to the people of Iraq in an attempt to quash attacks by Iraqi insurgents. Only thirty people attended the transfer-of-power ceremony.

JULY 9, 2004: Released by the Senate Intelligence Committee, the bipartisan "Report on Pre-War Intelligence on Iraq" evaluates the Bush administration's justifications for the war in Iraq, criticizing the CIA and other American intelligence agencies for the "mischaracterization of intelligence." According to the report, reports on Iraq's WMD were mostly overstated and unsupported by underlying intelligence. The report also questions the assertions that Iraq was producing nuclear, chemical, and biological weapons. And it states that there was no formal relationship between al-Qaeda and Saddam Hussein.

JULY 14, 2004: In Britain, The Butler Report agrees with the findings of the U.S. report from the previous week. It maintains that prewar intelligence exaggerated the threat posed by Saddam Hussein.

JULY 22, 2004: In Australia, The Flood Report characterizes the evidence of Iraq's WMD stockpiles as "thin, ambiguous, and incomplete."

AUGUST 2004: America's first nonprofit organization for veterans of Iraq and Afghanistan, Operation Truth (later renamed IAVA), is founded in New York.

AUGUST 2004: This month marks the highest number of attacks on Americans in Iraq since May 2003. On average, eighty-seven attacks occurred each day.

SEPTEMBER 7, 2004: Number of U.S. soldiers killed in Iraq reaches one thousand; some seven thousand have been wounded.

OCTOBER 14, 2004: The Green Zone, an affluent neighborhood housing many officials, as well as the American embassy, is bombed twice by insurgents.

DECEMBER 21, 2004: In Mosul, a bomb detonates inside a U.S. military tent. At least twenty-four people are killed, among them nineteen U.S. soldiers.

JANUARY 7, 2005: According to U.S. Lieutenant General Thomas Metz, nearly a quarter of Iraq's provinces are still too volatile to sustain peaceful elections. Baghdad is among those provinces.

JANUARY 12, 2005: The Bush administration announces that the search for WMD in Iraq has ended, having turned up nothing.

FEBRUARY 28, 2005: In Hilla, a suicide bomber kills some 115 people applying for employment with the Iraqi police force. This is the deadliest attack so far by insurgents.

MAY 1, 2005: Leaked to the press, the July 23, 2002, "Downing Street Memo" states that prior to the Iraq War, Blair and other British officials knew that "the case [for war] was thin," though "Bush had made up his mind to take military action." The U.S. wanted the war "justified by the conjunction of terrorism and WMD," and "the intelligence and facts were being fixed around the policy."

JUNE 23, 2005: According to Gen. John Abizaid, commander of U.S. forces in the Middle East, the Iraq insurgency has maintained the same strength for the past six months.

OCTOBER 15, 2005: Iraqis vote on a new constitution.

AUTHOR'S NOTE
AND ACKNOWLEDGMENTS

A portion of all my proceeds will be donated to the HOPE for New Veterans project, which works to prevent homelessness among Iraq and Afghanistan Veterans. More info online at www.hopefornewveterans.org. I humbly ask all my readers to help me *really* support the troops, by honoring our veterans. Please give what you can to this and other noble veterans' charities. You can also find more info at www.iava.org.

All events in this book are portrayed honestly and are, to the best of my knowledge, historically and factually accurate. This is the story of me and my platoon. It was our experience, at a certain time, in a certain place. It may be different from other soldiers' accounts of the war in Iraq, but I feel it is representative of the Iraq War experience. In writing this book, I relied heavily on my patrol notes, daily journal, letters home, news reports, and the recollections of my fellow soldiers.

I must disclose that I held back on some of what I wanted to write. If I hadn't, I'd probably be sued into oblivion right now. I had no idea creating a book was such an exercise in caution—until I tried it. I avoided using soldiers' names at times to avoid potential slander, and out of respect for the sensitivity of the subject matter to soldiers and their families.

Writing this book has been one of the hardest things I have ever done. It would have been impossible without the advice, diligence, and guidance of some critical people. Special thanks to Marvin Rydberg, Chris Stewart, Phil McQuaige, and Jack Taylor. The E-4 Mafia helped me to put all the pieces together again. Thank you to my editor, Mark Chait, who cracked the whip. Claire Zion and everyone at New American Library who believed in me and the importance of this project. Thanks to John Strausbaugh. You are a doctor with a truly exceptional bedside manner. You answered my questions, tamed my rage, and gave me focus when I had none. Thank you, Laurie Liss, my agent. You are as tactically proficient, fierce, and patient as the finest of warriors.

Balance is never truly achieved, and sanity is often precariously maintained. My gratitude to the people, places, and things that gave me solace and escape: Johnny Cash, System of a Down, Disturbed, Metallica, Citizen Cope, The Notorious B.I.G., Eminem, the City of New York, Café Pick Me Up, Tribe, 7A, Amherst College, Virgin Gorda, Chuck Palahniuk, John Fowles, Google, Bud, Diet Coke, the New York Giants, Jack Daniel's, Xbox.

Inspiration can come in many forms. Mine often came from the friends who engulfed me with support and kindness throughout difficult times in my life, and cultivated IAVA through the painful birth of a new movement. Thank you Todd Sutler, Scott Stanford, Kevin Kjellerup, Luis Sierra, Andy Berrey, Sergeant Grimm, Shad Meshad, Adam Thomas, Carol and Tim Thomas, Giovanna Torchio, Joe Sandler, Bruce Smith, POGO, Steve Robinson, Mike Atkinson, Charlie Fink, Jill Iscol, Dan Adler, Ben Mezrich, Gideon Yago, Arriana Huffington, Michael Franti, Catherine Enny, Rachel Maddow, Anthony Lappe, Nate Fick, Peter Klatsky, Dermond Thomas, Teddy

Sears, Danny Morall, Dan and Lazza Warnier, Warfield Price, Dan Lohaus, Patricia Foulkrod, FreeRange Graphics, Dave Russell, Devon Collins, Daniel Atwood, Les Gelb, Lynne Wasserman, Ed Vick, Chad Urmston, State Radio.

I am eternally grateful to my mentors: Max Cleland, Bobby Muller, Wayne Smith, Rosanne Haggerty, Coach James Hunter, Coach E.J. Mills. You are the oracles. I am humbled to have known you.

I am thankful for the strength and patriotism of my brothers and sisters in the next fight: Robert Acosta, Perry Jefferies, Herold Noel, Colby Buzzell, Andrew Borene, Jon Soltz, Todd Bowers, Dave Chasteen, Denver Jones, Jeremy Broussard, Rich Murphy, Ray Kimball, Sean Huze, Abbie Pickett, J.B. White. This is a marathon, not a sprint.

I am deeply grateful to my colleagues who have built IAVA and given of themselves in so many ways. Overworked and underpaid, you made a difference. If I go to war ever again, I'd be proud to have you by my side. Yannick Marchal, you are a genius and a dear friend who took a chance on a crazy idea and a crazier vet. Emily O'Brien, Joey Alley, Luci Canet, Andre Perez, Marco LoCascio. You gave us a summer of your life to build something. Eric Schmeltzer, thank you for working the mojo, training me, and making me better. Vanessa Williamson and Will Coghlan, your intelligence, diligence, and heart are inspiring.

The good people of Iraq are often the lost part of this complex equation. They were brave, kind, funny, and generous. Three men in Sector 17 embodied the best of Iraq and were citizen soldiers in the war for peace and understanding. Despite the risks, they rode and walked with us every day without hesitation. The American people owe them a tremendous debt of gratitude. As do the Iraqis. Heroes and patriots of exceptional courage emerged in this war. Esam Pasha, Mohamed al-Mumayiz, and Sid Al Khalily are three of them. You are my brothers. And I wish for you the strength to continue to lead your people through these tumultuous times. You are Iraq's finest ambassadors.

I thank the families of the soldiers of Third Platoon. You are the ones who never get the thanks from strangers. You served as the unsung rocks of stability for our platoon throughout the war, and will continue to serve beyond. Our platoon, and our country, are forever indebted to you for your sacrifice and selfless service.

I am most thankful to the soldiers of Third Platoon. We are family forever. You took care of me, and more important, you took care of each other. And we all came home alive—just like we said we would. We served honorably. We made a difference. Your professionalism, restraint, generosity, toughness, and benevolence were a demonstration of the best that our country can be. I am proud to have served with you.

Special thanks to Laura "Bama" Thomas. You are the best friend I have ever had, and you have given me more strength than I could ever deserve. You stood by me through a war in Iraq and the battles at home. And I am forever humbled by the depth of your love and the fire in your heart. Your presence in my life is a nonstop inspiration. You make every day fun.

I give great thanks to my family. My dad, Paul Rieckhoff, you have taught me the importance of hard work and quick thinking and motivated me to be a better man. My mom, Linda, you gave me the fire. My brother, Mikey Rieckhoff, this is just the beginning. Thank you for always keeping me in check. We are down for life. Carpe diem. Shawn Norton, you give me hope and joy. I expect big things from you. Nana, Grandpa, and Grandma, thank you for the gifts of your wisdom. You have given me curiosity and courage and have shown me the true meaning of patriotism. You taught me how to treat people and what is important in life.

I am indebted to you all.